MY LIFE AND TIMES
OCTAVE FIVE:
1915-1923

BY COMPTON MACKENZIE

Novels and Romances

SINISTER STREET
SYLVIA SCARLETT
GUY AND PAULINE
CARNIVAL
FIGURE OF EIGHT
CORAL
THE VANITY GIRL
ROGUES AND VAGABONDS
THE ALTAR STEPS
THE PARSON'S PROGRESS
THE HEAVENLY LADDER
HUNTING THE FAIRIES
WHISKY GALORE
KEEP THE HOME GUARD TURNING
THE MONARCH OF THE GLEN
THE RIVAL MONSTER
BEN NEVIS GOES EAST
THE RED TAPEWORM
ROCKETS GALORE
THE STOLEN SOPRANO
THE LUNATIC REPUBLIC
POOR RELATIONS
APRIL FOOLS
RICH RELATIVES
BUTTERCUPS AND DAISIES
WATER ON THE BRAIN
VESTAL FIRE
EXTRAORDINARY WOMEN
THIN ICE
EXTREMES MEET
THE THREE COURIERS
OUR STREET
THE DARKENING GREEN
THE PASSIONATE ELOPEMENT
FAIRY GOLD
THE SEVEN AGES OF WOMAN
PARADISE FOR SALE
MEZZOTINT
THE FOUR WINDS OF LOVE:
    THE EAST WIND
    THE SOUTH WIND
    THE WEST WIND
    THE NORTH WIND

Play

THE LOST CAUSE

Verse

POEMS 1907
KENSINGTON RHYMES

History and Biography

EASTERN EPIC. VOL. I

ALL OVER THE PLACE
GALLIPOLI MEMORIES
ATHENIAN MEMORIES
GREEK MEMORIES
AEGEAN MEMORIES
WIND OF FREEDOM
MR ROOSEVELT
DR BENES
PRINCE CHARLIE
PRINCE CHARLIE AND HIS LADIES
CATHOLICISM AND SCOTLAND
MARATHON AND SALAMIS
PERICLES
THE WINDSOR TAPESTRY
THE VITAL FLAME
I TOOK A JOURNEY
COALPORT
REALMS OF SILVER
THE QUEEN'S HOUSE
MY RECORD OF MUSIC
SUBLIME TOBACCO
GREECE IN MY LIFE
CATS' COMPANY
CATMINT
LOOK-AT CATS

Essays and Criticism

ECHOES
A MUSICAL CHAIR
UNCONSIDERED TRIFLES
REAPED AND BOUND
LITERATURE IN MY TIME
ON MORAL COURAGE

Children's Stories

LITTLE CAT LOST
SANTA CLAUS IN SUMMER
TOLD
MABEL IN QUEER STREET
THE UNPLEASANT VISITORS
THE CONCEITED DOLL
THE ENCHANTED BLANKET
THE DINING-ROOM BATTLE
THE ADVENTURES OF TWO CHAIRS
THE ENCHANTED ISLAND
THE NAUGHTYMOBILE
THE FAIRY IN THE WINDOW BOX
THE STAIRS THAT KEPT ON GOING
    DOWN

Autobiography

MY LIFE AND TIMES: OCTAVE ONE;
OCTAVE TWO; OCTAVE THREE;
OCTAVE FOUR

MY LIFE
AND TIMES

OCTAVE FIVE
1915-1923

Compton Mackenzie

1966
CHATTO & WINDUS
LONDON

Published by
Chatto & Windus Ltd
42 William IV Street
London, W.C.2

★

Clarke, Irwin & Co. Ltd
Toronto

Printed in Great Britain by
T. & A. Constable Ltd
Hopetoun Street, Edinburgh

To
JANET & REYNOLDS STONE
Affectionately

PLATES

*

APOLOGIA

THE handling of this fifth Octave has been a problem. Owing to the perhaps rash decision to relate the story of my life year by year I was faced with four long books of war memories the contents of which had to be compressed into three chapters. I was inevitably bound to be repetitive; yet I could not assume that more than a very small fraction of those who would read *My Life and Times* would have read my war memories.

When I started this fifth Octave *Gallipoli Memories* had long been out of print. Then to my great pleasure Panther Books decided to republish that book. However, I made up my mind to let the year 1915 remain as it is in *My Life and Times* with apologies to readers who were familiar with part of it.

Another difficulty, already faced in Octave 4, was what to leave out and whom to leave out if I was to preserve any kind of shape and avoid a scattered series of reminiscences. Critics who accuse me of a lack of selectivity must believe me when I assure them that from the very beginning of *My Life and Times* I have continuously refused to give my memory a loose rein. I have tried to keep every year as it came along as much in the mood of that year as if I had kept a diary.

As I write these words, half the task I set myself has been accomplished.

STILL THIRTY-TWO: 1915

T HROUGHOUT a long life from the time I taught myself to read
before I was two years old it has been my good fortune to become
completely absorbed, indeed I could say obsessed, by the ruling passion
of the moment, and in the course of that absorption or obsession to enjoy
a kind of Protean change through which I adapt myself to my circumstances and surroundings. By the time the S.S. *Roma* dropped anchor
in the harbour of Alexandria I was a young subaltern barely twenty,
acutely anxious to avoid disgracing the Royal Marines by lack of a
uniform. I have told in *Gallipoli Memories* about my desperate and
finally successful effort to acquire one.

The big Cunarder transport sailed on the afternoon of May 14th. I
found myself in the dining-saloon with three R.A.M.C. officers and
happened to ask why we had been given second-class cabins.

"I'll show you after lunch," said one of them.

Getting hold of a key from the steward, he took me along and opened
the door of what looked like a Bluebeard's Chamber. From floor to
ceiling the white cabin was splashed with blood.

"We brought back five thousand wounded in the *Franconia* and they
haven't had time to clear up the relics. The worst cases were in the
first-class cabins and there were only three of us to attend to them."

On the following evening the Colonel commanding on board handed
to me as the junior subaltern a packet of the men's letters to read
through and censor. Nobody in the various drafts for the Peninsula had
yet heard a shot fired in anger. I cannot resist reprinting one of those
letters sprawled in pencil over three or four sheets of toilet-paper:

Dear Perce, Flo and Susie,

*We have now been in the trenches under shot and shell for ten days, and its
something terrible I give you my word and no mistake—the noise is absolutely
deafning—enough to make your hair curl—we do not get a moment's sleep all
night.*

We are now well in for it with the Terrible Turk[1] *who by all accounts is a
proper Buger and no mistake. No more bloody armies for me—The next bloody
army I join is the Salvation bloody army and don't you forget it.*

Kind regards to Ma.
Yours sincerely,
Father

[1] Madrali the Terrible Turk was a professional wrestler who had toured the
music-halls before the war.

This is that unknown warrior's letter as he wrote it; I copied it out at the time, in the fern-filled ladies' saloon of the *Franconia*.

At six o'clock on Sunday morning, May 16th, we were anchored off Cape Helles.

All but fifty years have passed since I stood in the bows of the *Franconia* and beheld that incredible scene, but it is as clear as a chromolithograph in my mind's eye as I look back to contemplate it.

As I should write of it one day, I felt that I was watching in the window of a toy-shop an artful arrangement of toy soldiers and tiny tents in a martial scene; and just as the colours of the toys are a little brighter than nature, so were they here. The very puffs of smoke from the shrapnel-bursts seemed more like the cotton-wool with which a crafty salesman had imitated the real thing than the real thing itself.

"We don't seem to have advanced quite as far as they think we have in Alexandria," said one of the officers watching.

We looked at the hill Achi Baba which stood between us and Constantinople. Three-quarters of the way up those grey-green slopes was a large patch of poppies the sight of which set my mind back to the field-day at Aldershot and the scarlet of my volunteer battalion moving across Laffan's Plain in that August of 1901.

The only other person on board who was bound for G.H.Q. was a captain in the Royal Inniskilling Fusiliers called Kenny. He had had very little service with his regiment and was not in Crete or Malta with my brother Frank. He had been A.D.C. to the new Sultan of Egypt who, desiring to pay a compliment, had put him at Sir Ian Hamilton's disposal for the rest of the campaign. Owing to my wearing the Tommy's service-jacket I had acquired before we sailed, Kenny felt a little doubtful about my social status but made the best of the bad job of having to report to G.H.Q. in my company.

Nobody on Helles was sure where G.H.Q. was, but majority opinion favoured the island of Tenedos. After managing with great difficulty to reach Tenedos on the following day we were told there that G.H.Q. was still in the *Arcadian* anchored off the island of Imbros, twenty miles or more away. Kenny wanted to go back to Helles in the trawler which had brought us to Tenedos, but I persuaded him to agree to our hiring a caique to reach our objective. It was an exciting voyage next day. The engine broke down half-way to Imbros and we only just managed to make the westerly point of the island after missing by a few yards being run down by a French transport full of Senegalese soldiers, whose grinning faces I see still.

We managed to get a messenger to ride over to the other side of the island and slept that night upon the beach, to be taken off next morning in a torpedo-boat, and after a rough two hours' passage find ourselves alongside the *Arcadian*.

"Welcome indeed was the sight of Orlo Williams looking larger than ever in khaki when I stepped on to the deck of the *Arcadian*," I wrote. "It was due to him in the first place that I was here at all. Now he deepened my obligation by the trouble he took to introduce me to everybody on board, and for the kindness with which everybody made me feel at home I knew that I was also in his debt."

Orlo and I went on to talk about the mighty possibilities of the Expedition . . . an advance across the plains of Hungary after the fall of Constantinople . . . Breslau, the only really strong German fortress on that side . . . the war over by next year.

Presently Sir Ian Hamilton came striding round the deck and I was presented to him. He must have said something which allowed me without impertinence to ask him why Lord Kitchener did not grasp the difficulties of the enterprise and the full implications of its success, for his next words are cut with a chisel in my heart.

"Lord Kitchener is a great genius, but like every great genius he has blind spots."

As he spoke his eyes turned eastward to the long line of cliffs of the mainland; in one illuminating instant I divined that we should never take Constantinople. Yet at this date I had no reasonable grounds for pessimism. I had not yet experienced that *insurmountable mental barrier* of which Winston Churchill would one day write. *A wall of crystal, utterly immovable, began to tower in the Narrows, and against this wall of inhibition no weapon could be employed. The "No" principles had become established in men's minds, and nothing could ever eradicate it.*

I did not know on that May morning that two days ago Sir Ian had sent a cable to Lord Kitchener which owing to the political situation at home would not be discussed for another three weeks, although upon the answer to it depended the success or failure of our attempt to take Constantinople. I did not know that this very morning he had received a private cable from Lord Kitchener in which the word "withdrawal" had been mentioned for the first time. I did not know that Major John Churchill, our camp commandant at G.H.Q., had just received a cable from his brother to say he was to be driven from the Admiralty but that he hoped to be in a position to help the Expedition indirectly. I did not know that the leaders of the Unionist Party, barren of policy yet greedy of place and patronage, had taken advantage of this grave hour in their country's destiny to blackmail their rivals into surrendering to them an equal share of the responsibilities and emoluments of office. I did not know that in Paris Lord Bertie would be writing in his diary that night:

*How disgusting and disgraceful are all these intrigues and squabbles in the midst
of our life and death struggle.*

It would not be Gallipoli that would reveal to me the fearful pro-
fundity of those words Winston Churchill once wrote. I should not
appreciate them until I had played my part in the Greek tragedy, on
which the curtain had even then already risen. I should be at Gallipoli
a mere butterfly in a graveyard.

"I shall expect you at dinner to-night," Sir Ian rapped out, and that
thin eager form was off again on its restless promenading. North and
east the towering line of cliffs along a blue horizon. Southward the
rolling dunes on which presently the tents of G.H.Q. would be pitched.
Westward the soft sandy beach of Kephalo flounced with seaweed.
North-west the rugged hills of Imbros still green with the colour of hope.
All around that multiform flotilla in diverse shades of grey. And a
General striding round and round this deck like a squirrel in a cage.

At G.H.Q. St Omer the feeling was unanimous that whatever course
the war in France and Flanders took "Johnny" Hamilton and Winston
Churchill, like the Russians forty years ago, should "not have Constantinople". The state of mind at St Omer was well expressed by Sir
Henry Wilson who noted in his diary on July 17th that he had just
given Foch his latest Dardanelles news about the despatch of three
Divisions of Kitchener's Army for the Suvla landing, and had told Foch
that a success there would be a disaster.

In November 1937 I asked Sir Winston why he had not come to
Gallipoli as he had promised.

"George Curzon," he replied. "I was just boarding a destroyer at
Brindisi when George Curzon got me recalled to England."

When *Gallipoli Memories* was published in 1929 many of the reviewers
commented on the absurdity of my belief that the attempt to take
Constantinople if successful would have shortened the war by three
years. I recall one review which said: "Mr Compton Mackenzie has
some strange ideas of strategy, almost as strange as those of Mr Winston
Churchill, whom he seems to admire so much."

For many years the belief persisted in Australia that Winston
Churchill and Ian Hamilton had between them been responsible for
the sacrifice of so many Australian lives. Alan Moorehead, an Australian himself, in his excellent book about Gallipoli was completely at
sea when he tried to draw a portrait of Sir Ian Hamilton; it was a
caricature.

In July 1939 Mrs Churchill told me of landing on an island in the
Great Barrier Reef, from the late Lord Moyne's yacht, I think, and of
being met on the beach by an elderly man in tattered shorts with a large
unkempt beard and of his saying to her:

"Mrs Winston Churchill, eh? I've just been reading a book called *Gallipoli Memories* and from what I can make out your husband made a bit of a *faux pas* over Gallipoli."

I was less amused than I ought to have been by this story because I felt indignant with that aged beachcomber for misinterpreting my point of view about Gallipoli.

Even now in 1965 one or two reviewers in noticing the Panther paper-back of *Gallipoli Memories* seem to think that the attempt to take Constantinople was a *faux pas* of Winston Churchill. However, at eighty-two ignorance and stupidity no longer surprise me.

It was decided that the only place in which my services could contribute so much as a mite to G.H.Q. was in Intelligence. This was in charge of Colonel Ward, a delightful old Gunner who had never been out of England until he was sent with the escort to bring back Lord Roberts' body from France. Under him in I-a, information about the enemy, was George Lloyd,[1] a captain in the Warwickshire Yeomanry and Conservative M.P. for West Staffordshire. He had been cox of the Cambridge Eight which broke the nine-year sequence of Oxford victories in 1900 and was inclined to treat "Wardie" as a stroke with too many ideas of his own. Lloyd made me a confidant in his despair of the brains of professional soldiers, and the soldiers made me their confidant in their despair of the brains of politicians, or rather of bloody politicians because if one referred to a politician without the adjective they did not know about whom one was talking. George Lloyd and I were not on the same political side, but I had a profound regard for him as a man and an immense admiration of his ability. With Lloyd was Ian Smith, who had been Military Consul at Van. The head of I-b or counter-espionage was Wyndham Deedes,[2] a Rifleman who had held an appointment in the Turkish Gendarmery. "Jan" Smith, George Lloyd and "Dedez Bey" were all passionately pro-Turkish.

The pro-Turkish and pro-Arab proclivities of so many Englishmen deserve the attention of some exponent of psycho-analysis.

The cipher officer in I was Eddie Keeling, whom I had not seen since we played together in the *Clouds* at Oxford. He had recently been a Secretary at the Residency in Cairo but had contrived to escape for a while from diplomacy to become a temporary lieutenant. Our sense of the ridiculous was almost identical, which was lucky, for we were destined to share a tent when we all went ashore at the end of May. With his wide lofty forehead and baby's mouth he was like a benign infant Jupiter, and his serene detachment from the petty humdrum of mortal existence was hardly less Olympian. "These soldiers" among whom he

---

[1] The late Lord Lloyd of Dolobran.
[2] The late Brigadier-General Sir Wyndham Deedes, C.M.G., D.S.O.

B

found himself represented a more primitive society than any he had yet encountered; but his diplomatic training enabled him to deal with their taboos and totems without the least suggestion of superiority. He humoured their sense of their own importance as he would have humoured at the Foreign Office the dignity of a deputation of Fiji Islanders. Throughout his brief military career they remained as much a source of amusement to him as he was a source of amusement and sometimes of perplexity to them.

It is tempting to go on evoking from Operations and Intelligence those figures of fifty years ago with so many of whom I enjoyed an intimacy much cherished in memory, but in *Gallipoli Memories* and *First Athenian Memories* this thirty-third year of my life was allowed 800 pages to relive itself; in Octave Five of *My Life and Times* it has to be compressed into a chapter.

The first thing which had to be done after my arrival on board the *Arcadian* was to "regularize" my position and off I went to Helles in a trawler with a note:

To G.O.C.
     R.N.D.
    The services of Lieut. E. M. C. Mackenzie, R.M. H.M.S. Victory can be usefully employed in G.H.Q. (I) if you have no need for them.

When I reached Lancashire Landing people were as vague about the whereabouts of the Royal Naval Division as they had been about the whereabouts of G.H.Q. However, at last I managed to get directed to my destination, and leaving behind me the noise and confusion of that dusty amphitheatre by the sea, I found myself on a road that led toward a grey-green expanse of flat empty country across which I walked on until the road came to an end. The aspect of Achi Baba from here gave it a much more gradual elevation; the poppies which had reminded me of the field-day at Aldershot had within a week been dulled into the dingy brownish crimson of an old blood-stain.

At this moment the empty air suddenly became full of whispers; the whispers turned to attenuated Aeolian whinnyings, a half-melodious sound rising and falling. I stopped and listened anxiously. Was this the noise of shells? Yes, but whose shells? I should look such a duffer if I even started walking faster than usual to avoid shells intended to burst two or three miles away on Achi Baba. I tried to determine from which direction the whinnying came; it was circumambient, ubiquitous, inestimable. The larks went on singing away overhead; the telephone wires running along near the ground hummed as peacefully as a kettle on the hob. A tortoise crawled clumsily through the dwarf scrub at my feet. I told myself that, if this tortoise had been crawling about here for the past month without suffering any harm, it would be deliberate cowardice on my part to quicken my pace, however much I might feel inclined to do so. I reminded myself that if destiny intended me to be killed at Gallipoli it would mean that I had done the work required of me in this world and that for me to desire to prolong my stay here would be ignoble. I decided then that nothing would ever shake my conviction that no human being's existence depended upon blind chance; nothing since has shaken that conviction.

I walked on to Divisional Headquarters at the same pace I had used since I started to ascend from the noisy beach to this sage-green solitude; I felt curiously invulnerable, for the self-confidence or vanity of the artist had by now decided he had not outlived his capacity for valuable work. The shells continued to whinny past; now and then one presumably nearer to myself seemed positively to neigh, while others farther off seemed to give the same kind of sibilant chirrup that goldfinches utter in their dipping flight toward some distant paradise of thistledown. At the moment of achieving that comparison the hell of a bang went off quite close and made me jump, and in spite of my reflections on destiny set me running for about a hundred yards. I might have gone on running all the way to Divisional Headquarters had I not sighted a long double line of mules with men in shirt sleeves moving about their business. There was another bang, at which all the mules started to fling their hindlegs in the air. I hurried on, thinking I would as lief be hit by a shell as by the hoof of a mule. After another quarter of a mile of walking in a style that would have disqualified me in a walking race I reached the outskirts of a small olive-grove, and seeing a man in shirt-sleeves strolling along with two buckets I called out to ask him where exactly Divisional Headquarters were. For answer he sat down abruptly in a bush. I thought he had tripped over something until I found he had been hit in the forearm by a shrapnel bullet.

"These Turks are proper blighters, sir," he observed, clicking his tongue reproachfully at the wound. "But this don't mean Alex. Or I don't think so," he added, yet with a note of optimism in his voice as the blood gushed encouragingly.

A minute or two later I was saluting in the entrance of General Paris's[1] dug-out.

"You'd better come inside," said a burly, florid man with a white moustache, who was sitting at a camp-table some two yards into the earth. "A fellow was hit in the foot yesterday just where you're standing now."

After I got back to G.H.Q. Colonel Ward was doubtful of being able to invent any work for me when I presented myself in the ship's gym-

[1] The late Major-General Sir Archibald Paris, K.C.B., R.M.A.

nasium where I branch of G.H.Q. was housed until we went ashore on May 31st. It was George Lloyd who solved the problem by handing over the Intelligence Summary which he had not kept up to date since the beginning of the month; that meant an abstract of all the information about the enemy which reaches the Intelligence of a General Staff during a campaign. It was dull work, and when Deedes came back from the Peninsula I was glad to start the compilation of a list of suspects and hand the summary to somebody else.

On Whit Monday, May 24th, I went over to Anzac, where there was a truce of eight hours for the Turks to bury their dead. While the preliminaries were being discussed in a tent on the beach by officers of high rank on both sides, all of them a little more anxious than usual to uphold the dignity of their respective nations, a ludicrous incident occurred. The flap of the tent at the back was suddenly lifted and an Australian or New Zealand batman put his head through to call out in a voice of indignant contempt:

"Heh! Have any of you effers pinched my effing kettle?"

On that damp hot airless morning I landed with Major Jack Churchill from the torpedo-boat on a narrow beach running along the base of the steep towering cliffs. As we turned the corner and started to walk up the Valley of Death a stretcher came rapidly past, on which I was horrified to recognise, with head thrown back and mouth agape stertorously breathing, the prostrate body of my old friend Harry Pirie-Gordon, with whom I had shared rooms at 43 High Street, Oxford; he was suffering from acute ptomaine poisoning and was being hurried away to a hospital ship. It was a tremendous shock to meet like this a man whom I had known intimately since we were eighteen but of whose presence out here I was completely unaware until I saw his body sweep past me in the swirl of that crowded narrow beach.

It had been hot enough down by the water's edge; the further we penetrated up the Valley of Death the hotter it became. Almost to the very top the steep slopes were riddled with dug-outs, some as apparently inaccessible as sand-martins' holes in the face of a quarry. Outside a dug-out beside the path a couple of tall Australians were sitting with nothing on but shorts. One of them was holding up the pannikin that held his restricted allowance of water.

"Now, if I was an effing canary," he was murmuring pensively, "I might have an effing bath in this."

The splendid appearance of these Australian troops had become a commonplace of war-correspondent journalism, but a splendid appearance had seemed to introduce somehow an atmosphere of the parade-ground. Such litheness and powerful grace did not suggest the parade-ground; their beauty, for it really was heroic, should have been celebrated in hexameters, not headlines. As a child I used to pore for hours over those illustrations of Flaxman for Homer and Virgil which simulated the effect of ancient pottery. There was not one of those glorious young men who might not himself have been Ajax or Diomedes, Achilles or Hector. Their almost complete nudity, their tallness and majestic simplicity of line, their rose-brown flesh burnt by the sun and purged of all grossness by the ordeal through which they were passing, all these united to create something as near to absolute beauty as I shall ever hope to see in this world. The dark glossy green of the arbutus leaves made an incomparable background for those shapes of heroes, and the very soil had taken on the same tawny rose as that living flesh; one might have fancied that the dead had stained it to this rich warmth of apricot.

On and on we walked. Major Jack Churchill was setting a cracker of a pace. He was a beefy man, and by now his round cheeks were wet and as crimson as the cistus flowers in the scrub. At last, dripping with sweat, we reached an almost perpendicular cliff up which it was difficult enough to scramble by that narrow zigzag of sticky mud with only a cane. What it must have been for men in full equipment to storm the face of that cliff at the bayonet's point . . . or for wounded men and stretcher bearers to descend . . .

Somebody turned round to offer me a cigar.

"You'd better light up this."

As I paused for a moment to wonder why I should exhaust by smoking what wind I had left, the smell of death floated over the ridge above and settled down upon us, tangible it seemed and clammy.

Along the top of the ridge were the trenches of Quinn's Post, with the Turkish trenches hardly twenty yards beyond. I clambered up on the parapet to stare at the forbidden land which rolled away in grey-green bosky undulations as far as the eye could reach. In the foreground was a narrow stretch of level scrub along which flags were stuck at intervals and a line of sentries, Australians and Turks, faced one another . . . and everywhere Turks digging and digging graves for some four thousand of their countrymen who had been putrefying in heaps along this narrow front for nearly a month of warm May air.

"You've got your foot in an awkward place," one of the men in the front trench called up to me. Looking down, I saw squelching up from the ground on either side of my boot like a rotten mangold the deliquescent green and black flesh of a Turk's head.

In that Whit week a German submarine arrived off Gallipoli. On Wednesday H.M.S. *Triumph* was torpedoed, and on the following day H.M.S. *Majestic*. Ellis Ashmead-Bartlett was in the latter; he lost his kit and went back to England to get a fresh one and poison Fleet Street with his tales about the muddle that was being made of the Gallipoli campaign. Sir Ian Hamilton, who hoped he had seen the last of Ashmead-Bartlett, asked if I would like to take on his job as official Eyewitness. I told him I should prefer to stay as I was if it meant giving up my commission. He said there was no question of giving up my commission and telegraphed to Lord Kitchener that he had appointed me to be official Eyewitness pending the decision of the Newspaper Proprietors' Association whether they would keep me or send out another correspondent. He was not prepared to have Ashmead-Bartlett back.

Sir Ian told me to have a talk with Maxwell,[1] who in addition to acting as official Censor and running the O I Mess was editing a daily sheet called *The Peninsula Press* which was served out to the troops as a supposed tonic. He was a veteran war correspondent and had been with the Japanese in the Russo-Japanese war. He was a self-important little man, more like Tweedledum than anybody I have seen except the picture of Tweedledee. As soon as he heard my news his wattles reddened.

"Sir Ian should realise," said Maxwell, "that he cannot behave in this high-handed way. The Newspaper Proprietors will strongly resent having an amateur foisted upon them in this way. Why did he not consult me before he took this extraordinary step? This will do him a great deal of harm with the Press. And I'm afraid it may be rather unpleasant for you."

"Why don't you go and explain this to Sir Ian, Maxwell? Perhaps he'll ask you to act as correspondent. Only don't suggest that I should edit your *Dardanelles Driveller*."

The poor Newspaper Proprietors had to put up with my amateurish efforts in two despatches before an arrangement was reached by which Ashmead-Bartlett came back with two other correspondents. One of these was H. W. Nevinson; I dip my pen to salute him with a sense of privilege in having seen that paladin in action.

My first despatch was about the Battle of the Fourth of June; I print it as an appendix.[2]

During that month I corrected the proofs of *Guy and Pauline*. Somebody suggested that the least return I could make for the trouble the General Staff had taken over my punctuation was to dedicate the book to them. I went to Sir Ian Hamilton, feeling a little nervous beforehand about the way he might receive the proposal, to ask leave to inscribe the book to him and the Staff. He accepted the dedication in the kindest

[1] The late Captain Sir William Maxwell, K.B.E.
[2] Appendix A.

way and contrived to make me fancy, whatever were his own vexed thoughts at that time of endless anxiety, that the suggestion pleased him. Two or three reviewers were to find that dedication a bit of showing off on my part. Well, well . . .

About the time I was sending off those proofs I had a letter from Henry James:

> 21 Carlyle Mansions,
> Cheyne Walk, S.W.
> *June 18th 1915*

My dear Monty,

All this while I have remained shamefully in your debt for interesting news, and I am plunged deeper into that condition by your admirable report from the Dardanelles in this a.m.'s Times. I am a backward being, alas, in these days when so much is forward; our public anxieties somehow strike for me at the roots of letter-writing, and I remain too often dumb, not because I am not thinking and feeling a thousand things, but exactly because I am doing so to such intensity. You wrote me weeks ago that you had finished your new novel—which information took my breath away (I mean by its windlike rush)—and now has come thus much of the remainder of the adventure for which that so grandly liberated you and which I follow with the liveliest participation in all your splendid sense of it and profit of it. I confess I take an enormous pleasure in the fact of the exposure of the sensitive plate your imagination, your tremendous attention, to all these wonderful and terrible things. What impressions you are getting, verily—and what a breach must it all not make with the course of history you are practising up to the very eve. I rejoice that you finished and snipped off, or tucked in and wound up, something self-contained there—for how coould you ever go back to it if you hadn't?—under that violence of rupture with the past which makes me ask myself what will have become of all that material we were taking for granted, and which now lies there behind us like some vast damaged cargo dumped upon a dock and unfit for human purchase or consumption. I seem to fear that I shall find myself seeing your recently concluded novel as through a glass darkly—which, however, will not prevent my immediately falling upon it when it appears; as I assume, however, that it is not now likely to do before the summer's end—by which time God knows what other monstrous chapters of history won't have been perpetrated! What I most want to say to you, I think, is that I rejoice for you with all my heart in that assurance of health which has enabled you to gird yourself and go forth.

If the torrid south has always been good for you there must be no amount of it that you are now not getting—though I am naturally reduced, you see, to quite abjectly and helpless and incompetent supposition. I hang about you at any rate with all sorts of vows and benedictions. I feel that I mustn't make remarks about the colossal undertaking you are engaged in beyond saying that I believe with all my heart in the final power of your punch. As for our news here the gist of that is that we are living with our eyes on you and more and more materially backing you. My comment on you is feeble, but my faith absolute, and I am, my dear Monty, your more than ever faithful old

Henry James

P.S. I have your address, of many integuments, from your mother, but feel rather that my mountain of envelopes should give birth to a livelier muse.

To my mother he had written from Carlyle Mansions on June 8th:

Dear Virginia Compton,

I thank you very kindly for your luminous statement of Monty's complicated accessibility. I shall follow your indications to the letter—that is for the letter— and I meanwhile rejoice in what you tell me of your tidings of him and of his tone and condition. These and his whole undertaking do him the greatest honour and I feel well nigh as proud of him as you and his Father must be. The beauty is, too, that we shall have it all from him (D.V.) in some admirable work of images. For myself, the hideous interest of the general situation sustains me almost as much as the constantly renewed horror beats down yours ever

Henry James

Reluctantly I pass over the details of what for me was that enthralling summer. I was on the Peninsula at H.Q. of the Eighth Army Corps commanded by the unforgettable Hunter-Bunter.[1] Here I wrote my second despatch as official Eyewitness. Then Ashmead-Bartlett came back and I was relieved of a task I had never wanted. I dealt with Ashmead-Bartlett in *Gallipoli Memories*, but I cannot resist re-telling one incident. I was on my way with some despatches to Army Corps Head-quarters. The shrapnel started, but I was not in the mood to be frightened by it; it was only when I reached General Hunter-Weston's camp that I began to feel some qualms. There was not a living creature in sight. Evidently a bombardment by that infernal Asiatic gun was expected. I waited, embarrassed by the silence and emptiness and wondering with a perceptibly increasing woolliness about the knees which way to turn for cover. Just as I was preparing to dive into the first hole I could find and escape from those big shells the head of Carter, Hunter-Bunter's A.D.C., rose slowly and cautiously from the ground almost at my feet. Save that his countenance was as always cheerful and ruddy he might have been a figure in Dante's *Inferno*.

"Oh, it's you, Mackenzie," he exclaimed. "We thought it was Ashmead-Bartlett, and we didn't want to ask him to lunch."

He shouted jovially, and from other dug-outs emerged the relieved faces of the Army Corps Staff.

Deedes sent me over to Tenedos to organize a cutting-out expedition by Greek irregulars in an attempt to silence that nine-inch Turkish gun.

[1] The late Lt.-General Sir Aylmer Hunter-Weston, K.C.B.

I was glad indeed to see again that island beloved by Apollo, which with Imbros was disgracefully handed over to the Turks in 1920 and is now profaned by being called Bozcaada. I had a wonderful time with "Kiddy" Loring,[1] who had commanded the *Ocean* when she was sunk in March during the attempt to force the Narrows. He was now Governor of Tenedos.

"The finest little fellow God ever made," said Jack Higgins to me. Higgins had been surgeon in the *Ocean* and was a brother of Kevin O'Higgins, the strong man of the Irish Free State Government, who was assassinated by the Republicans.

Jack Higgins had to deal with one of my acute attacks of pain and after trying every analgesic in his stock he had decided that morphine was the only alleviation, giving me a note to this effect which I was to show to any doctor when necessary.

Soon after I left Tenedos Loring was given command of H.M.S. *Albion*. In November he would be writing to me:

You heard of course that Tenedos is no longer ruled by a British Governor— Well, since the poetry of our life there was wrecked I do not grudge the French their possession, but the memory of it all is still green.

And for me some fifty years later the memory of those days I spent with "Kiddy" Loring is still green.

In July I was sent to Mytilene to start a rumour that we intended to make a landing by Smyrna; the idea was to keep Turkish troops away from Suvla, where our landing was planned for the first week of August. I was to enquire about possible camping sites for 40,000 troops, look for water, enquire about food and fuel, and perhaps about suitable guides for the Smyrna district. Of those magical days and nights on Lesbos I have written at length in *Gallipoli Memories*. I was told to put up an extra pip to lend some probability to my mission.

Heathcote-Smith,[2] who had been Vice-Consul at Smyrna when war broke out, was now in charge of all espionage as Vice-Consul of Mytilene. He was not unnaturally staggered when I told him in strictest confidence why I had arrived in Mytilene. Words for the folly of soldiers in sending somebody as ignorant of the country and language as myself on such a mission left him with nothing but indignant gasps. The final proof of such folly came when I told him I felt I ought to let the Nomarch know what I was doing in Mytilene. The Nomarch was a bitter enemy of Venizelos, he declared, and would certainly warn the pro-German Royalists in Athens of what was going on.

As this was just what I wanted, I insisted, and I can see now the

[1] The late Vice-Admiral G. K. Loring, C.B.
[2] The late Sir Clifford Heathcote-Smith, K.B.E.

expression of despair on dear Heathcote's face when he heard me "blowing the gaff" in that great Genoese castle to that little Nomarch with a pasty porous face, who said he must go to Athens next day and let M. Venizelos know about the outrageous breach of neutrality that was contemplated.

"Now you've done it," said Heathcote-Smith when we left the castle.

"Yes," I said humbly. "I'm sorry I didn't listen to your advice, Heathcote."

The Nomarch went to Athens and told Venizelos what we were preparing to do. Venizelos went round to the British Legation to remonstrate with the Minister and beg Sir Francis Elliot to let him know beforehand about such British intentions. The British Minister sent an indignant telegram to the Foreign Office. Sir Edward Grey protested to Lord Kitchener about military plans being made without reference to the Foreign Office. Lord Kitchener sent a rocket to Sir Ian Hamilton to ask him what he thought he was playing at. Wyndham Deedes explained to Sir Ian about my mission to Mytilene and Sir Ian was so pleased with the strength of the rumour I had started that he decided to come to Mytilene himself in the cruiser *Chatham* with George Lloyd and inspect the troops of the Tenth (Irish) Division who were diverted from Mudros in the transports *Andania* and *Alaudia*. Luckily they were missed by a German submarine which, thanks to the rumour, had been waiting for them off Port Iero in Lesbos.

Sir Ian congratulated me on the success of my rumour-spreading.

"But I'm afraid I shan't be able to mention you in my despatch," he said. "I've made a rule that none of you temporary officers will be mentioned in my despatches. It's not fair, you know, to the professionals."

However, I should one day have the satisfaction of reading in the book written by Liman von Sanders, the German General, that he had been perplexed what to do about rumoured landings at Smyrna and Aivalik; there had not been a glimmer of a notion that Suvla was our objective.

When I returned to G.H.Q. some of the generals of the three Divisions of Kitchener's Army were at lunch. At that lunch Brigadier-General Reed, V.C., who was Sir Frederick Stopford's C.R.A., was holding forth almost truculently on the folly of the plan of operations drawn up by the General Staff. He was not going to advance a single yard until all the Divisional Artillery was ashore.

"Stopford, Sitwell, a Brigade-Major called Bask and a broken Reed of a C.R.A. It sounds ominous."

Little did I realise when I made that crack to young Val Braithwaite how bitterly prophetic it was.

In spite of a bad go of dysentery coupled with cystitis, the latter including an unpleasant operation by lantern-light when the sand blowing into the tent put one catheter after another out of action by sticking to the vaseline, I wrote a long letter to Faith on August 9th:

> *It has been a day of disappointments. The IXth Army Corps failed to push on . . . Sir Ian went off to curse the General commanding . . . he actually let his men bathe when by an effort the Peninsula could have been straddled. It's really heartrending. We still hope they'll get to a certain ridge, but there is no news, and in military operations no news is bad news. . . . The Australian and New Zealand casualties are about 6000; they have done splendidly.*

> *Later*
> *Still no good news of the IXth Army Corps. I'm afraid they've ruined the show. It's absolutely damnable. Guy Dawnay was almost weeping when he came back from Suvla to-day. There were only 800 Turks and we had more than 15,000 men. They actually bathed and George Brodrick told me that on one beach, whenever a shell burst within 400 yards, all the men lay down. If this is Kitchener's Army (and the best three Divisions at that) give me the good old Territorials. . . . Hunter-Weston has been invalided home. If he had commanded that Army Corps we should have had the Bulair lines by now. . . . There were forty ships with their guns pointing at the Anafarta ridge, and the General wouldn't advance because there had been no artillery preparation. He had been reading about artillery preparation in France, and his men were digging themselves in 300 yards from the shore. There was the chance of open fighting, there was no need of artillery preparation; there were no Turks to fire at, and the aeroplanes said only three guns, which could have been captured. It's a tragedy.*

> *August 10th*
> *Feeling pretty rotten. I've done a cross reference index raisonné of 370 names of suspects to-day.*

> *August 12th*
> *No grouse except a mental one. Some sickness in O to-day. A Brigade-Major called Bask had wired his Brigadier:*
> *"Two Turkish shrapnel burst over the battalion this morning. Glad to report that battalion kept quite calm and there were no casualties."*

I wonder what they would have said to this telegram at Lancashire Landing!

That twelfth of August was to be a critical day for my future. I had finished some pages of I-b stuff and was taking them across to the office tent to be typed out, when, in the short space between it and the tent in which I worked, I met Sir Ian face to face as he was hurrying across probably to consult the C.G.S. about a cable from Lord K. to ask him why he could not ginger up the Tenth and Eleventh Divisions! I had saluted and was passing on when he stopped me.

"You're looking very ill, Mackenzie."

"I'm not absolutely fit, sir."

"The usual trouble out here?"

"Yes, sir."

"You're looking wretchedly ill," he repeated. "I'll tell you what you'd better do. You'd better go to Athens for the week-end. The *Imogen* leaves to-night. Take the whole of next week. I dare say Sir Francis Elliot will ask you to stay with him out at Kephissia. Do you no end of good. I don't want to lose another of you young writers."

With this allusion to the death of Rupert Brooke, he hurried on.

Had I left the tent a couple of seconds later, I should not have met Sir Ian face to face like that and I should not have gone to Athens that week-end. I was not two seconds later, and so out of those two grains of mustard seed grew like a mustard tree the next two years of my life.

After dinner that night I walked down with Patrick Shaw-Stewart to the landing-pier. He was on his way to the Rest Camp on the other side of Kephalo beach. That brilliant Fellow of All Souls had taken advantage of being in the Royal Naval Division to grow a long pointed red beard. We sat there talking about Oxford and books. He told me how much Rupert Brooke had been looking forward to *Guy and Pauline*.

"And Charles Lister is always asking when your next book is coming out and to hurry up with it so that he can read it before he's killed," he added.

But Charles Lister was killed before *Guy and Pauline* reached Helles.

The young moon had set and we sat there in a cool gusty wind talking about Oxford, of Ronnie Knox and the Grenfells and "Oc" Asquith and many another, the thought of whom glowed in the darkness. Patrick Shaw-Stewart would command his battalion and be killed in France two years later. I should live on to hear Rupert Brooke and his peers sneered at as romantics by the prematurely weaned young sucking-pigs of the next generation.

The *Imogen*, which had been the yacht of the British Embassy at Constantinople, was commanded by Captain Potts, a brother-in-law of Lord Northcliffe. He was the strongest man I have known and could tear a pack of cards twice across with his fingers. The other passengers were Commander W. F. Sells, the Naval Attaché of our Legation in Athens,[1] and Lieutenant H. A. Simpson, R.N., who, although only twenty-one, commanded a torpedo-boat. Apart from his professional abilities he had a tremendous zest for life, a sense of humour, and to the

[1] Vice-Admiral W. F. Sells, C.M.G., R.N.

gaiety of youth he added sympathy and charm. My meeting with
"Bill" Sells was the beginning of an association which was never marred
by a single misunderstanding throughout two topsy-turvy and difficult
years, and of a friendship that has lasted until to-day.

I was feeling pretty rotten on that voyage, but at dawn on August
14th, too much on fire with the thought of at last beholding Greece to
care about illness or pain, I dragged myself up on deck, and was
granted the perfect expression of a lifetime's dream.

The *Imogen* was passing below Cape Sounion and there, white and
light as a sea-bird on the cliff's edge, I saw the marble columns of the
Temple of Poseidon, a legend-haunted world of famous mountains
beyond. I stood there and watched in a rapture the white columns grow
warm as ivory when the great sun came glancing up out of the sea. Two
or three hours later the *Imogen* berthed at Phaleron. The first view of the
Acropolis glittering in the morning sunlight four miles away set my
pulses racing again, for it too was fulfilling the fancies of years in a way
I had not dared to hope would ever really happen; and to the Acropolis
was added the first vision of the hill Lykabetos, the shape and height of
which I had never pictured to myself. The glory of the Acropolis has
always been so bright that the value of Lykabetos to that classic landscape has not been sufficiently emphasized.

In spite of the dysentery and cystitis I managed to have two good
days with Simpson in Athens before Dr Aravantinos, to whose care I
had been recommended by George Rendel,[1] then a Third Secretary in
the Legation, insisted on my spending a fortnight in a clinic, eating
nothing but boiled rice, to which after a week was added boiled chicken.
With such a diet and without even as much stimulant as a cup of coffee
I did not think it surprising my temperature should remain two degrees
below normal; it would not have surprised me if it had been five below
normal.

By now I had made up my mind that there was no chance of our
reaching Constantinople before next spring and the prospect of winter
in a tent at Kephalo was not encouraging. It might end in my being
sent to Alexandria in a hospital ship and spending the rest of the war in
a Cairo office. I had conceived as strong a prejudice against Egypt as
the Jews had; somehow I must find a good reason for being kept in
Athens through the winter.

Our Intelligence in Athens was centred in Major Samson, who since
February 1915 had been obtaining military intelligence about the
Turks under cover of administering a fund for the relief of refugees from
Turkey and Asia Minor. Samson's mysterious initial was R, not V as I
called him in my *Athenian Memories*. He had been Military Consul in

[1] Sir George Rendel, K.C.M.G.

Erzerum before the war and was a devout lover of the Old Turks. He worked under C or Captain Mansfield Cumming, R.N.,[1] the head of the secret service, M.I. 1 (C), who was responsible for espionage and in neutral countries counter-espionage, deriving his funds from the Foreign Office. Elsewhere counter-espionage was under K or Colonel Vernon Kell[2] of M.I.5, whose funds came from the War Office.

At this date I had no idea who C was. All I heard from Major Samson was that he grudged money for counter-espionage, which only fed his rival K. Certainly the counter-espionage in Athens was at present a joke, run by Major Monreal, a Regular Army officer of Maltese extraction, under R. It had been my job at G.H.Q. to extract as much sense as possible from R's telegrams about suspects, out of which I had made that index raisonné which I was compiling after Suvla.

If every little biography had been as colourful as that of Captain Hawkyard Hinde it would have been a more amusing task.

" 'Captain' Hawkyard Hinde, left Birmingham in 1897 where he was employed as a clerk at Messrs——, brass-founders. Suspected of I.D.B. in the Transvaal. Expelled from Pretoria. Smuggled ivory from Abyssinia. Arrested for an unnatural offence at Durban. Involved in several frauds in the U.K. Served sentence of three years' penal servitude. Served sentence in Queensland for stealing opals. Expelled from Tripoli by Italians during Turko-Italian war for suspected espionage. Ran a Seaman's Rest House in Smyrna. Arrived in Anzac as Interpreter. Arrested and sent to Malta for the remainder of the war."

Alas, most of the entries in that list of mine were as dull as a directory. When R visited me at the clinic I suggested that if Deedes could provide £150 a month I should set to work seriously on counter-espionage in Athens. R, who was anxious to get rid of Major Monreal, said he would support such a suggestion.

Sir Francis Elliot, who came to see me three or four times, thought I might do a good job for propaganda in Greece by acting as liaison with the editors of the Venizelist Press. He suggested this to the Foreign Office, but they had already appointed Gerald Talbot.[3]

Another visitor was Admiral Mark Kerr, who was head of the British Naval Mission but would be leaving Athens in a week or two for a Command. He was anxious to make me grasp King Constantine's point of view and was eloquent on the subject of his bad treatment by us. I am not going to argue the case for or against King Constantine in *My Life and Times*. When *Greek Memories* was prosecuted in 1932 two

[1] The late Captain Sir Mansfield Cumming, K.C.M.G., C.B., R.N.
[2] The late Maj.-Gen. Sir Vernon Kell, K.B.E., C.B.
[3] The late Commander Sir Gerald Talbot, K.C.V.O., C.M.G., R.N.V.R.

serial translations of it were published by the Royalist and Liberal Press to show how well justified both sides had been. I ask for no better testament to the fairness with which I presented their opposite points of view.

Admiral Kerr's indignation about the treatment of King Constantine was strongly supported by our Military Attaché.[1] Argument with "Tommy" Cunninghame was a difficult business because he heard little of what was said to him, and of what he did hear he usually barked a scornful contradiction. He was the pragmatical Lowland laird whose portrait might look down from the walls of an old Ayrshire house. Centuries of struggles with the English; years of dusty theology from which the habit of disputation had remained; a readiness to feel himself affronted, which seemed an inheritance from the affronts offered to Scotsmen who came south with James VI, had combined to make a man of long and illustrious lineage, with much more brain than the average Rifleman, present himself to the world as a querulous, obstinate, and disappointed soldier. His wife was a tall woman whose dark beauty seemed out of place with her fondness for fox-hunting. Unable to hunt out here, she had become absorbed in politics and believed she was able to undo some of the harm that in her opinion the attitude of the Legation toward the King, the Court, and the Greek General Staff was doing.

Lady Cunninghame was another of my visitors and preached fervently the gospel of keeping in with the King. Sir Francis had been here too long; he looked at things too much from the point of view of a native. It was a mistake to identify ourselves with what was merely a political party. The King could not help feeling this. Only last week he had said quite bitterly that the members of the British Legation seemed to think they were election agents for Venizelos. Her only reward for trying to convey this information to the Legation was to be told that Sir Francis objected to ladies always going in and out of the Chancery.

I was as ignorant at this moment of Court intrigue as young Fabrice del Dongo, and had no Count Mosca to give me the essence of Stendhal's profound and lifelong study of the ways of the world. I was only too ready to fancy that Lady Cunninghame spoke with the wit and wisdom of the Duchess Sanseverina in that immortal guide to worldliness, that supreme novel of manners, *La Chartreuse de Parme*. It was flattering to be told that my arrival in Athens had created curiosity. I did not know then that in a Balkan capital the arrival of a commercial traveller at a time of political excitement was capable of producing the wildest speculation. My sense of the ridiculous was at this moment lying dormant in the trappings of romance.

[1] The late Col. Sir Thomas Montgomery-Cunninghame, Bt., D.S.O.

While I was still in the clinic a letter came from R. C. Gunstone (Gunner), the old steward of Magdalen J.C.R., which filled the white rooms with Oxford ghosts.

August 9th 1915

My dear Sir,
    At last you have sent me an address I can use. . . .
    I do not go often into College. Mr C. R. Carter (Bursar) sent an invitation to the Wife and I to go to Service in the College Chapel in commemoration of all ours who have fallen in the War. We went, it was a very solemn affair. I could not sleep that night for thinking of all those fine young fellows I had parted from only a short time before. Over thirty names read out, and since then many have to be added to the list. . . .
    Mr Benecke is the only Don up, the place is deserted, only 30 undergraduates out of our usual 150 came up last term. I think it will be worse in October. I went to see my old room the other day. "Oh my," what a change. The wall-paper you mentioned[1] (as brownish-yellow) is all gone, it is no longer like an office but a Chocolate shop in Bond Street, it may be better? But the old charm of the place is gone for ever.
    I have been looking at your portrait [postcard] you look ill. . . . Day after day I find Magdalen men in the list of killed and wounded. . . . How is "Sinister Street" going? The Pre and Lady Warren are away, the last time I saw him he was very lame and old. I still keep very fit for my age. The Wife is in splendid form, she joins with me in wishing you a safe return. And with many thanks for your letter and P.C.

I am, dear Sir,
Ever yours faithfully,
Gunner

Enclosed in the old man's letter was a half-sheet of that so familiar College note-paper on one side of which Gunner had copied for me what may have been the only poem he had ever written.

Magdalen College,
Oxford.
Deserted
No sound across the Cloistered quad
As daylight fades away,
No laughter borne upon the air,
No light with cheerful ray.

Where are the sounds of long ago
That echoed through these halls?

[1] In *Sinister Street* when writing of Venner.

Nought but silence now is found
Among the old grey walls.

The heavy doors look sinister,
Deserted is the stair,
Stilled are the steps for evermore
That used to enter there.

On the back of this half-sheet the old man had written the names of some of the killed—about forty already, a dozen of whom were contemporaries of my own. The white room in the clinic was thronged for a moment with shapes and rich with colours . . . Leander pink, the scarlet and lilies of the Magdalen cox, Authentic blazers, vivid Rambler ties, the black and white of the Soccer team . . . and the white room again.

I had received by the same mail a list of Oxford men now serving. Magdalen was third with 670, Christ Church and New College being first with 700. But then those two colleges could count on an average of 300 undergraduates and Magdalen on no more than 160, so that proportionately Magdalen was far ahead of any. Such a figure as 670 meant that practically every Magdalen man for twenty years was in the Navy or the Army. In this letter of Gunner's I heard for the first time of the deaths of many old friends. With some bitterness of spirit I feel that if the war had come to an end in that autumn of 1915, as well it might but for that *insurmountable "no"*, the sacrifice which those contemporaries of mine had made would hardly have been appreciated. It was not until the material discomfort of the war began to affect the civil population that there was induced a state of mind which was to respond to the obscene horrors of post-war books written with a self-pity that expressed the self-pity of their readers. Those who volunteered to give their lives and gave them without complaint were not praised in such books, lest a hint of admiration should render to war one tattered shred of the glory that was once believed to enfold it. There may have been nothing heroic in the readiness of those young men of 1914 and 1915 to volunteer. There may have been nothing behind that impulse except a desire to do the right thing. However, since none of them considered himself a hero and since none of them made a book about his sufferings, those still alive in the twittering 'twenties might have spared them at least as much respect as they gave to writers by whose sufferings some of us might have felt more pitifully moved if they did not seem to have lavished all the pity in the world upon themselves.

The morning after I emerged from the clinic at the beginning of September Eddie Keeling arrived in Athens, having been posted to the

C

Legation in Nish. He told me that Princess Nicolas commanded him to bring me to tea at Kephissia. I protested I had nothing to wear but a ready-made suit I had bought in Athens. Keeling was firm. Her Imperial Highness had expressed a clear desire to make my acquaintance, and go I should. So I went, feeling as timorous and not nearly so well dressed as the White Rabbit on his way to the party of another Duchess. I need not have worried; the grace, the charm and the beauty of the Grand Duchess Helena, a first cousin of the Tsar, would have made the folds of that ready-made suit unnoticeable. When we were sitting in that room in the Kephissia villa where the sunlight was tempered by great pine-trees and civilization seemed to have expressed an ultimate perfection of type in the great lady who was our hostess, two little girls called Olga and Marina came in with their governess, full of an adventure they had had in meeting a cow somewhere during their walk.

Two days later Keeling went northward to encypher some of those desperate telegrams for help from Serbia and then to suffer the ordeal of the retreat as escort of the British nurses; his last behest to me had been to be sure that a pair of riding-breeches I was to get cleaned for him in Athens were sent on to Nish promptly. I did not hear from him until the following May, when he wrote from our embassy in Rome:

After unspeakable horrors in Serbia, I am now happily established here. . . . My breeches arrived just before the Bulgars, and were much admired by the 150 virgins whom I conducted intact across the mountain passes of Montenegro and Albania.

During that fortnight after I came out of the clinic I made up my mind I would transform that comic apology for counter-espionage in Athens into efficiency. Luckily R found an excuse to get rid of Major Monreal when the latter nearly gave him a heart attack by telling him he had arranged for somebody to be killed. It was poppycock of course, but the Major rejoined his regiment and I now had for my Number Two Charles Tucker, to whom I took an immediate liking. His father had a sanitary engineer's business in Constantinople but was at present a refugee in Athens with the rest of his family, of which Charles was the eldest. Although he spoke Turkish, Greek and French as fluently as English there was nothing about Charles Tucker to suggest the Levantine Englishman. He was typically the Cockney business man. His cheeks were as pink as a wild rose; his full, fair moustache was Saxon to the last hair; there was not an angle in his body. His main object in life was to feel that things were going smoothly; his defects sprang from the qualities that made him such a good companion. He was too pliant and too supple; a downright "no" would have saved him and me many a difficult moment during the next two years.

I went back to G.H.Q. exactly a month after I had left it and was depressed by the change of atmosphere. There seemed to have been a great deal of getting on one another's nerves since I had been absent. The social diphthong which had been created by the amalgamation of the Operations Mess and the Intelligence Mess had suffered a diæresis; instead of the big marquee where we all used to eat together the O people were in one small marquee, the I people in another. Although I felt guilty to have been enjoying myself so much during the past fortnight, my tales of the absurdities of Athenian counter-espionage in its present state were welcome and I was granted the sharpest of pleasures in the assurance of people I admired and loved being really glad to see me again. I had had several letters to tell me that my tales were missed, but paper cannot smile nor ink light up like the eyes of friends. Yet the dead hand of failure was heavy upon that camp at Kephalo.

Guy Dawnay had gone home at the end of August; but his brother-in-law, my old friend Robin Buxton, had come out to take up a job as Staff Captain. The shelling on the beach at Suvla was getting worse and worse. When he came back to Kephalo in the evening after his round of visits, the way he would be telling of how he had just failed to stop this or that shell used to sound like some mad inversion of a sportsman's return home, for, instead of having to excuse himself for missing his bird, he was the bird.

The day after I got back Sir Ian Hamilton sent word that I was to have tea with him and give him the news from Athens. I was shocked by the change in him this month had wrought. The disappointment of Suvla followed by days of uncertainty about the future of the Expedition had told heavily upon the Commander-in-Chief. That fly-blown arid little hut among the fretted shadows of a few starveling trees was become a prison. That poor impermanent little shelter, which was meant to be left behind here so soon as of no more importance than the dry pod of a locust-bean, had taken root. It was become immovable as the War Office itself. I did not know when I sat at tea with him that afternoon how near he was to receiving that fatal telegram from Lord Kitchener which announced the postponement of the promised new Divisions and foreshadowed the Salonika landing. It would be decyphered before dinner to-night.

Lord Bertie had just written in his Diary:

"There are rumours well-founded of a large French Expedition to the Eastern Mediterranean. I suppose that the 'political' General Sarrail will command it independently of Sir Ian Hamilton."

Deedes promised to maintain his monthly allowance of £150 for as long as he could, even if circumstances should take G.H.Q. to Egypt.

"Do you mean there is any thought of evacuating the Peninsula?" I exclaimed.

"It may be the only thing to do, but whatever happens Athens will become more and more important as a centre of enemy activities. If you take my advice you'll try to get your services definitely asked for by R. Then you could be seconded for service under the Foreign Office, and when the situation is clearer next spring we can get you back if you want to come back."

"Here?"

Deedes did not answer; but his long upper lip lengthened a little.

The night before I was to return to Athens in the *Imogen* General Braithwaite, the C.G.S., asked me to dine with him in the Operations Mess. About six o'clock I had that shuddering stab in the heel which portended a bad attack of sciatic neuralgia. By the time I sat down to dinner the tendons under my left knee were contracting in spasms of intolerable agony. I sat on through the meal, trying to amuse my hosts about Athens; but my face was growing greyer and greyer every moment, and my forehead was dripping.

"You're looking very seedy, Mackenzie," said the C.G.S. suddenly. "What's the matter?"

I gave up and retired from the table, muttering the silly excuses one does when fighting acute pain.

"You'd better lie down," General Braithwaite advised.

I stretched myself out on a wooden bench which ran along the side of the marquee and lay there, listening to the talk and feeling a nuisance.

Hare, the Doctor, was sent for and prescribed morphine; his last hypodermic syringe had been broken and he was still waiting for a new supply, so he had to give me a morphia pill instead, which he warned me would not work as quickly as an injection. General Braithwaite suggested I should be sent on board the *Imogen* as soon as possible, and about nine o'clock, when the bitter pill was still slowly dissolving under my tongue, two orderlies came with a stretcher and carried me down that sandy slope for the last time.

"This means being invalided out anyway," I muttered to myself.

Hare, who had come down to see me aboard the *Imogen*, agreed.

It was eleven o'clock before the morphia pill began to work, but although the pain was less I could not sleep. I opened a parcel which had been put with my kit and saw two copies of *Guy and Pauline*, which I started to read through and discovered a maddening misprint where a printer's reader had substituted "oilily" for "olidly". It was already light when at last I fell asleep, to be wakened by the noise of every gun in the harbour firing; G.H.Q. was being attacked by three German planes. Pain returned after the *Imogen* weighed anchor, and its obliterating egotism engrossed me for the rest of the day. At last the sickness of morphia was succeeded by the sickness caused by the rolling and plunging of a small pleasure yacht in a heavy sea. I was pitched out of my bunk several times and my leg resented it, but with daylight we ran into kinder waters and I escaped from the self-centred whirlwind of intense pain.

For a fortnight after that visit to G.H.Q. my leg behaved badly, but except during violent pain I was able to move about and recovery was hastened by new quarters in the British Archaeological School, which I owed to the Director, A. J. B. Wace, who himself was doing Chancery work at the Legation. Wace provided a delightful combination of great scholarship and worldly humour. He invited me to join him and "Willie" Erskine,[1] the Counsellor of the Legation, at lunch in the Director's house. That Mess of ours provided every day an opportunity to slip back out of the war into a civilized existence. The renown of Magdalen College in the 'nineties was greatest on the river, but with that pre-eminence of the oar went an attitude which made a Magdalen man of that decade as unmistakeable as a vintage wine; Erskine had belonged to that period.

The British School standing in its own garden above the glittering garish streets of Athens was as quiet as an Oxford quadrangle in the Long Vacation. The tranquil statues and viewless busts upon their pedestals had taken this house for their own; sharp was the reminder of art's length and life's brevity.

It was appropriate that R should hand over F. W. Hasluck to work with me at the British School, for he was the librarian of it, and summed up in himself the essence of its present abandonment. He was my chief mental consolation during the fever of 1916. On that index raisonné I started at G.H.Q. he built up a card index at which he worked on those figures who flitted like shadows across our inquisitiveness; it was a model of really fine scholarship. Hasluck's health grew worse throughout 1916; finally he had to go to Switzerland, where in 1920 he died in a sanatorium at the age of forty-two. I owed him a great debt. By the time Hasluck left us there were well over 12,000 cards; by the time I finished in September 1917 there were 23,000. I quote these figures to show the rate at which our work grew; the details of it may be read in my *Memories*.

At the beginning of October 1915 I received a long letter from Eddie

[1] The late The Hon. Sir William Erskine, K.C.M.G.

Marsh, now in the Duchy of Lancaster Office, from which I quote a few extracts:

I look on you with great pride as a sort of Marine godson and read your descriptions with enthusiasm . . . I'm about ⅓ through Guy and Pauline . . . so far it's one of the most delicious books I ever read. You have got hold of some heavenly minor characters . . . and your mise en scène is exquisite. . . .

I was very nearly wiped out by the Zep, or should have been if I'd been at home (in Gray's Inn), as bombs fell within a few yards on both sides of my rooms and smashed most of my windows. . . .

I'm having rather an unsatisfactory life just now, as there is very little to do, and I regret the time when I used to be at the Admiralty till 1 or 2 o'clock every night. Of course I must stick to Winston while he wants me, he has plenty to do, but not much that he can pass on to me. It's an awful waste of him, too. . . .

I'll tell you the only amusing story there has been lately—about the King visiting a hospital for wounded. One man was in a very bad state of nerves and suddenly hearing the K's voice talking to a patient in the next ward he flew into a panic and screamed "the Germans are on us, the Germans are on us".

What a waste indeed of a Winston Churchill in the Duchy of Lancaster Office!

The insensate muddle of the Near East that was being made by the Coalition Government was making us despair in Athens.

On October 7th a terrific thunderstorm accompanied by a shrieking wind and torrential rain broke over Athens; a few sentences from a letter written while the lightning was turning blue my room at the British School and while the thunder was crashing peal upon peal almost without a break may reveal the mood most of us were in.

The situation is desperate. The Germans have crossed the Danube at two points. The Bulgarians will attack the Serbian flank. Greece is paralyzed with fear . . . it looks as if we may have to leave at any moment . . . we are as near to ruin at this moment as ever during the war . . . the Bulgarians may attack our positions in Gallipoli . . . and a really dreadful disaster is imaginable . . . and yet these bloody optimists at home prattle of all going well . . . you can absolutely smell the lightning.

Two days before, Venizelos had resigned in despair at the inadequate force the Allies were sending to Salonika to meet the Bulgarian threat; and all through October Tucker and I were being pestered by R to discover German officers that were supposed to have arrived in Athens preparatory for the now mobilized Greek army's being put into the field against the Entente.

Poor R was getting into a more acute state of nerves all the time. He was worrying about the prospect of being kidnapped and tortured by the Young Turks. On November 4th I was down with a bad attack and I was still feeling pretty rotten when a week later R arrived about midnight in my bedroom at the British School.

"You will leave for Naples to-morrow morning at eleven o'clock, Z," he announced in a voice of portentous solemnity.

By this time Z had become my mysterious letter in the alphabet of the Secret Service.

I protested that I had been in bed for a week and could still hardly walk. Argument was useless; R had decided that the dissolution of the Greek Chamber had made it unsafe for any of the people in my organization to remain in Athens.

"And I want all your papers brought down to Academy Street by nine o'clock so that they can be burnt."

"Not the cards! Hasluck will go mad if you burn all our cards."

At last I managed to persuade R to let us leave the cards in the safe keeping of the Legation, and made one more attempt to get him to let me stay in Athens.

"Now, don't argue about it any more, there's a good fellow," said R. "I really must put you under orders to leave by the *Spetzai* to-morrow morning. In any case you have been overdoing yourself far too much since you came out of hospital, and a compulsory rest will do you good. And I want Hasluck to go with you."

The *Spetzai* was a typical steamer of the Eastern Mediterranean, with a dark and stuffy saloon out of which the cabins opened. I had telegraphed Faith, who was in London, to join me in Capri, but when we reached Naples she had not arrived. We just managed to catch the afternoon boat for Capri and reached the island about seven o'clock of a chill dank evening. Capri was in the depth of gloom, for the war had struck a mortal blow at the gay life of the island. Greetings from old friends were warm, but the cry was always "*O signore mio, che miseria! Questa bruta guerra quando si finirà?*" To complete the evening's depression the fire in the *salone* at Casa Solitaria smoked and poor Hasluck's cough was incessant.

The next day Faith arrived, and with a few lunch parties we tried to pretend it really was Capri again. One day my boatman Vincenzo came up to see me. This was his first leave from the Italian navy.

"*Ah, signore,*" he sighed, "you were right when you said in June last year that the murder of that Austrian would bring war to the world. How many times since have I thought about what you said that evening, though at the time I thought you were joking."

On November 26th a telegram came from Athens through the

Consul-General in Naples telling Hasluck and me to return as soon as possible; but it was the beginning of December before we were able to get a steamer. This was the *Athenai*, a sister ship of the *Spetzai*. The voyage to Messina was stormy. I was flung out of the upper bunk twice, and both of us were very sea-sick. By the time we reached Messina I was walking on white-hot spikes and had no heart to explore the place. Not that Messina offered any encouragement to sight-seeing; it was still a nightmare city of huts and façades, of rubbish heaps and jumbled masonry, the aftermath of the great earthquake.

As I was crossing the gang plank to go on board the *Athenai* one of the port officials shouted out and waved. He hurried along to tell me the *Spetzai* had just arrived with the news that she had been stopped by an Austrian submarine yesterday afternoon and that two British officers had been taken prisoner. We were no sooner out of harbour than the Captain came down to our cabin to say that if the *Athenai* were stopped by a submarine he should be obliged to hand me over at once. I had a sharp argument, Hasluck translating, and said I should resist arrest by shooting any of the enemy who came down the companion to take me. The Captain said such behaviour by me might lead to the submarine's sinking his ship. Finally he agreed to take the names of Hasluck and myself off the passenger list.

The voyage was much too rough for submarines to play any tricks. The Ionian was like the English Channel at its worst. That night was an inferno. I can still see the emaciated figure of Hasluck in his vest as he held on to the side of the bunk and tried to get into an overcoat to go in search of something to alleviate my pain. He was no longer sea-sick, but I was still retching from time to time. Presently Hasluck came back with a small bottle of laudanum which the Chief Officer happened to have as a souvenir of toothache. Sixty drops of laudanum on a lump of sugar was the most revolting meal a sea-sick creature could attempt. Ugh! For the next half-hour I played yearningly with the hope that a German submarine was soon going to sink the *Athenai* without warning. There was a story told of A. J. Balfour's crossing the Channel late in the war and asking what chance there was of being torpedoed. He was warmly assured that with the escort they had there was no chance at all. "Oh," said Balfour, "I'm sorry to hear that."

Yes, that laudanum had the same effect on me as the nightingale on Keats; it really was seeming rich to die.

We reached Patras early in the morning, a cold rain drenching down upon the dark deserted quays. Nothing I could say would stop dear Hasluck from dressing himself and going out to try to find a doctor who might give me some relief from pain. The *Athenai* waited for only an hour, and during that time he was unsuccessful. In the calmer water of the Gulf of Corinth I was able to sleep a little; by the time we reached the Piraeus I was much better.

Tucker was down at the quay, beaming; we drove directly to 3 Visarionos Street where Tucker had made arrangements for me and himself to live at present.

On going to the Legation I found that Lord Kitchener's visit had only confirmed King Constantine in his neutrality; the costly British retreat from the River Vardar in face of the invasion of Serbia from Bulgaria, the evacuation of Monastir on the southern border of Serbia, the occupation of Salonika as a base, and the imminence of new elections, had all taken a back place for the time in the news of the capture by that Austrian submarine of Colonel Napier, our late Military Attaché in Bulgaria, and Captain Stanley Wilson, M.P., a War Office Messenger, and not merely of the two officers but of the Legation mail bags as well. Poor R was nearly distraught, for among his despatches had been a list of all our agents in Constantinople. Later on, news had come that only one bag had been captured and that an American woman had taken charge of the others, refusing to deliver them up to our Embassy in Rome, refusing indeed to deliver them to anybody except Lord Kitchener himself in person.

When the *Spetzai* came back I sent down Tucker to see the captain and I wrote a confidential report of what had happened. As the *Spetzai* was passing out of the Gulf of Corinth into the Ionian Sea an Austrian submarine had fired a shot across the bows of the Greek steamer and indicated his intention to stop her. Colonel Napier had gone down calmly to his cabin and destroyed some papers; Captain Stanley Wilson had been in a state of nervous agitation and had flung a large bag overboard from the stern of the *Spetzai*; this bag had drifted about without sinking. The commander of the submarine had called across through a megaphone for the captain of the *Spetzai* to lower a boat and bring the passenger list. It was then sent back for Colonel Napier and Captain Wilson, who were told they must consider themselves prisoners of war, but were allowed to go back to the steamer to fetch their suit-cases. The captain had been much impressed by Colonel Napier's calm demeanour but obviously surprised by Captain Wilson's undignified agitation. It was while the two officers were packing their suit-cases that the commander of the submarine had noticed the floating bag and sent a boat to hook it up; there had been no search of the steamer. The American lady had stood over the two small heavily weighted crossed bags like a hen over her chickens.

Why Wilson had not flung these weighted confidential bags overboard was a puzzle only to be solved by attributing it to the state of his nerves. As a young man of twenty he had been the chief witness against

Sir William Gordon-Cumming in the Tranby Croft baccarat scandal of 1891. At G.H.Q. Kephalo, we had thought Stanley Wilson an unreliable chatterbox; his behaviour on that Greek steamer confirmed the belief I had already formed that his evidence against Gordon-Cumming was worthless.

In due course excerpts from the captured letters were published in the neutral Press, and the originals were sent by the Emperor Francis Joseph to King George V. In a letter to his mother, Lady Mar and Kellie, Erskine had written that the only solution of the Greek situation was to kick "Tino" off the throne. This letter was sent to the Foreign Office with an observation by King George to say that Mr Erskine should not be employed any longer. However, he was not moved from Athens till the end of 1916, when he became Counsellor at our Embassy in Rome, after which he went as Minister to Havana, then to Sofia, and finally to Warsaw. When the Poles made their Legation in London an Embassy the Foreign Office had to make Erskine an Ambassador in spite of that bad mark.

The Athens Chancery was in disgrace over the captured bag, and the amount of lead used thenceforth to weight Foreign Office bags left nothing to chance.

We were much amused in Athens when early in 1917 a crossed bag to Russia was captured in the North Sea. The contents were published in the neutral Press, among others a confidential letter from Lord Hardinge, the Permanent Under-Secretary, to Sir George Buchanan, our Ambassador in Petrograd, which began something like this:

Dear George,
These damned revolutionaries are going to spoil everything. . . .

This was embarrassing at a moment when we were pretending hard that we welcomed the Revolution.

The possibility of that list of agents having been captured finally shattered R's nerves. One night when Erskine, Sells and myself were discussing what my position would be in Athens if R decided to go to Alexandria, as softly and silently as the Boojum he vanished away.

Scares about the future were rife toward the close of 1915; one of the most persistent rumours was that the Germans intended to concentrate the whole force of the Turkish Empire upon an invasion of Egypt after driving the British troops at Gallipoli into the sea.

The authorities in Egypt began to get nervous about the ease with which agitators and spies were passing to and fro between Alexandria and the Piraeus. The High Commissioner asked if something could be done in Athens to regulate the passenger traffic. One day toward the end of that December Wace took me aside in the hall of the Legation to propose what he hoped might be a helpful plan and give him something positive to do. The suggestion was that he should examine personally all the applicants for Egypt, and if he was not satisfied with the *bona fides* of the intending traveller that he should be empowered to notify the various British Consuls that visas should not be granted. I was to supply him with the information he wanted about doubtful cases and to provide him with a clerical assistant.

One of our problems in Athens was what to do with the half-dozen or so of R's compromised agents from Constantinople, now useless but to whom we were paying a salary. I saw an opportunity of using them and managed to persuade Sir Francis Elliot to notify their names to the Greek police as members of an authorized Bureau of Information.

"In other words I am to tell the Consuls in my zone that they have no right or power to visé a passport without your permission, Mackenzie," he said to me drily when I put forward the plan.

"I wasn't proposing we do anything at present except about passports for Egypt. After all, sir, if the Commercial Department of the Legation can exercise absolute control over exports and imports between Egypt and Greece, why may not the Legation institute a department for controlling travel?"

We were lucky to have a Minister like Sir Francis Elliot who was not frightened of making exceptions or setting precedents; he agreed to this experiment in passport control. There was no separate room available for Wace in the Legation; he used to sit at a table in one of the corridors from which a trail of waiting applicants sometimes stretched right across the marble entrance hall and even out into the street. This crush of applicants became a nuisance. The staff of the Legation on their way to the Chancery found their odour almost overwhelming. Early in 1916 an opportunity arose to acquire commodious premises next door for what presently became the Intelligence Department of the British Legation, and not the least of its triumphs was the extraction of 200 francs a month from the Foreign Office toward the rent of those premises.

In the spring of 1916 a telegram from the Foreign Office announced that in accordance with the new passport regulations Lieutenant Compton Mackenzie was to be Military Control Officer in Athens.

To this Sir Francis Elliot asked:

What are the new passport regulations and what is a Military Control Officer?

The Foreign Office replied that by mistake the new regulations had been omitted from the bag but would be sent by the next bag. It added that the new regulations had been largely based on those already operating in Athens.

So from that practical and simple suggestion of Wace's about Egyptian passports sprang the control round the world which would serve as a cover for Intelligence, or more crudely espionage, and add to travel the annoyances still plaguing us to-day. When Franklin D. Roosevelt enunciated his four freedoms he omitted to include freedom of travel in times of peace. Alas, no insecticide has ever been discovered for the parasites of bureaucracy.

By the end of the year the financial problem of what was now a sub-bureau of R's Eastern Mediterranean Special Intelligence Bureau in Alexandria—E.M.S.I.B. for short—became acute. R was dependent on C, about whom we knew nothing except that he was head of the secret service. Sir Francis told me to write a full report of the Intelligence situation in Athens.

Luckily before R left I had got him to agree to our taking on Erskine's Sunbeam for £400. By swift action I also got hold of the Ford which had been at the disposal of our Consul in Canea. This was intended for service with the Commercial Department who got their funds from R, but I bluffed them out of it. More valuable than the Ford was its driver, Adam Robertson, a private in the Army Service Corps who became my driver in the Sunbeam, Erskine's chauffeur Markham being given the Ford. Robertson became a valued friend and remained with me in close attendance until I left Greece in the autumn of 1917. He was at the wheel during many an exciting quarter of an hour, and during several that were rather too exciting to be pleasant; but there was never a sign on Robertson's countenance that he was not driving the Sunbeam at a leisurely pace along a wide country road on a fine afternoon in England. In 1922 he was engineer of my motor-boat *Aphrodite* when she was second in the race from London to Cowes.

In that December the French started a Bureau de Renseignements presided over by Captain de Roquefeuil, the new French Naval Attaché. He told Sells and myself about the grandeur of his proposed organization. It would occupy the French Archaeological School, which would be made extraterritorial. Wireless was to be installed which would connect the School directly with Salonika and the Greek islands. There would be a photographic studio, a chemical laboratory, half a dozen automobiles and unlimited funds. The two French Military Attachés would be installed at the School in direct communication with Grand Quartier Général of Salonique. De Roquefeuil himself with the Assistant Naval Attaché, Hector de Béarn, would direct a large Bureau of Naval Intelligence with agents everywhere to deal with submarines and contraband. There was to be a propaganda service to counterbalance the activities of Baron Schenck. Finally, under Engineer-Captain Ricaud, there would be a *service de contre-espionage*; it would be a pleasure to present him to me.

I had made up my mind while De Roquefeuil was enunciating the glories of the new French Bureau that a close alliance must exist between it and the Z Bureau.

"It will give me much pleasure," I said quickly, "to put all our available information about the enemy's activities in Athens at the disposal of M. Ricaud."

De Roquefeuil thanked me, but I could see he did not suppose my offer was of the slightest practical value.

Then Sells sailed in.

"Vous savez, cclui est un auteur."

"Ah, non, par exemple, il n'y a pas d'hauteur. Au contraire j'estime beaucoup la bonne volonté dont il a . . ."

"Non, non," Sells interrupted. "Auteur! Ecrivain! Raconteur! Il écrit livres."

De Roquefeuil responded at once to this, and even when he heard my books were novels remained impressed by what would finally have damned my pretentions in the eyes of an Englishman in his position.

"I think the little man was shaken," said Sells when the new French Naval Attaché had left us.

"Not till you told him I was a novelist."

Sells grinned.

"Queer birds the French. Still, I think he's going to make things buzz in Athens."

I agreed, but neither Sells nor I had the ghost of an inkling at that moment how loud a buzz it would be.

The secret of de Roquefeuil's plenipotentiary powers was his intimate personal friendship with Admiral Lacaze, the Minister of Marine in Briand's Government. He had married into the Mumm family and, being a man of considerable means with wide social connections, he was able to wield an influence and an independence far beyond that of the average *capitaine de frégate*.

Presently Ricaud came to 3 Visarionos Street for the first time, a little shy and somewhat overcome by the exuberant cordiality of Tucker's welcome. He was in appearance a characteristic Frenchman of the Midi, small and dark and finely made with long-lashed eyes that were normally sombre, but the brown depths of which could blaze with fury and sparkle a moment after with their owner's exquisite sense of the ridiculous. Perhaps it was our common pleasure in absurdity which first made us friends; it was certainly that which above everything else prevented our disagreement.

Ricaud was at this time hardly thirty, but with his scrubby dark moustache, his pallid lined forehead, and a certain grave maturity in his manner he seemed older. He preferred to speak French with me, only retaining the habit of using a few English expressions of which he was fond. One of those was "I concur" delivered with a roll of the final "r". It is pleasant to remember how many times I heard Ricaud say "I concurr", for it may be accepted as the symbol of our agreement.

On that December afternoon Tucker took me aside.

"You don't want me to give him *all* our stuff, Captain Z?" he pleaded in obvious perturbation.

"Why not?"

"Well, look what it's cost us. And what are we going to get in return?"

"The confidence of the French."

"Well, of course, you may know best, Captain Z," Tucker replied doubtfully as he opened the door of the safe and took out the files.

Ricaud was astonished by our files and that card-index, which already contained 1500 names.

"I had no idea you had done all this work," he said. "I assure you I appreciate excessively what you are doing for us. I shall come with your permission every evening to work at these papers. Would you object if I bring one of my assistants to copy what I tell him?"

"Not at all. He will be French, of course?"

"*Ah, ça va sans dire.* A French officer of the Marine, Jehan Heurtel."

"To-morrow," I promised, "I will give you an idea of the system on which my organization is arranged. Of course, we shall keep to ourselves our own secret agents?"

"I concurr."

"And if I might make a suggestion it is that you will occupy yourself more particularly with Schenck and the German Consul at the Piraeus, leaving the German Legation and Hoffman to me. I am in a good position now to get good information about both, and it would be a mistake, I think, to run the risk of spoiling our game by both of us tackling the same places and people."

"I concurr."

"At present we have very little money. So, I cannot do as much as I should like, but I am always hoping to enlarge our scope."

"I shall be excessively delighted to ask M. de Roquefeuil to contribute from his funds whenever you find yourself in any difficulty. If it is a matter of 20,000 francs I can assure you he will be very pleased to place the money at your service."

I gasped. £800 was more than twice the amount I was allowed with which to carry on for a month and I feared that the £150 contributed to that by Deedes would not be available presently.

"You are very kind, but I hope that will not be necessary. Still, perhaps we might sometimes share the expenses of a coup?"

"You will always find me ready to share anything with you."

And he always was.

Few men during that First World War can have had the fortune to work with such a profoundly loyal colleague of another nation, and I still resent the failure of the British Government to accord him any recognition by decorating him with one of those strips of ribbon that were showered like confetti at a wedding on so many onlookers during the war. Ricaud died when he was hardly forty; it was Robertson who sent me his brief obituary cut from a French newspaper he had seen on the Riviera.

I had been anxious to keep the German Legation for myself because I had bought the services of the Greek porter whom I called Davy Jones. As soon as I met him I recognised in him the authentic spy, the spy by nature, with his very pale blue eyes filmed with suspicion and furtiveness almost as if by a visible cataract. At that first interview it was evident he was in a class apart. His character sketches of the Legation staff were on a different level from any I had heard hitherto and his physical descriptions were brilliant in their capacity to provide the essentials. He treated his sorry material in the spirit of an artist. Nothing escaped him, from the effect of a visitor on the Military Attaché's mood to the way in which that visitor had rung the bell and enquired if Major von Falkenhausen was at liberty. Nothing escaped him, neither the minutest shred of paper in the Minister's wastepaper-basket nor the nail print of the Marine Attaché's forefinger upon a map.

For over six months I interviewed Davy Jones three evenings a week, never once in the same place; through him we kept ourselves well-informed of the most intimate details of existence at the German Legation. It is difficult to avoid a suggestion of complacency in pointing out the tremendous difficulty of keeping an agent like that uncompromised in a city of 200,000, which was then the population of Athens, where public attention, official attention, police attention and hostile attention were all concentrated upon our work. Yet I managed to keep Davy Jones a secret from everybody except Tucker. In this I was of course enormously helped by the cleverness of Davy Jones himself, whose acting at the German Legation must have been superb, to enable him to carry off the excuses which his frequent entrances into the various rooms of the Legation entailed. He spoke English with enough fluency to give me all his facts and descriptions with the help of a little French;

but he spoke German perfectly, and he understood Italian. So he was able in passing through a room to pick up what was being said, and he had such an accurate memory that I always received word for word what he had overheard without any embroidery. He knew I should welcome the dull truth more warmly than the exciting lie. He had, indeed, for me the cordial devotion of an artist for a critic who, he feels, appreciates his work and understands the fatigue and patience and care which have gone to the production of it. Thanks to Davy Jones I learnt during that last week of December more about the German organization of espionage in Athens than we had learnt during the preceding nine months, and it was due to the solid facts he provided for me that I was able to make the co-operation of our ill-equipped, ill-defined sub-Bureau indispensable to the grand new French Bureau des Renseignements which was now to be installed in Athens and by its installation leave an indelible mark upon the history of modern Greece.

The Manager of the company engaged upon the draining of Lake Copais had invited Sells and myself to spend Christmas with them. I could not spare more than two days off, so with Robertson and the Sunbeam I drove Sells there on Christmas Eve and came back on Christmas Day to meet Ricaud in the afternoon and eat a jolly Christmas dinner which Sir Francis and Lady Elliot gave annually to the various people connected with the Legation.

One last tribute I must pay before Lisa brings me my coffee and wishes me many happy returns of my thirty-third birthday and that is to Lisa herself. When Tucker and I went to live at 3 Visarionos we found that the tenants were looked after by Lisa, an old lady who inhabited the basement, where she received many visits from friends and relations, but not in the least so as to interfere with the floor above. I have called Lisa an old lady, and inasmuch as she had almost white hair and was well over sixty I suppose she was an old lady. Yet she had grown old so exquisitely that she reminded me of the fairy godmother who assumes the appearance of age, but whose eternal fairy youth, one feels, must have been perceptible to those she favoured with her patronage. Lisa's cheeks had the delicate bloom of an autumnal rose and her face was still as demurely pretty as a china shepherdess, with a delicately moulded profile and clear blue eyes. Her figure was as trim as a girl's, and she had beautiful little feet of which more than anything she was really vain, always buying for herself the neatest shoes and the best black silk stockings. About the house she used to wear black dresses with frilly aprons in the evenings like the French maid of bygone farces; but she dressed herself gaily when she went out, and the first time I met her coming home from market on a sparkling winter's day and saw her blushing beneath a flowery hat she might have been a Greuze. She may sound as I have described her like an old woman coquetting with her former self; this was not so. She talked of herself as an old woman, and used the privilege of age to speak her mind or tell a worldly tale not fit for the lips of a maid.

Conversation between Lisa and myself was never fluent, because, though she was under the impression that she spoke French well, her French consisted of about fifty words without ability to put together a sentence of any kind. As for my Greek, it remained in much the same state as Lisa's French, and though I could soon understand most of what was being said I never admitted I could; in any case Lisa was much too proud of her French ever to condescend to talking to me in her own language. Yet her devotion to myself was so complete and my gratitude to her so constant that, looking back across half a century, I am aware of a perfect intimacy, little as either of us could ever say to the other by the world's standard of intercourse.

Lisa stayed with me all the time I was in Greece. She moved with me in Athens to every house in turn; she came with me to Syra. She never seemed to sleep. If I arrived home at 3 in the morning, worn out by some long expedition over vile roads, I would hear underneath faint sounds as of a mouse moving in the wainscot, and a minute later Lisa in a saxe-blue velvet dressing-gown and a lace nightcap would put her head round the door and say:

"Cocoa. Toute suite. Cocoa très bon."

When I was racked with neuritis she would search Athens for unguents and medicaments, and occasionally even bring strange women with a reputation for magic and herbs to see what they could do.

It was Lisa who brought me coffee and wished me the first many happy returns of my thirty-third birthday.

D

THE Minister decided to send that report of mine he had asked for to the Foreign Office, through Sells. That report may be read in *Greek Memories*. Sells suggested Blinker Hall[1] as the best man to hand it to.

"What's he do?"

"He's the D.I.D."

"What's that?"

"Director of the Intelligence Division, my dear ass," Sells replied, a little shaken by my ignorance of such an important Admiralty personage.

Thus lightly was made the fatal suggestion that was to impede our work for nine months, at the end of which time I was to meet C personally and find him henceforth a supporter and a friend, too late, however, to undo the harm which was done by unwittingly putting into the hands of his superior officer a report which C considered a reflection upon himself.

I regard your behaviour in sending a report over the head of your superior officer and, over my head, to my superior officer as a gross breach of discipline, and if it occurs again you will be immediately recalled.

Two days earlier Sir Francis Elliot had sent a telegram to Sir Arthur Nicolson,[2] the Permanent Under-Secretary, earnestly hoping that the suggestions in my report would be accepted.

From Sir Arthur Nicolson came a private telegram in reply to Sir Francis Elliot:

Authorities here think that however clever Mackenzie may be he has neither the knowledge nor the experience to direct the whole of the Intelligence of the Near East.

When Sells came back I asked him what C meant by my going to his superior officer over his head.

"Blinker holds senior rank to him in the Service."

"Is C a Naval man?"

"Yes, but he's apparently attached to the War Office, though he gets his money from the Foreign Office."

---

[1] The late Admiral Sir Reginald Hall, K.C.M.G., R.N.

[2] The late Lord Carnock.

"What's he like?"

"Funny old boy with a wooden leg," said Sells.

Early in March Sells went to the Naval Conference in Malta. It augured ill for the financial future of the Intelligence Department of the British Legation. C had conceived an irremovable prejudice about myself, and kept asking Sells what I was trying to get out of it. Nothing Sells could say availed to shake his conviction that every word and every action of mine were prompted entirely by personal ambition.

"He's as obstinate as a mule," Sells told me, "with a chin like the cutwater of a battleship."

Somebody had told Sells the story of how C lost his leg. In the autumn of 1914 his son, a subaltern in the Seaforths, had been driving him in a fast car on some urgent Intelligence mission in the area of operations. The car, going at full speed, had crashed into a tree and overturned, pinning C by the leg and flinging his son out on his head. The boy was fatally injured, and his father, hearing him moan something about the cold, tried to extricate himself from the wreck of the car to put a coat over him; struggle as he might, he could not free his smashed leg. Thereupon he had taken out a penknife and hacked away at his leg until he had cut it off. After which he had crawled over to his son and spread a coat over him, being found later lying unconscious by his dead body.

"That's the sort of old chap C is," said Sells.

I enquired after R.

"Just the same as ever, lad. Couldn't be nicer, of course, but absolutely incapable of making up his mind and frightened to death of C."

"They'll damn well have to settle something soon, because by the end of this month we shall have spent all the money we have and the whole of the April money as well," I announced.

The political situation in Athens and the military situation in Salonika remained more or less static during the first three months of 1916. Yet they seem a nightmare to look back at. I was working ten hours a day at my desk, writing telegrams and reports without proper clerical help. I was interviewing secret agents, Venizelist officers and politicians, diplomats and sundry observers from other Mediterranean Intelligence centres. I had been asked by the Serbians to take over their counter-espionage, to which I had rashly agreed without realising in what complicated plots that would involve me. I was starved of money to run the Intelligence Department of the British Legation. I was asking myself whether anybody could be more stupid than Colonel Fairholme,[1] the new Military Attaché, who when Military Attaché in Brussels at

[1] The late Brig.-Gen. W. E. Fairholme, C.B., C.M.G., M.V.O.

the outbreak of war had left behind in a Belgian hotel the plans made by us with the French and Belgian General Staffs before the war for an offensive against Germany. They had thus fallen into the hands of the Germans, who had published them as evidence of our hypocrisy about the violation of Belgian neutrality.

Fairholme's mother had been a Baroness Poellnitz-Frankenberg of Bavaria. She had been one of three beautiful and romantic sisters, all of whom had married Scotsmen and one of whom was the mother of Norman Douglas. I did not know this when I asked "Fairy", as we called him, to support my endeavour to get Norman Douglas out to Athens for Intelligence work. His rubicund heavy-jowled face darkened to the colour of a mulberry.

"That blackguard," he exclaimed. "Never! Do you know I've just heard that his unhappy wife whom he treated so abominably was burnt to death recently in a Munich brothel?"

"There are two sides to the story of Douglas's marriage," I objected.

"Damn it, do you realize that Norman Douglas is a first cousin of mine? I'll see to it that *he* never comes out to Greece."

Colonel Fairholme was one of the stupid people chosen to represent the brains of Great Britain in time of war. I used to wonder why the English had such reverence for Alfred the Great, when Ethelred the Unready would have been such a more suitable king for them to venerate.

Toward the end of March Major Eric Holt-Wilson,[1] one of the original builders of M.I.5, arrived in Athens on the way to Alexandria to report on my show. The shock of meeting somebody connected with Intelligence work who could understand immediately what was wanted and why it was wanted began to dispel the nightmare. Holt-Wilson reported to Alexandria and London so enthusiastically about our work that on April 1st the following telegram arrived:

£1800 has been sent to you through the Minister, £600 to cover last month's deficit and £1200 to cover expenditure for current month.

After the nerve-racking financial anxiety of March we could hardly believe we were not being made April fools with the announcement of such wealth on the way.

It was as fortunate for Great Britain as it was for Greece that there was a Minister of the calibre of Sir Francis Elliot representing us in those difficult days. His grasp of the situation must have been embarrassing. I remember hearing a Foreign Office critic say the trouble with poor old Elliot was he had been so long in Greece that he always saw the Greek point of view.

[1] The late Brigadier Sir Eric Holt-Wilson, C.M.G., D.S.O.

Lord Grey in his book *Twenty-five Years* showed clearly how remote he was from any earnest attempt to understand the state of affairs in Greece. All he says of the year 1916 is that his last days of office were made tiresome by Greek complications; the mental weariness of a fine mind is obvious in every word of that chapter entitled "The End of Office".

At the end of May came the ignominious surrender by the Greek government of Fort Roupel to the Bulgarians; if the Foreign Office or Quai d'Orsay had offered solid support Venizelos would probably have moved against the Greek Government then in power, but he still hesitated. There was trouble now between the French and British Commands in Salonika; General Sir Brian Mahon had been recalled, presumably because he was suspected of being too much in sympathy with the French point of view.

The French put pressure on the Greek Government to be less amenable to the Central Powers by imposing a blockade of which the British Legation had not been notified, and in the course of the telegraphic exchanges that followed Sir Edward Grey instructed Sir Francis Elliot to issue a proclamation to the Greek people which would state among other things that we had only sent troops to Salonica because Mr Venizelos had invited us to send them there. In fact the French had merely announced that they were using Salonica and almost simultaneously a Sapper Brigadier-General had arrived to measure the harbour without previous notification. Venizelos had accepted this with a formal protest. I wrote a full account of this business in *Athenian Memories*. What seemed to us a flat lie by Sir Edward Grey created consternation in the British Legation, for it seemed to us a betrayal of our friend Venizelos. Elliot telegraphed a strong protest to Grey against carrying out his instructions, and I was told to send a telegram to C giving the arguments for a British ultimatum in the Entente's interest, with a request to show it to the Foreign Office.

On reconsidering the telegram I had drafted I felt that it lacked a final and convincing argument and it occurred to me that if an act of violence could be committed against a fairly prominent individual such an act might be the spur to prick the Foreign Office into firmness. I was living in a small villa in Old Phaleron and an attempt had been made to put me out of action by loosening the wheel of a big Lancia that had been lent to us. Robertson heard something which made him slow down when we were tearing along the Phaleron road at about sixty miles an hour and just as the car stopped the wheel came off. The fact that already Greek Government supporters had tried to eliminate me made it obvious that the only person to be shot at and wounded was myself. It would be unpleasant, but if I were shot through the forearm on my way back to Phaleron it would be less painful than the agony of acute sciatica in this heat. I could rely on Robertson's nerve; could I rely on the accurate eye and aim of the man I had in mind to entrust with this "outrage"? I did not feel it would be playing the game to provoke an ultimatum merely by having a few shots fired at the car. I must be hit and have the moral satisfaction of feeling I had done all I could to justify such provocative action. Meditation on the pain a bullet wound in the arm would cause drove the pain of my leg away. I was just going to ring the bell for Robertson with a feeling of delicious freedom when Tucker came in to say that a mob had smashed up the offices of the *Patris* newspaper and was now wrecking the *Ethnos* building. I hurried to the front office, threw open a window and listened to the dull roar of the mob in the direction of Stadium Street.

At this moment a white-faced agent came in breathlessly to say the mob had broken up the offices of the *Astir* and were on their way to smash up the *Nea Hellas*. The noise of the mob was now much louder and when they reached the corner of Dragatzani Street some of the rioters turned aside and came hurrying along toward the Legation. About fifty disreputable vagabonds stopped outside and booed for a few minutes, after which they went on to overtake their companions and help to smash up the *Nea Hellas* offices. I sent a car at full speed to Kephissia with a message to tell Sir Francis Elliot what was going on in Athens, leaving it to him to take what action he thought best.

It must have been now about half-past seven. I was getting into the Sunbeam to drive round the city, when there was a sound of firing and I was persuaded not to go out for the present. I sat listening to those sounds of riot and destruction that were like music to my ears. All this must persuade the Foreign Office to agree to the stipulations in the ultimatum we had asked for.

When Sir Francis arrived from Kephissia we drove him round to look at the damage, after which he went back to the Chancery and sent off a rousing telegram to the Foreign Office *en clair*.

Next morning there was a telegram from Sir Edward Grey to insist on the publication of his announcement that Venizelos had invited Allied troops to land at Salonika. Such capacity for self-deception made us despair. In the Annexe I found de Roquefeuil marching round and round my desk and waving a telegram from Briand to say that in spite of every argument he had used in London Grey absolutely declined to yield; therefore he was instructing the French Minister to associate himself with the British in the announcement about Venizelos.

I told de Roquefeuil that the only thing he could do was to ask to be recalled and persuade M. Guillemin, his Minister, to do the same rather than betray such a devoted friend of the Entente as Venizelos.

This he dashed off to do; presently the French Minister and his Naval Attaché arrived at the British Legation to acquaint Sir Francis with their decision. The latter suggested that before taking such a grave step they should wait to hear Sir Edward Grey's reply to the *en clair* telegram he had sent last night. Meanwhile, another protest, with which Prince Demidoff, the Russian Minister, would associate himself, should be sent, to which in postcript was added an appeal from Mr Venizelos to the personal loyalty and political honesty of Sir Edward Grey. At last on the following afternoon Grey telegraphed that he supposed the Entente Ministers would have to do as they thought best.

The original terms agreed between them for the Note had included the demobilization of the Greek Army but had not demanded the dissolution of the Chamber and new elections, by the result of which the Entente in its future policy promised to abide. I had suggested to Sir Francis Elliot this clause and, convinced by my arguments, he had persuaded the other two Ministers to agree.

The Allied Fleet kept postponing its arrival at Salamis and so the delivery of the Note giving the Allied conditions for ending the blockade kept on being postponed, but at last it was presented without the Allied Fleet. That was an anxious day, with the thermometer going up to 109° while Greek troops in full equipment were marching down to the Piraeus. I had staked everything on the terms of the Note being accepted. If the information I had given to Sir Francis Elliot should prove wrong the most trivial incident in the present state of tension might provoke a massacre of Venizelists. What a relief it was when at half-past eight on that June evening Sir Francis came into my room at the Annexe, a flush on his pale cheeks, a brightness in his eye as he waved a paper and exclaimed that the Greek Government had accepted everything. Elliot was congratulated by the Foreign Office on his diplomacy; if at that moment Great Britain had taken the Greek situation firmly in hand, the open split between the King and Venizelos might have been avoided.

I asked Sir Francis if he could not extract from Sir Arthur Nicolson what our policy was in the Near East. Were we or were we not justified in encouraging Mr Venizelos? Sir Edward Grey replied personally to Sir Francis Elliot in the most confidential cypher that we had no policy in the Near East except to use a restraining influence upon the French. This may seem incredible, but it is sadly true. Sir Edward Grey was indeed a tired man, and the danger of allowing foreign affairs to be handled by tired men would be evident forty years later to all of us.

At the end of June Lord Denman[1] visited Athens. He was not one of those peripatetic amateurs of diplomacy who were sent out from time

---

[1] The late Lord Denman, G.C.M.G., K.C.V.O.

to time to tell them at home what was going on; he did not think that within 24 hours of his arrival he was in a position to telegraph to London a solution of every difficulty in the Balkans. He took the trouble to master the intricacy of the situation and spent a great deal of time with me. I put all our papers at his disposal and when he went home he gave the Foreign Office the most accurate estimate of the situation they had received from anybody who had visited Athens.

The disappointment of the French that the Note was presented and accepted before the Fleet arrived was acute, and they were not happy until they did succeed in getting the Fleet to Salamis two months later.

On the morning of September 1st de Roquefeuil arrived at the Annexe, portentous with unrevealed secrets. After wandering up and down my room for a minute or two, he suddenly stopped and asked for my promise not to mention a word of something until that something was a *fait accompli*. When I gave him my promise he announced that at four o'clock that afternoon the Allied Fleet would arrive off Piraeus.

"But what for?" I gasped in utter surprise.

"Come round to the French School as soon as possible and we shall have a consultation."

I told him he could not include Sir Francis in that promise I had just made him; after a momentary hesitation de Roquefeuil agreed to my telling Sir Francis. When he left the Annexe I hurried round to the Legation.

The British Minister, who had just come back from an audience with the King, was upstairs in the library, his top-hat on the desk. My news surprised him as much as it had surprised me. He was so angry that he picked up his top-hat and threw it on the floor.

Sir Francis Elliot had reason to be angry. He had just come up from an hour's interview with the King, feeling hopeful that all misunderstandings would soon be removed and that Great Britain and Greece in perfect harmony would move forward along the road to victory. He had assured the King he would do everything to discourage any more humiliating Notes; in his anxiety for that reconciliation between the King and Venizelos on which he had set his heart he half-believed that the reconciliation had been almost effected. Now the King would suppose that throughout the audience he had been aware of this demonstration; he would never believe the British Minister had been in complete ignorance that the British Squadron was on its way to the Piraeus.

Sir Francis Elliot went fuming to the Chancery to draft an exasperated telegram to the Foreign Office, asking why the Fleet was coming to the Piraeus and why he had not been advised beforehand of its coming. He asked for the whole operation to be cancelled if possible

in view of the fact that the King had never shown himself so amenable
as this morning. He had just finished a draft of this when Reuter's
correspondent sent in his card to ask if the British Minister could give
him any information for the Press about a large fleet of warships which
had arrived off the Piraeus. I left Sir Francis dancing about the Chancery and drove up to the French School where de Roquefeuil told me
what demands the Admiral intended to impose.

"The Admiral intends to impose?" I asked sharply.

"It is time to finish with these diplomats," said de Roquefeuil. "From
now on we shall always demand everything through the Commander-
in-Chief of the Allied Squadron, Admiral Dartige du Fournet."

It began to look as if the French design to establish a political and
commercial supremacy over Greece had taken a long step toward
accomplishment. No wonder the Foreign Office had felt too sheepish to
notify Sir Francis Elliot of this intention to exchange diplomacy for
action.

The French demands were accepted, but the Royalists had a dis-
agreeable counter-stroke waiting. On September 11th eight thousand
men of the Kavalla garrison surrendered to the Germano-Bulgarians
with all their arms, guns, munitions and stores. Most of the troops of the
Serres Division refused to surrender and, retreating to Salonika, joined
the revolutionary movement which had just begun there, but with
which Venizelos had not as yet identified himself.

The invasion of Macedonia was a deliberate electioneering device to
deprive Venizelos of some sixty safe seats when the new elections were
held. The Kaiser wrote a letter to King Constantine to tell him that
within a month the Germans would have finished with Rumania and
that they then intended to throw Sarrail and his army into the sea.

On September 22nd the Foreign Office telegraphed to Athens that
the British Government had proposed to Paris that the King should be
warned that if he did not declare war by October 1st the Allies would
not be answerable for the consequences. This proposal was made at the
instance of Sir Francis Elliot and the consequences for which responsibility was to be declined were the proclamation by Venizelos of a
Provisional Government. The first positive step forward by the Foreign
Office toward a solution of the situation in Greece alarmed the French
with the idea that Venizelos was to move under British auspices. The
proposed ultimatum was held up for discussion and meanwhile the
French redoubled their efforts to spur Venizelos into immediate action.
He can hardly be blamed for not waiting any longer for open British
support. Yet, by moving when he did without guarantees of goodwill
from Great Britain, he gave the King an opportunity to maintain that
such precipitate action had prevented his joining the Allies because it

showed the movement headed by Venizelos was primarily anti-dynastic.

About now two French naval officers came to visit me at the Annexe. One of them was a small shrivelled man, Capitaine de Frégate Viaud, with brightly rouged cheeks which made him look even older than he was. He waited with the distrait look of extreme boredom while his companion discussed with me some technicalities connected with the Controls; at the end of the interview when shaking hands he asked if it was true I was a *romancier*. On hearing that I was, he wished me success and turned quickly to leave the office. Next day I asked Ricaud who was the little old man with rouged cheeks. It was Pierre Loti. For a moment I was back in the Upper Fifth A at St Paul's, sighing over the annotated school copy of *Pêcheur d'Islande*.

At five o'clock in the morning of September 20th, 1916, M. Venizelos and Admiral Koundouriotis set out for Crete from the terrace of a restaurant by the sea at Old Phaleron. Their reception at Canea was inspiring, and the scenes of enthusiasm there were repeated in Chios, in Samos and in Mytilene.

Two days later General Danglis came to the Annexe to ask if I could make arrangements for him to join Venizelos. The political and naval creators of a great Greece had already set out in the high hope of creating an even greater Greece, and it was appropriate that one of the chief military creators should form the third of that triumvirate. It was not my privilege to make the actual arrangements for the General's embarkation; the official attitude of the British Government toward the Provisional Government had not been discovered yet, although in the Islands the Navy had already committed British policy to the open support of what soon became a revolutionary movement.

When Venizelos left Athens he was followed by many patriots; every night the Annexe was full of officers and soldiers bivouacking in the various offices. The selflessness of their patriotism was complete, for at this date there was no guarantee of any future for them. They hazarded their chances of promotion. They forsook their homes, their families and their friends. They wanted nothing except the honour and the glory and the greatness of their country. Naked, as it were, they went northward, and they flung the world away for an ideal.

It was not to be expected that the sailors to whom the universally beloved and respected Admiral Koundouriotis had set such an example would be content to linger. His lead was followed by Lieutenant Voulgaris, who had taken Admiral Miaoulis in T.B.14 to shoot quail on the island of Poros. When he went ashore Voulgaris gave the order to steam away to Salonika and left the Admiral marooned. Lieutenant Vouvoulis, in command of the destroyer *Thetis*, was suspected of intending to join Venizelos and was ordered to moor alongside the *Arethusa*. The lieutenant on the deck of the *Arethusa* saw the *Thetis* getting up steam and called out through a megaphone to know the reason. Vouvoulis shouted back that he was coming alongside; putting on full steam he made straight for the open sea. It looked as if the guns of the *Hydra* and the *Arethusa* were going to open fire on the *Thetis*, but our Military Control boat deliberately got in the line of fire and before anybody could make up his mind to take the risk of firing on the blue ensign the *Thetis* was gone, the cheers of the crew floating back across the harbour.

Public opinion at home was unanimous in supposing that we had tacitly encouraged Venizelos to commit himself and his fellow-patriots and that expediency brightened by honour demanded we should see him through. Now was the moment to assert Great Britain's claim to guard the threshold of the East by becoming the instrument of Hellenic power. If once it were understood in Greece that Great Britain and not France stood solidly behind Venizelos his opponents would shrink to a handful of disappointed politicians supported by a comparatively minute fashionable and aristocratic clique.

At the end of August I had asked Sir Francis Elliot to support my request for £3,000 to meet our expenses in September. The Foreign Office apparently thought this extra money was to be used for bribing the Greek electors, and demurred at the amount. Sir Francis telegraphed back that in June the German Legation had drawn 803,000 marks and in July 750,000 marks through the National Bank.

Similar encashments were made at the Popular and Commercial Banks. Besides the above about 6,000,000 marks have been paid out this year. I think Mackenzie's modest demand for £3,000 monthly might have your support. The expenses of the Passport Office and Control work are growing very heavy and stationery alone costs £40 a month.

The reply to this was a telegram to say it was now felt in London that the Athens organization had grown too large and too important for an officer of my rank and that Lieutenant-Colonel Plunkett[1] was being sent out to take charge. This was not intended to reflect in an way on the services of Captain Compton Mackenzie, who would remain in Athens as Assistant Military Attaché.

Colonel Plunkett had been Military Attaché to the British Legations in Greece and Serbia when war broke out, and Sir Francis had never forgiven him for going up to Belgrade to watch the Austrian bombardment and getting a stray bullet in his behind. For my own part, if anybody was going to supersede me, I would be superseded by "Plunks" more willingly than by most. He was a kind and lovable man of whom

[1] The late Brigadier-General E. A. Plunkett, C.B.E.

I had affectionate memories from Gallipoli. Sir Francis, however, was determined if possible not to have Plunkett. He telegraphed to say that it had been pointed out as long ago as January how important Athens was bound to be as a centre, that most of what I had asked for then had only been obtained by me now after eight months of very arduous work, that the large size of the organization was entirely due to my energy in building it up, that the rank of Lieutenant had been considered good enough for me up to the end of July, and that the simplest thing to do was to grant me the rank of Lieut.-Colonel immediately.

To this the Foreign Office replied that War Office principles of seniority must be respected and that Colonel Plunkett would arrive in September.

Sir Francis sent a private telegram of protest:

God help us if mediocrity is to supersede talent to gratify War Office principles of seniority. The new arrangement shall be given a fair trial and there will be a loyal attempt to make it work. A change of status for Mackenzie will cause confusion. His signature as Military Control Officer is known all over Europe. Why should not he and Colonel Plunkett both be Military Control Officers?

A week later Lord Hardinge, who had succeeded Sir Arthur Nicolson, telegraphed that the last suggestion was approved, adding that except for an application for £2,000 a month referred to him and not sanctioned (with the Secretary of State's approval) because it seemed to be required for election purposes he was not aware that any application for funds had been refused.

Colonel Plunkett reached Athens early in September and at once showed himself cordially appreciative of the work we had done. He told me he was determined to get our position in Athens fairly represented at home. To an ambitious man the post in Athens would have seemed a wonderful chance for self-aggrandizement. It would have been perfectly easy for Plunkett to make my position intolerable and drive me to ask for a transfer; instead of that he took advantage of every occasion to give me the credit for anything I had done. "Decent" may seem a poor hackneyed epithet, but from the heart I say that Plunkett was "decent"; it was the kind of modest epithet that "Plunks" himself would have preferred me to write.

Plunkett's arrival gave me the chance of a month's rest, which I badly needed. In London I might hope to present a different view of what was happening in Greece from that which evidently prevailed. It seemed vital to obtain the support of C for the ever-increasing demands made upon us. I now had the responsibility of visas for all British passports in Greece, of port control at the Pireaus and in the Peloponnese, of control of the Greek police, and of sitting on the board of control with my French, Italian, and Russian colleagues who were all Generals. To these administrative activities were added the responsibility of keeping the Minister informed of what was going on; of telegrams to London, Alexandria, Salonika, Malta, Marseilles, Berne, Rome and Gibraltar, and of long detailed reports of every aspect of our work. I needed urgently more officers, more clerical staff, and more money. I could only hope to get them by personal influence. Any further hesitation about leaving Athens was removed by Sir Francis Elliot's telling me he would ask Lord Hardinge to make a point of seeing me in London so that I might explain orally much about the Greek situation that was impossible to explain in writing. But the last thing Lord Hardinge wanted was to be given first-hand information about Greece; he did not send for me.

On Wednesday, October 4th, I went on board the battleship *Exmouth* which was proceeding from Salamis to Malta. After the hectic, anxious, and incessantly busy life of which I have given the barest outline in this Octave, it was like a progress in sleep to glide with such an air of stately leisure past the line of Allied battleships moored against that classic background. It was almost to a day the anniversary of the Battle of Salamis; I did not dream for a moment that within fifty years the naval scene of 1916 would be almost as unimaginable as the Persian fleet of nearly twenty-five centuries earlier. The crews of every ship were standing at the salute; white ensigns and tricolours were dipping. A Marine band was playing in the Rear-Admiral's flagship. On the quarter-deck of the *Exmouth* we stood in ceremonious and rigid farewell. The glare of Athens was forgotten in that great blue and white October sky.

It was fair-weather sailing all the way, and in a battleship one was very near to the sea. I spent an idle but ineffably rich day, travelling with no more sense of effort than the great swan-breasted clouds high overhead. There was a rumour of a submarine waiting for us off Matapan, but the two destroyers that escorted us could look after that. The idleness and azure were exquisite. As we drew near to Malta the propinquity of enemy submarines was signalled and we began to zigzag while the two destroyers steamed round and round us as a couple of collies run round a flock of sheep. *Exmouth's* sister ship *Russell* had struck a mine and gone down just outside Malta not so long before, and we seemed the easiest of marks on that velvet sea.

We reached Valletta safely, and as we glide through the narrow entrance of the harbour we stand at the salute while the ship's band plays "*Here we are, here we are, here we are again!*" Everything is moving past us in music and colour; gun crews salute from the shore batteries; flags signal our arrival; flags dip in salute; sentries are presenting arms.

Fortifications, houses, faces at windows, bright curtains are swimming past us on either side until we reach the inner harbour where the battleship will spend some weeks refitting. The band has ceased to play its jaunty tune. The scene no longer moves. The world seems to have come to an end for a moment, and then begins again in the bustle and noise of disembarkation.

I was being depressed by that empty lost feeling while everybody was hurrying ashore with such familiarity when I saw a Marine officer coming along the quayside, obviously on the look out for somebody. I had a hopeful notion he might be that Captain Farmer with whom for many weeks now I had been in close and friendly communication over Intelligence matters; and Farmer it was, as delightful in reality as the picture I had formed of him from our correspondence. He had booked rooms for me in an hotel until the mail ship sailed for Taranto two or three days hence, and presently we were walking through the arched vault of the old bagnios hewn out of the rock which once housed the stores of the Knights, but which were now mostly used for naval stores. In one of them was the office of Major Lampen, the Naval Staff Officer for Intelligence. Lampen was just as cordial as Farmer and I realized why intercommuncation between Athens and Malta had never been marred by a single misunderstanding, whereas Gibraltar, with another Marine major, had been continuously unco-operative.

Much of my time in Malta was to be taken up with going into various questions in connection with the prisoners interned there, from whom I had brought a packet of petitions to be investigated. The internment camp was on the top of a hill with a perfect view of all the harbours and shipping. Many of the prisoners had spent their time in making rock gardens, and the recreation ground resembled the beach at Margate. Shortly before I arrived the German prisoners had presented a petition to have Captain Müller, the famous Captain of the *Emden*, removed on account of the way he bullied them; he had just been sent off to Alexandra Palace in the battleship *London*. Müller had been selected by popular opinion in Great Britain as the type of a sporting and chivalrous opponent. In fact he had regretted his sportsmanship when he was damaging British commerce and leading the Navy such a dance. "I wish I had known then the way the war was going to be fought by us," he used to sigh. One of Captain Müller's amusements had been photography, and in order to indulge in this hobby he was always laying in supplies of a certain chemical, a property of which was that when used as a secret ink it would react only to photography. From the camp he was able to note the movements of every ship and with the help of Maltese agents he had tried to communicate the information to the German Admiralty.

One prisoner I was glad to meet was Captain Alfred Hoffman, the cleverest by far of all the German agents in Athens. He had surrendered to me personally when German agents were expelled under the terms of our Note. He was comfortably installed with his wife in a pleasant row of cottages near one of the harbours. He had a piano and plenty of beer, and I spent an hour with him, drinking beer while he played Schumann. Both Hoffman and his wife expressed their appreciation of the kindness shown to them in Malta, and I parted from them as one parts from old friends.

After interviewing various interned suspects, the release of many of whom I afterwards recommended and was successful in obtaining, I visited the M.I.5 centre in one of the glorious Auberges of the Knights of Malta which in time of peace was the Mess of the Royal Artillery and Royal Engineers. Genial Major Haldane in charge was very proud of the perfection to which the indexing system had been brought. I looked enviously at the filing-cabinets with thousands of cardboard folders all beautifully lettered and numbered, and even more enviously at a dozen or so rosy-cheeked young English indexing clerks who were doing their bit to show in the stock cliché of the time how splendid the women were during the war.

"Any name you want, Mackenzie," said Haldane, beaming. "Ask me for a name."

I felt like the member of an audience called up on the stage to assist a thought-reader as I asked for the dossier of some rascal, the details of which we had supplied from Athens. One rosy-cheeked young woman hurried off to the boxes of the card-index, and returned presently to equip another rosy-cheeked young woman with the necessary clue to send her scurrying across to an enormous chest of drawers whence with another clue she hurried over to a third rosy-cheeked young woman, who with the final clue to the whereabouts of the required dossier opened a filing-cabinet to bring the culprit's misdeeds to light.

"Magnificent system!" Major Haldane exclaimed.

"It seems rather elaborate," I commented.

"But it's foolproof, that's the best of it. It takes twelve index-clerks to keep our lists."

I thought of the huddle and muddle of papers in the Annexe of the British Legation in Athens and reflected how easy clerical life was in Great Britain and her dependencies compared with life in a neutral capital disturbed by political faction and hostile propagandists.

"I'm so sorry, Major Haldane," said the rosy-cheeked young woman in charge of the *sanctum sanctorum* of filing-cabinets, "but I don't seem able to find the man you want."

"Can't find him?" the Major gasped. "What an extraordinary thing!

Well, this is the first time, my dear fellow, that our indexing system has gone wrong. Miss Smith, are you sure you gave Miss Jones the correct details from your cupboard?"

"Yes, Major, quite sure," Miss Smith declared, firmly.

"Then perhaps Miss Brown was wrong?" Major Haldane suggested, turning to the first rosy-cheeked indexer.

"No, Major, I don't think so," she insisted primly. "I think this is the name Captain Mackenzie asked me for."

I confirmed Miss Brown's confidence; but, search though they might, neither Miss Smith nor Miss Jones could find any details about the gentleman in question. His misdeeds were buried beneath thousands of cardboard folders.

"I assure you, Mackenzie," said the Major, "this is the very first time in my experience that our system has gone wrong. It's most extraordinary!"

I decided that our system in Athens, with myself damning, with Tucker vowing he had never seen the bloody paper, and with Hasluck, his head on one side like a duck's, suggesting various reference numbers, was not so much inferior after all.

After Mass on Sunday I drove out to lunch with Lord and Lady Methuen. It was a hot dusty drive between checkers of dry stone walls; but the Governor's country house was set in an oasis of trees and the shadowy green-lit dining-room was cool as a country house in Hampshire. The other guest at lunch was Lady McMahon, the wife of the High Commissioner for Egypt. Lord Methuen was then over seventy, tall and spare and handsome and as upright as a subaltern. His voice was more like a poet's than a soldier's, and the crimson velvet tabs of a Field-marshal gave a kind of softness and romance to his khaki uniform. I do not remember any of the conversation at lunch. I think I must have been too much carried away by admiration of that great gentleman who was already a soldier ten years after the Crimean War. What I do remember is his telling me when I was leaving that if ever I was in a difficulty where Malta was concerned to telegraph him personally.

Another experience I enjoyed in Malta was dining in the Mess of my own ship, H.M.S. *Egmont*, to the strength of which I had been transferred from H.M.S. *Victory*. *Egmont* consisted of a series of buildings on shore. Farmer himself lived aboard her. Soon after my visit to Malta he was sent to Jamaica as Naval Intelligence officer, but he left a tradition behind him of alliance and friendship with Athens, and when the Military Control Office moved to Syra in the Cyclades we always had the support of Malta in various difficulties.

On October 9th I left Malta for Taranto in the mail ship, a very fast packet with a vicious motion. She was full of officers of both services,

C.M.

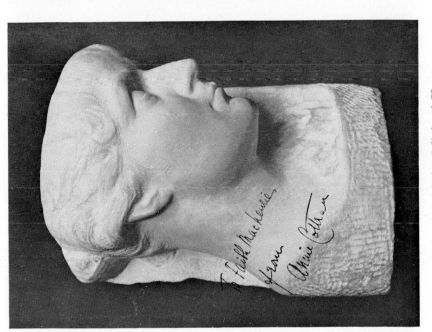

Statue of Faith by Michael Katz

Venizelos

C.M. in uniform

most of them going home on leave. While we steamed up the Sicilian coast I was leaning over the port rail, pondering upon the sublime shape of Etna, when a sudden gust of wind seized my cap and flung it into the sea. This was disaster. Not only was it the best cap I found during the war; it was the only cap I had with me at the time. It was a cap made by Lock of St James's Street which I had bought from Eddie Keeling at Gallipoli. My problem was really appalling. There I was, bound for London with no prospect I could see of obtaining another cap, at any rate until I reached Taranto; the notion of going aboard Admiral Kerr's flagship *Queen* without being able to offer or return a single salute except by bobbing my head like an actress taking a call pierced my soul. I consulted a kindly padre and begged him to take advantage of his sacred office to ask in turn of every officer on board whether he had a spare cap. It was fruitless. There was nobody on board with a spare cap, and I had to accept the kind offer of a naval officer to lend me a white helmet he had. It looked hideously inappropriate with a khaki uniform, and it wobbled about on my head owing to the removal of some of its inside, but at least it would enable me, however sheepishly, to salute, and I buoyed myself up with the hope of borrowing a cap from some Marine officer at Taranto.

We reached Taranto in a drench of rain; I felt the incongruity of that white naval helmet more than ever. Admiral Mark Kerr had sent across to ask me to lunch with him; I encouraged myself to believe that in such weather there would be nobody on the quarter-deck except the officer of the watch and a ship's corporal, whose glassy eyes I nerved myself to brave. Luck was against me. In spite of the rain the awnings were out. As I went up the ladder, feeling as if I was balancing a blancmange on my head, I saw that the quarter-deck was thronged not merely with the officers of the *Queen* but with Italian officers as well, for Admiral Kerr was entertaining an Italian Admiral and his Staff. I could fancy I had saluted half the armed forces of Europe before I managed to reach the ward-room and divest myself of that infernal helmet.

The Captain of Marines in the *Queen* kindly offered to lend me a cap if it fitted me; it was just too small, and it was also very stiff, so that when it was pressed down in order to hide the smallness I felt as if my head was enclosed in an iron band.

Preoccupation with the problem of headgear must have obliterated all impressions of Taranto, for the next thing I remember is lunch in Rome with Eddie Keeling and Gerald Tyrrwhitt[1] in Eddie's delightful rooms where we were waited upon by a butler with the manners and appearance of a Cardinal. It was all exquisitely civilized and pleasant,

---

[1] The late Lord Berners.

E

for there was little in the atmosphere of Rome to remind one that Italy was at war. Rome preserved her calm; those sun-browned streets seemed thoroughfares to peace. I failed to visit Vienna before the First World War; I am grateful to Providence that I knew Rome before it became the noisiest city in Europe instead of the quietest.

After two days in Rome I went on to Paris, where I hoped to find a cap that fitted me; by now my head seemed to be taking on the shape of an Aztec's. I visited the Inter-Allies Bureau, which was in charge of Clive Bigham,[1] whom I had last seen when he was Provost Marshal at Gallipoli. Working with him was my old friend Henry Lygon.

"Ah, Henry," I said, "you'll be able to tell me where I can get a cap."

The most earnest enquiries could not discover any shop in Paris where one could buy a British military cap.

"But I'll drive you to Boulogne to-morrow," Henry offered. "The boat leaves at two, and we must start from Paris at ten sharp."

What a drive! It was an open car and the chauffeur had but one eye. Henry's luggage was excessive and every time we turned a corner his bags leapt about in the car like performing animals; even the lead-weighted crossed bag I was taking to the Foreign Office jumped about. It rained and it blew hard. I had no goggles. Then we punctured, and I stood miserably by the road in a whirl of dancing poplar leaves. After the puncture was mended the one-eyed chauffeur drove faster than ever. We reached the quayside at Boulogne just as they were taking up the gangway.

"We should have done it comfortably," said Henry, "if it hadn't been for that puncture."

"Not comfortably, Henry," I said. "It could never be comfortable to travel at sixty miles an hour in an open furniture van."

As soon as I reached London I left my bag at the Foreign Office and then drove straight to Hilhouse in Bond Street.

"The cap you're wearing, sir, is just a leetle bit tight," said the assistant. "It's left a regular mark on your forehead."

"I wonder it hasn't cracked my skull," I told him.

I gave the address of the kind Captain of Marines who had lent me his cap and asked for it to be posted back to Taranto at once. Then I drove to Bury Street to be greeted by Faith in the service-flat she had taken. A light khaki uniform was cold in the autumnal weather of London, and I lost no time in getting equipped at Forster's with a blue Marine uniform. Braced by the prospect of that enviable uniform I felt better able to face the ordeal of my first meeting with C.

In those days taxis were very hard to find. So when I reached White-hall Court I told the driver to wait; I fancied that ten minutes would be

---

[1] The late Viscount Mersey.

the extreme limit of the interview. The voice on the telephone which had informed me that the Chief would see me at half-past five that afternoon had sounded ominous. When I enquired for the whereabouts of "Captain Spencer's" flat I was directed up the familar staircase which led to the Authors' Club. I debated for a moment when I reached the first floor whether I should turn aside into the club and have a strong brandy before going up to C's headquarters at the top of the building; I decided I might need one even more acutely ten minutes hence and went on up.

The attitude of subordinates always indicates what is likely to be the attitude of the head man in any show, and my reception by various young R.N.V.R. lieutenants was ambiguous. There was that air of nervous anticipation with which schoolboys watch the victim who has been sent for by the Head. Even the pink-faced lady secretaries came fluttering on some excuse into the room where I was waiting, to take a quick glance at the man who had ventured to defy C for nine months. After about ten minutes of this embarrassed waiting a young lieutenant came in to announce gravely that the Chief wished to see Captain Mackenzie immediately. I followed him into C's private room tucked away under the roof, crowded with filing cupboards and shelves, and with the rest of the space almost entirely filled by C's big table. I saw on the other side of it a pale clean-shaven man with a Punch-like chin, a small fine bow of a mouth, and a pair of very bright eyes. This was Captain Mansfield Cumming, R.N., in naval uniform.

C paid no attention when I came in, but remained bent over the table, perusing some document through a pair of dark horn-rimmed spectacles. I stood watching through the dormer window the blue dusk and tarnished silver of the Thames until presently C took off his glasses, leant back in his chair, and stared hard at me for a long minute without speaking.

"Well?" he said finally.

"Mackenzie, sir. Reporting to you from Athens."

"And what have you to say for yourself?" he asked, putting in an eyeglass and staring at me harder than ever.

Somehow I suppose I must have embarked on my tale in such a way as to win his attention; after a few minutes he murmured in those faintly slurred, immensely attractive accents of his:

"There's no need to tell me all this standing up. There's a chair beside you."

So I sat down and went on talking until about a quarter to seven when a pink-faced secretary with a bundle of papers put her head round the door. She conveyed an impression of having been deputed as the least likely person to have her head bitten off if she was interrupting. C held out his hand for the papers and signed one C after another in the bright green ink he always used. Presently we were left alone again.

At half-past seven he said:

"Well, you'd better stop and have some dinner with us."

"Thank you very much, sir," I said. "Would you mind if I went downstairs and sent away my taxi?"

"Have you been keeping a taxi waiting two hours?"

"Yes, sir. I thought you would probably be finished with me in a few minutes."

"My god," C exclaimed. "No wonder you're always asking for another thousand pounds every month."

I went down to pay off the taxi; when I came back the offices were empty. C took me into the dining-room, where I was introduced to Lady Cumming as the man who had given him more trouble than anybody in his service.

After dinner C showed me various books he had been buying; they were mostly sets in bright leather bindings.

"These ought to be in your line," he said. "You're a writing fellow, aren't you?"

Those books and the full length oil-painting of a young officer in the uniform of the Seaforth Highlanders were the chief features of the room. I remembered the tale of how C had cut off his leg with a penknife to reach his dying son and put a greatcoat over him; the little room filled with that large portrait expressed how large a place the original must have held in his heart.

It was after eleven when I got up to leave. C stumped along with me to the door of the flat.

"You'd better look in every day while you're in London," he told me. "I thought this would happen."

"You thought what would happen, sir?"

"Why, I intended to make myself extremely unpleasant to you, but I said that when I saw you I should probably find you a man after my own heart and fall on your neck. We'll have dinner at the Savoy one night soon."

I felt as I walked down the marble stairs of Whitehall Court that we should get a real move on in Athens presently.

Principal R. M. Burrows of King's College, a great philhellene and a devoted champion of Venizelos, wanted me to have an interview with Sir Edward Carson, who had resigned from the Cabinet over the Salonika muddle a year ago and was now inclined to interest himself in the Greek question. I said that before seeing Sir Edward Carson I ought to wait until Lord Hardinge sent for me; after waiting some time C told me definitely that Lord Hardinge did not wish to see me. After that I no longer had any hesitation about putting the state of affairs in Greece before Carson. Burrows took me along to the Law Courts where we found him in a dark little room, his wig on the table beside him. His large swarthy face looked larger and swarthier in the dimness and dinginess of his surroundings. A sombre and impressive figure he seemed, as he sat there nursing a knee and listening to my appreciation of Greek affairs.

"Well," he said in the end, "I might overthrow the Government if matters grow worse in Greece. I have the support of 153 members."

"The miraculous draught of fishes," I murmured.

He smiled severely and I quickly went on.

"But, Sir Edward, the situation may develop rapidly at any moment. The lives of Allied subjects in Athens, not to mention the lives of Venizelist Greeks, may be in danger while they are waiting for you to overthrow the Government. What is required is a positive assurance that the British Government will support Venizelos. The moment that is made clear we shall have no more talk of Royalist violence."

"Well," said Carson, "if you find the situation becoming really grave you can communicate with me through Professor Burrows and I shall probably decide to act."

We talked a little more about the muddle last October which had led to the overwhelming of Serbia, for which Carson blamed Kitchener. He told us about a Cabinet meeting at which the despatch of troops for the Suvla landing was being debated before Lord Kitchener arrived.

"I was about the only member of the Cabinet who wasn't frightened of him and I was urged to get his views. 'Mr Secretary of State for War,' I said when he arrived, 'could you indicate to the Cabinet whether you think this projected new landing at Gallipoli is likely to be successful or not?' Lord Kitchener snapped back. 'How do I know? I've never been there.' "

Perhaps if the disastrous events of the First of December in Athens had happened a fortnight earlier Carson might have succeeded in overthrowing the Government before those tortuous negotiations which ended in the supplanting of Asquith by Lloyd George.

I had more hope of what Lord Denman might be able to do for us with searching questions in the House of Lords. A vivid and pleasant memory of that October is of Faith and me lunching with Lord and Lady Denman. The other guests were a major in the Black Watch who had lost an eye in Flanders and a pretty fair-haired young wife. This was Major Archibald Wavell, M.C., who would almost at once be leaving London to be attached to the Russian armies in the Caucasus. He was a first cousin of Raymond Wavell-Paxton, who I heard was one of the British officers the Germans had put into solitary confinement as a reprisal for Winston Churchill's provocative announcement of the more rigorous treatment we should give to U-boat commanders taken prisoner. Raymond was a captain in the Coldstream who had been Assistant Military Attaché in Vienna when war broke out.

The "guinea a word" Archie of the future was as talkative as myself in those days and we monopolized the conversation at lunch, discussing Gallipoli, Salonika and the Near East. After he had left with his young wife, who had presented him with a son six months ago, Lady Denman asked me what I thought of Archie Wavell.

"I think he's terrific. He's the first fellow I've met from the Western Front who realizes that there is such a sea as the Mediterranean, let alone that there's a war going on at one end of it."

"I'm glad you feel like that about him because *we* think Archie Wavell will go a long long way."

I should not meet the future Lord Wavell again for thirty years.

Faith was much bucked by Lord Denman's telling her that the organization in Athens was the most dramatic Intelligence achievement of the war. She felt that a testimonial like that from a former Governor-General of Australia and Captain of His Majesty's Honourable Corps of Gentlemen-at-Arms was a testimonial indeed.

By now C was wholeheartedly with us in the effort to hold our position in Greece. I had outlined for him my scheme for a check on contraband going northward to the enemy by establishing posts between Janina and Volo. This proposal of mine was to be brought up at an Intelligence conference of top brass to be held shortly.

On the morning of the conference, a drenching October day, C told me that if I wanted the money for those places of mine with unpronounceable names I'd better buy a half-crown map of Greece from Bartholomew's and mark each place with a cross before I started arguing. This I did.

The conference in the War Office began, various generals and colonels being seated round a table in the War Office. Colonel French, my sponsor, told the D.M.I. that I had a proposal to make and had bought a map to show what I required. There was a murmur of satisfaction when the generals and colonels heard that a map was available, and there was almost a buzz of excitement when they leant over and saw my red crosses presenting an apparently impenetrable barrier from sea to sea against the most intrepid and resourceful contrabandist.

"I see he's got it right across Greece," said one general. "That should be very effective. How much do you think this scheme of yours would cost, Captain Mackenzie?"

My original request had been for something under £600, but seeing the enthusiasm those crosses had aroused I quickly doubled it.

"I think I ought to be able to do it for £1,200 a month, sir."

"That sounds very moderate," said another general. "Don't you think you'd want rather more than that?"

"Well, sir," I replied, judiciously, "with the gradual extension of our Controls I should like to be able to call on £2,000 a month, though of course I don't anticipate spending all that on this northern chain; I'm hoping to make the Peloponnese completely secure also."

To make the Peloponnese secure on paper I had drawn a red line right round it; not even during the most favourable moments of the Lacedemonian War can Sparta ever have looked so secure as it looked on that map of mine, guarded by a pencilled ring.

One afternoon at Whitehall Court I went into C's room and found a cheerful young man with him to whom I was introduced. This was Wiseman,[1] who was running C's show in New York and just leaving again for America. He showed me a photograph from one of our illustrated weeklies of the German Ambassador at Washington in a bathing-dress with two ladies also in bathing-dresses.

"This is going badly against him in New York," Wiseman said with a chuckle.

I replied with a sigh that only in Great Britain or the United States could such a photograph have been expected to influence public opinion against the war aims of Germany; I was depressed by the civilization we were fighting such a great war to preserve. Contemporary readers may be unaware that the official name for the First World War was "The Great War for Civilization": at any rate the Second World War escaped the humbug of being called "The Great War for a Free World", however many avenues in it politicians might explore.

C had promised me all the new officers he could get hold of to extend our scheme of port control; after meeting Edward Knoblock at some party I suggested he should come out to Athens. Knoblock at that time was working with the Indian Secret Intelligence, housed somewhere near Sloane Street. Somerset Maugham was also engaged in that branch of secret activity. C agreed to get Knoblock a lieutenancy in the R.N.V.R., but no sooner had Knoblock procured a naval uniform than it was discovered he could not be a lieutenant in the R.N.V.R. because he was still an American subject.

"However," said C, "I believe we can get him a commission in the R.N.A.S."

So Knoblock rushed out and bought a woollen bird to sew on his uniform. No sooner had he equipped himself as a naval airman than he was told he would have to be a second-lieutenant in General Service.

[1] The late Sir William Wiseman, Bt., C.B.

So Knoblock rushed out again from those wonderful Regency rooms of his in Albany and equipped himself with a khaki uniform and the green tabs of an Intelligence officer.

We were due to leave England on November 3rd, and as Knoblock's commission could not possibly be gazetted until long after that he thought it would be safest to take all these uniforms out to Greece and possibly dispose out there of any superfluous equipment when it was settled which service he was to join. In his enthusiasm he even bought two swords, a naval and a military one.

I did not forget Tucker's longing for the executive curl when commissions were being discussed and before I left London I was able to secure his commission as Lieutenant R.N.V.R. instead of Assistant-Paymaster R.N.V.R.

Remembering Private Robertson's desire to be a Corporal in the Army Service Corps, I put in for his promotion when I reached London and after some dogged correspondence managed to achieve those two stripes for him before I left London, but only as an honorary rank. In other words he was to be allowed to call himself Corporal, but he was not to get any extra pay.

The day before we were to leave for Greece, C presented me with the swordstick he had always carried himself on spying expeditions in time of peace.

"That's when this business was really amusing," he said. "After the war is over we'll do some amusing secret service work together. It's capital sport."

Word had been sent from the Foreign Office that I was to carry some bags for them to Rome and Athens. The two bags for Rome were enormous affairs, both uncrossed; the bag for Greece was very small but what it lacked in size it made up for in weight; there seemed to be enough lead inside it to cover a roof. It was crossed and I had been given to understand that it contained an extremely confidential dispatch for M. Venizelos. So heavy was it that there were moments on that journey when I felt I was carrying M. Venizelos himself.

At Boulogne, which we did not reach until after dark, we found that the train was about a mile from the boat and separated from it by an overflow of mud from Flanders. We could not get hold of a porter and when at last Knoblock and I reached the train after dragging the bags and some of our own luggage through that infernal mud we found that no compartment had been reserved for the King's Messenger. The train was already crowded, and whatever happened to the rest of the luggage the bags had to go with me. Finally, in the forefront of the train we found an empty first-class compartment and I settled down inside with the bags while Knoblock went back to fetch the rest of the luggage.

While he was gone a French official put his head round the door of the carriage to say that the whole of this part of the train had been reserved for Mr Pierpoint Morgan and that the compartment I was in was reserved for his valet. I told him I was a *courrier du roi* and that if Mr Pierpoint Morgan's valet tried to get into this carriage I should push him out into the mud, and Mr Pierpoint Morgan as well, unless another compartment was found for me. The official retired and presently Knoblock arrived with the rest of the luggage. When two officials came along to renew the argument about our right to occupy the compartment we had by this time filled with luggage Knoblock, whose French was as fluent as my own, joined in; when we had finished with Mr Pierpoint Morgan there was hardly an unused opprobrious epithet in the French dictionary. The officials retired discomfited by the vigour of our duet and we settled back in our corners, undisturbed again all the way to Paris.

We dined next night at the Gare de Lyon, and I thought how often I had dined here, with one eye on the big clock, on the way to Italy by this very train, the time of whose departure at 8.25 not even war had changed.

We were kept two or three days in Rome waiting for news of a passage from Taranto to Greece. I forget at which hotel we stayed but I remember being awakened on a topaz-bright November morning by the chattering of multitudinous swallows gathering for their flight across the Mediterranean. In Rome I met Ivor Novello for the first time; he had been in Sicily with Phyllis Neilson-Terry, acting in a film made from some book by Robert Hichens. On one evening at a party Phyllis Neilson-Terry recited a poem about Verdun, the refrain of which was "They shall not pass".

At Taranto I was lucky enough to get a passage in a French destroyer immediately after lunch with Admiral Kerr. The Captain signalled there was room only for me; Knoblock had to wait for the French packet-boat.

When we were about ten miles out of Taranto I saw a mine floating past us on the port side hardly a couple of yards away from the ship. I shouted a warning. Everybody got much excited and it was agreed that the mine must be destroyed. Rifles were taken out of the armoury, and the ship's officers and myself went up on the bridge to shoot at it. The destroyer had been put about; the mine, looking like a giant sea-urchin, was bobbing about some fifty yards to starboard. I was invited as the guest to take the first shot. I had an idea that it was usual to be further away than we were before shooting at a mine, but not liking to disgrace my new blue uniform by betraying too acute a nautical ignorance, I blazed away and missed. After me the Captain took a shot and missed. The Lieutenant took a shot and missed. The Enseigne took a shot and missed. Others fired and missed. Then it was my turn again and—if anybody ever really has nearly jumped out of his skin I did when that mine went off. A great column of water quite 200 feet high spurted up. A lot of glass on the bridge was smashed by the force of the detonation, and there descended upon us a shower of broken bits of metal. The crew started scrambling about the deck on all fours for souvenirs in the shape of old iron. After a signal had been sent to the Admiral announcing the destruction of the unpleasant monster the occasion was celebrated with red wine. That red wine did not go well with the motion, and when I began to feel sea-sick the Captain decided I must have all my meals on deck. I could have done without any meals at all, but as the ship's cook had been making special dishes at the Captain's instigation I had to eat them. In the intervals of eating and being sick the Captain talked to me about Alphonse Daudet's books. His kindness to that guest of fifty years ago is still remembered. I hope that after the First War his life in some sunny garden in the heart of France was placid and that he was able to fish in a stream as serene as his own blue eyes.

Gradually the sea-sickness passed; by the time we were running down between Kephallonia and Ithaca I was able to contemplate the beauty of a sunset that was turning the grey rocks of Ithaca to amethyst. Next morning I woke to see the embanked cliffs of the Corinth canal gliding past. That afternoon I was back in Athens.

I was amazed to find that during my five weeks' absence the French attitude to King Constantine had changed. They were now convinced that he was their friend and they were prepared to let down Venizelos and the Provisional Government if it suited them better to establish their political and commercial supremacy in Greece with the King's help. He had suggested they should ask for some arms and the French Admiral, who was an ingenuous snob, had fallen into the trap. He made his claim; the Greek Government rejected it. The Admiral then demanded the delivery of ten mountain batteries by December 1st, 1916.

And if I do not receive satisfaction, he concluded, I shall be obliged to take any measures which the situation may demand.

While the French were getting ready to sell out the Provisional Government our own military authorities up in Salonika were trying to tempt the Bulgarians to make a separate peace at the expense of Greece. Not only that, but they were trying to negotiate a separate peace with Turkey, again at the expense of Greece. I was asked to look out for a

possible envoy to Constantinople; my refusal was as offensive as I could
make it to Army Headquarters at Salonika.

I was convinced that trouble was in store for us on December 1st and
I had to make up my mind whether, if the worst came to the worst, I
should surrender to what was coming to seem the impossible task of
persuading the people at home to handle the Greek situation with
common sense and ask to be recalled, or whether I should try to keep
our organization together in the hope of its being of service to the
Provisional Government.

The great ship *Britannia* had been torpedoed off the island of Zea and
the *Braemar Castle* had been torpedoed in the Mykonos Channel within
sight of Syra. The latter had been brought into port because the torpedo's effect had been spoilt by hitting her where she was carrying a
large store of toilet-paper which swelled in the water coming in and
plugged the leak. Ricaud brought me four coded telegrams from the
German Consul in Syra with letters to the German Legation which
proved he was communicating the movements of Allied ships. The
members of the four enemy Legations had been expelled from Greece in
the previous week, after I had secured documentary evidence of
espionage against the German Marine Attaché and the Turkish Military Attaché. Consular officials in districts outside Athens had been
granted an extension of time, but obviously the consuls at Syra must be
removed at once. I had decided that if events took the bad turn I
expected after that foolish Note of the French Admiral we would go to
Syra and make the enemy consulates our headquarters.

Sir Francis Elliot agreed with me that the enemy consuls should be
got rid of but asked how I proposed to do it. I reminded him that
Engineer Lieut.-Commander Knox was at Syra in charge of repairs of
His Majesty's ships in the dockyard there. Sir Francis telegraphed
Consul Hastings to authorize Knox to arrest the enemy consuls and
send them up to Salonika with their staffs. Thirty-four hours later the
German, Austrian and Turkish consuls had been expelled and their
consulates taken over.

All through that Saturday, November 25th, prominent Venizelists
had been coming to the Annexe and imploring me to obtain some kind
of protection for them; they were convinced the Royalists meant to
resist the French demands and take the opportunity to level up old
scores with their political opponents. I told Sir Francis that, unless
immediate steps were taken to secure hostages from the Royalist party,
trouble was inevitable. He agreed and tried to persuade the Admiral,
who insisted that such action was unnecessary. During that night all
shops belonging to avowed Liberals were marked with crosses of red
paint as an indication of those suitable for looting in the riots which

were to be stirred up a week hence. It was certain that the Admiral's Note would be rejected and I was able to say exactly where every Greek detachment would be placed and every gun.

Sells was sending urgent telegrams to his Chief at the Admiralty; I was sending urgent telegrams to my own Chief for passing to the Foreign Office; the Minister was sending urgent telegrams. Not the faintest attention was paid to them. The struggle in London for political power was then coming to a climax. The French Admiral was not the only man with an ultimatum for delivery on December 1st, Mr Lloyd George had one in his pocket for Mr Asquith, and he was showing himself a better hand at taking precautions.

On November 29th Plunkett went home. He said he felt rather worried about going off at such a critical moment but that there was nothing for him to do in Athens, and that even if he stayed he should leave the sole command to myself.

Captain Leo Amery[1] came through Athens on his way to Salonika. He had just crossed from Corfu and seemed to fancy he was completely *au fait* with the situation in Greece from a conversation with one of the Ministers in the late Government whom he had met on the boat. By now I was incapable of being shocked by the ignorance of professional politicians of everything except professional politics. Over coffee at the Grande Bretagne Hotel I tried to present him with a few realities but did not expend much energy on trying to penetrate the impenetrable. He was extremely genial and reminded me of a friendly bulldog.

On the day Plunkett left, Ricaud lunched with me at my house in Ghizi Street. I asked him if he would co-operate with me in seizing a few prominent Royalists to hold as hostages for the safety of their political opponents. Ricaud felt it would be too grave a breach of naval discipline to disobey the Admiral's orders. At that moment I noticed his knives were crossed and leant over the table to put them straight, telling him I did not want to quarrel with him at this critical moment. He laughed at such superstition.

"You can laugh," I said, "but in moments of crisis I do believe in omens. There's only one thing left now to make me feel finally convinced that the worst is going to happen the day after to-morrow, and that is for me to see a peacock."

At this Ricaud roared with laughter.

"*Un paon*! An intelligent man like you to be frightened by a peacock? *Ah, non, par exemple!* But you can be quite tranquil because you will not be seeing any peacocks to-day."

At that moment there was a tap on the door and Robertson came in to say that my agent Davy Jones had returned from his mission to

----

[1] The late Rt. Hon. L. S. Amery, M.P.

Sparta with two peacocks as a present from the Mayor of Sparta. And down in the garden there really were two superb peacocks, one of which immediately jumped on Robertson's back. I told Davy Jones to take the birds away at once, which he did, protesting that the Demarch of Sparta had sent them to me as an expression of goodwill. What happened to the peacocks I never heard. There were enough omens of disaster coming in every hour without auguries from birds.

I spent the rest of that evening and half the night in taking down reports and in trying to establish an atmosphere of calm among our people in the Annexe, who were getting more and more badly rattled all the time. When I drove back to Ghizi Street at three in the morning I had my final omen from Josephine, my Constantinople cook, who emerged from a kind of cupboard under the stairs where she slept with her child.

"*Josephine voulez faire cartes,*" Lisa announced.

To humour her I agreed and cut the pack in three. When the cards were turned I saw two black cards and the ace of spades upside down.

"Treachery, violence, death," Josephine proclaimed in Greek.

This was the message from Fate, pondering which I turned over to sleep that night.

Next morning as I drove down to the Annexe I noticed bands of Reservists being cheered by the crowd on their way to the barracks. Information came in that 150 rounds were being served out to each man with or without uniform. That evening Sells and I got hold of Rear-Admiral Hayes-Sadler, who was commanding the British squadron with the French fleet, and begged him to be prepared for the worst to-morrow. He assured us the French Admiral had positive pledges from the King that no violence would happen. Then Major Huntingford, R.M.A., the liaison officer on board the flagship *Provence*, came along for final news. He showed us the operations order and I warned him that the Royal Marine company which had been told to occupy the powder factory would meet with strong opposition there. I was only too sadly right; thirty of them were to be killed the next morning.

There was now nothing I could do except concentrate on providing as far as I could for the safety of those under my orders. For the last ten days I had noticed on the way back to my house an increasing number of scowling Reservists sitting about outside the nearby cafés; after those peacocks and those cards I decided I should be safer sleeping out of the house for the present. It occurred to me, however, that if it were known I was in the Annexe it might provoke an attack there to-morrow.

Knoblock was now in the khaki of a 2nd Lieutenant G.S. and at nine o'clock that evening I told him to put on my big military greatcoat, pull my Marine uniform cap well down over his face and drive back to the house in Ghizi Street with Robertson in the Sunbeam. I had already sent Lisa down to the Piraeus to be stowed away in some safe place; Josephine had gone off to spend the week-end with friends.

It had been a habit of mine since I was twice shot at in the car to sit as low as I could in the seat beside Robertson, and I showed Knoblock how to copy my posture. I told him to hurry inside as soon as he reached the house, which was detached and surrounded by open waste ground, and to leave again immediately by the back door, get inside the car and lie down on the floor covered with a rug so that the Sunbeam would drive back at once to the Annexe, apparently empty. I hoped this ruse would secure the Annexe against attack.

I had given orders that all our own men were to spend the night in the offices. There were about fifty of them there, and this number was increased gradually throughout the night by the arrival of Venizelists in fear of violence. By morning there were over 120 people in the Annexe.

I had an hour's uneasy sleep toward dawn on a table in the main office, the longest sleep I was to get for many hours.

Next morning we watched from the balcony of the Annexe French sailors on the skyline of the hill Philopappas below the Acropolis and lines of Greek soldiers advancing against them. We had watched the Greeks open fire and the French replying. We had watched silhouettes falling dead or wounded. For the rest of the morning we could obtain no news; there was intermittent firing all this time, both close at hand and far away.

At a quarter-past one the Military Attaché came round to the Annexe to say he had had word from the commander of the Athens garrison that everything was over; he hoped I could drive him to the Grande Bretagne because he had a bridge date after lunch.

Against my better judgment I agreed to go to the hotel. The crowd in Stadium Street was excited; but there was no sign yet of any rioting. Sells was at the Grande Bretagne and I heard from him about the events of the morning. The French Admiral, convinced that the mere sight of him would be enough to cow the Greeks into surrendering the batteries, had driven down to the Zappeion, a building in the Park. Here he had been immediately surrounded by Greek troops, and machine-guns in the shrubberies—of the whereabouts of which I had notified the pompous little man—started firing, though they had stopped at half-past twelve. I asked what had been finally settled between the King and the Admiral.

"Nothing apparently so far," said Sells, "but over fifty of the French sailors were killed in the advance this morning." I asked about our Marines; there was no news of them.

While Sells and I were talking, Robertson came hurrying to our table to say the Legation was being attacked and that he thought I ought to come at once. Sells and I rushed along; as we passed Fairholme's table I stopped to ask him if he wanted to come with us. The Military Attaché assured us we were probably being taken in by one of the "wild rumours" that my "ruffians" were always starting. Besides, he had an appointment for bridge in the hotel at a quarter to three.

We had to move very slowly along Stadium Street, which was now filled with a murmurous crowd. J. M. N. Jeffries of the *Daily Mail*, the only newspaper correspondent in Athens who could be trusted not to disseminate rumours, jumped on the running-board of the Sunbeam and clung on. About halfway down Stadium Street a seedy-looking blackguard spat into the car, but at the same moment the car bumped over another man's foot and we passed on. When we turned the corner out of Stadium Street we saw on the left, outside the Ministry of Finance, about half a dozen Greek sailors kneeling on the pavement with rifles held ready to fire. Sir Francis Elliot hatless, but carrying an umbrella, was walking off in the direction of the Legation. Two of my men were standing on the balcony of the Annexe with revolvers; several others were carrying a body through the gates into the courtyard. We jumped out, eager to hear the explanation of this strange picture.

Zammit, our chief Maltese agent, had seen a wounded French soldier being dragged along by a Greek patrol. On Zammit's calling for volunteers to rescue the French soldier two or three of our porters had rushed out with revolvers and freed the Frenchman from the patrol. They were getting into safety, when some sailors covered by the sentry-box of the Ministry of Finance opposite had opened fire on them. One of the porters had been shot through the lungs and Zammit himself was wounded in the shoulder. When the firing started two more of my men had fired back at the sailors from the balcony of the Annexe. Sir Francis on hearing the noise had run out of the Legation, waving his umbrella, and ordered everybody to stop firing at once. His appearance as he hurried into the line of fire was described to me afterwards as like that of an elderly gentleman waving his umbrella to stop a bus.

The behaviour of the sailors outside the Ministry of Finance was symptomatic of what was to come. By 3.30 p.m. the Legation and the Annexe were completely surrounded by Greek troops. A machine-gun was mounted on the roof of one of the houses looking down into the courtyard of the Annexe; this was removed later when its presence might have been awkward for the Government contention that their revenge upon the Liberals was self-defence against a revolutionary outbreak.

At 4.30 p.m. we could hear the sound of firing from the direction of

Constitution Square, and a number of soldiers came running into the Square in front of the Legation; a violent fusillade broke out a few minutes later. There was a shout that they were attacking the Annexe. Everybody rushed in a panic to close the shutters of the front windows; I had to use some rough language before I could restore calm. Finally I allowed the shutters in front to be closed, for I discovered that darkness had a tranquillising effect upon the men; it reminded me of putting a cover over a cockatoo's cage to stop its screaming. The firing we heard at half-past four was a fresh bombardment of the Zappeion; this spurred the Admiral at last into ordering the guns of the Fleet to open fire.

Just before dusk two shells landed by the Palace without bursting, and they may have helped to persuade the King to agree to an armistice. The garrison of the Zappeion marched back to the Piraeus, three hundred of them escorted by sixty Greek soldiers and followed by the Admiral in his car.

At 6.30 p.m., being still without news and fearing an attack upon the Annexe during the night, I gave orders to burn certain papers and to take the most important documents over to the Chancery.

There seemed little hope that Francesco, the wounded porter, would live until morning. The haemorrhage was heavy; the two nurses we had got for him were pessimistic. Venizelist refugees were still creeping in one by one to get the protection of the Annexe; the Venizelists, for whose immunity no provision had been made in that precious armistice, had been having a bad time of it during the afternoon. Many of them had been badly mauled by the mob, some having been actually bitten as though by real wild beasts. The Annexe was a nightmare.

I walked round to the Legation for news. As I stepped outside two rifles went off in the dark a few yards away. Then I heard running footsteps and a cry of "Halt!" from a sentry in the square. The running footsteps continued. There was another shot followed by silence and a low moaning. I walked across the road to find out what had happened; a couple of soldiers sprang out from the darkness and forced me back, sticking the muzzles of their rifles into my ribs. I gave up being inquisitive and retired into the Legation, where I heard the story of the King's conference with the Allied Ministers.

At 11 p.m. word was brought up to my room that Francesco was going fast. A messenger had volunteered to find a priest, but none of those he asked would venture forth. One of the Maltese had given Francesco a crucifix to hold as a light for the soul about to depart into the darkness. He was lying in a corner of the passport office on some coats, a handsome fellow with clear-cut features, now white as marble. In the other corner of the room four or five of his companions were squatting over a card game which was being played by the light of two

C.M. and Clifford Heathcote-Smith

Martin Secker

D. H. Lawrence

guttering candles stuck on the floor. Francesco, still in his early twenties, had already fought in the Balkan wars, where he had been shot through the forehead, the hole in his skull still visible.

"I am going to die, my captain," he whispered.

"Rubbish," I told him. "A Cretan who has been shot through the head by a Bulgarian bullet will be ashamed to die from the bullet of a Boeotian Reservist in his lung."

Francesco Manoussaki smiled, and from that moment he began to recover. Indeed, he was so much better by morning that I felt justified in letting the two girls who were nursing him go back to their house for clothes. When they arrived home they were attacked by Reservists, treated with the vilest indignities and dragged off to jail, where they were kept for thirty hours without food, shut up in one of the latrines; their house was looted.

The rest of that long night passed without further disturbances. By this time nearly 200 Venizelist refugees were sleeping all over the Annexe on the floors. Everybody was tired, hungry and depressed. Athens was black and silent. The Allied Ministers were conferring at the Legation until 2.30 a.m. I rested on the table in the front office as I wished to be at hand in case of panic among the mixed crowd we were harbouring; one shot from an imprudent pistol might bring the whole place about our ears.

About five o'clock in the morning I was wakened from a brief uneasy doze by a dishevelled young Marine.

"I heard there was a Marine officer here, sir," he panted, "and having got cut off from my detachment I wish to report. God, sir, it was awful yesterday. We'd only just sat down to have a bit of lunch by the side of the powder magazine near the cemetery, and we were just getting up when they opened fire on us over the wall and shot us down just as we were, sir, without a chance to reply. There's about thirty of our poor fellows gone, sir." With these words he burst into tears. "I don't know how I ever got away myself, sir, I've been wandering about all night."

I told the boy to get a rest and report later in the morning to the Naval Attaché, who would tell him how to get back to his ship.

Later that morning Ricaud arrived to say that all of them at the French School had been ordered to go on board at once. I asked his authority to destroy the French papers in the Annexe if I thought it prudent. He told me to act as I thought best and said how badly he and the others felt about leaving me in Athens.

Then he grasped my hand and said that it would perhaps be a pleasure for me in this *mauvais quart d'heure* to hear that the Legion of Honour had been granted to me. He hurried away downstairs. His blue

F

boat-cloak was fluttering in the wind as he crossed the courtyard to the car.

We felt a little quiet and lonely after the French drove off; but at 10.45 a loud fusillade broke out close to the Legation. The bullets were whistling constantly over the back garden. From one of the houses just behind the Annexe the shooting was so furious that somebody cried out a machine-gun had been turned on us, which set up another panic and our chaps began pulling out pistols and revolvers. I said I was tired of these panics and that everybody must give up his arms. I was never free from the fear that one of our fellows would start firing from the Annexe and provoke an attack. When I ordered the arms to be brought into my room I was met by an excited refusal. They did not mind fighting, but they were not going to be butchered like sheep. If the Annexe was attacked they wanted to put up a show.

"If the Annexe is attacked, you silly fellows," I exclaimed irritably, "of course I'll let you have your pistols, but you must hand them over to me meanwhile so that they can be locked up in my room until I give the word to use them."

Still they would not obey.

"Look here," I urged, "the only person in this building of any real importance to the other side is myself. You don't suppose the Royalists are going to risk the unpleasant results of attacking the Legation merely to frighten a lot of sheep like you? And now as you won't believe me, I'll prove to you how unlikely they are to attack the Annexe by proving that they dare not attack me."

With this I walked downstairs and out through the gate. Lighting a cigarette, I then strolled up the street out of the Square into Stadium Street, where I stood for about five minutes on the edge of the pavement, watching the mob swaying now this way, now that. One wretched Venizelist, a fat man, was being dragged along by half a dozen monkey-faced Reservists. Every time he stopped some of them hit him in the face, which was streaming with blood; others prodded him in the back with their bayonets. Presently I became aware that the mob was beginning to notice my presence and, when I heard my name called out, I thought it was time to retreat. I had not felt at all frightened while I was standing on the pavement with my eyes on them; yet as soon as I turned round to walk back the hundred yards to the Annexe my knees began to get woolly. The noise of the mob growing quieter as I left them behind me was eerie. I began to wonder if I should get a bullet in my back before I reached the gates of the Annexe; nothing happened.

When I reached my room again the floor was covered with revolvers, daggers and cartridge belts; the rifles were stacked away in a corner. One or two of my much loved "ruffians" were in tears, and I was assured they would never again disobey an order of mine. In the words of one of them "This must not be again, my captain. Not at all, no. The pistols are now for you to say, for we to use."

The firing and mob violence went on all day in Athens on that Saturday; many bullets struck the Legation and the Annexe. King George V was being told by King Constantine that the Greek Government had irrefutable proof that the Venizelists had planned to make themselves masters of Athens at 3 p.m. on December 1st. King George V believed that twaddle, which was afterwards given currency in print by the late Sir Basil Thomson who was paid out of the million pounds that Prince Christopher could command by marrying the wealthy American widow, Mrs Leeds, to write a book called *The Allied Secret Service in Greece* with a lie on almost every page.

The house of Venizelos, after a stout defence by a few Cretan guards, had been sacked; news had come that my own house had been looted, and the indomitable Knoblock went off to investigate. When the Reservists saw me enter the house and the car drive away empty, as they thought, they had surrounded it. Early on Friday morning, before the rejection of the Admiral's ultimatum, a Greek sailor had ascended the back staircase and knocked at the door. When there was no answer he had forced open the door, gone along the passage to the front room, stepped out on the balcony and fired a pistol shot into the air. The Reservists surrounding the house had been so anxious to start firing that they had wounded the sailor in the leg before he had time to get off the balcony. After making the house look like a pepperpot they had broken in. They had found a signed photograph of Venizelos on the wall and chewed it to pieces with their teeth. Then they had destroyed all my clothes and belongings, including the typescript of a novel called *No Papers* I had laboured to write at intervals during the feverish year of 1916. They had decided that I must have escaped by a secret passage to the Annexe and tore up the floorboards in an effort to discover it.

There was still no indication on Sunday morning that London was aware of what was going on in Athens. Sir Max Aitken after an "exhausting" Saturday had woken "feeling weary"; the war everywhere was forgotten in the struggle for political power. As London was too much preoccupied even to offer advice, let alone instructions, I decided to move first and ask afterwards where I was to go.

Sir Francis Elliot approved of my suggestion to take over the enemy consulates in Syra. In the event of war with Old Greece the island would be an ideal centre for Intelligence. I drafted a letter to the Greek Prime Minister for him to sign, in which the Greek Government was called upon to provide our organization with transport to the Piraeus and suitable escorts. I then telephoned to commandeer the steamer

Thessalia, which had just unloaded at the Piraeus, and ordered the staff to begin dismantling the offices of the Annexe.

The answer of the Greek Government to the proposal that I should leave Athens was the promptest ever received to any diplomatic Note sent to them. Government lorries should be put at our disposal; escorts should be provided for our men. A safe conduct should be accorded to myself, and a Greek officer of equal rank unarmed should accompany me in the Sunbeam from the Annexe to the Piraeus.

The Venizelist refugees were in despair when they heard of our departure; so I put them down on my list of agents, secured a Greek escort and had them all marched down to the Piraeus with a promise that I would take as many of them as I could in the *Thessalia*.

I left the Annexe in the Sunbeam with Tucker. The unarmed Greek captain sat in front beside Robertson. We were stopped several times by patrols, but after the password was given and the safe conduct shown we were allowed to proceed. As we were driving round the curve of the small bay Kastella beyond Phaleron I was looking at the little house where I had visited King Peter of Serbia two or three times. He used to sit over a brazier, rubbing his ancient hands upon his knees and recount to me vague rustic tales of the remote past like a village gaffer. In a corner of the room was a sleek nurse, eyeing us from time to time over a book she was reading. Thinking it was probably a French novel I looked to see its name; to my astonishment the book was Baudelaire's *Fleurs du Mal*. As I was seeing again those visits to King Peter I heard my name being shouted from a roof to right of us on the other side of the road; glancing up, I saw half a dozen Cretans of the Royal Guard with their rifles levelled at the Greek captain in the car.

"Come up here and join us, Captain Mackenzie," they shouted. "We will shoot that poor rat for you first."

I told Tucker to explain that we were not prisoners and that the Greek captain was a hostage for our safe conduct; the Cretans lowered their rifles reluctantly. I asked them how they came to be on the roof like this. They said they had been on the way into Athens to protect the house of Venizelos but had been driven back and compelled to take to the mountains, as they put it. They had been here since Friday afternoon and boasted that they had kept Kastella clear of traitors to Greece and stopped any attempt to report to the Piraeus what had happened in Athens.

"We shot a few of them on their way down, and since yesterday not a Reservist has dared to come by here. We'll soon be on our way to Salonika."

I told Robertson to drive on, waving the Cretans fortune and farewell. Those mountainy men had made the chimney-pots seem rocks and boulders and turned that suburban terrace into a precipice on Ida.

The Greek captain looked round, mopping his forehead to express his gratitude.

"I thought I was dead," he said, with a sickly smile.

A few minutes later we reached the quayside at the Piraeus and went on board the *Thessalia*.

The confusion on that vessel was indescribable, with 108 members of our Service, their wives, children and various friends and feminine relations, to whom were added about 150 panic-stricken refugees of mixed age and sex. Finally there were seven or eight French cabaret girls; these were credited to me as mistresses by the Royalist Press.

Luckily Admiral Hayes-Sadler had granted Sir Francis Elliot's request for a destroyer to escort us to Syra; otherwise I doubt if I could have persuaded the crew to sail.

On Tuesday afternoon, December 5th, when I hoped that at last all our troubles were over and that we should get away punctually, the crew refused to sail because there were not enough life-belts on board. We managed to secure a hundred from the *Vassilefs Constantinos*, the 14,000-ton liner which was housing the British residents of Athens and their families.

By now the commander of the destroyer was getting impatient over the delay, and just as we reached the boom a signal was made to stop. I was rowed ashore to find Sells waiting for me. The Minister had just had a telegram from Syra to say I might not find things so quiet as I had hoped, but that Sir Francis left it to me to decide what to do. I said that things could not be worse in Syra than they were in Athens. Sells thought I was doing the right thing and wished me luck. I jumped into the cutter and was pulled off to the *Thessalia*; looking back I could see Sells driving back to Athens in his blue boat-cloak.

As we left the land behind us a fine rain came on and there was a ground swell which made the *Thessalia* roll unpleasantly, for she was steaming in ballast only and riding very high in the water. Every time a chain rattled or a block creaked the women would scream and the children would cry and the men would run about yelling: "Submarine! Submarine!"

I ordered everybody below, and sat on the deck wrapped in rugs, with a pistol on either side of me. We were so high in the water that a sudden rush of passengers to the side might easily make the ship turn turtle; I had to announce I would shoot the first man who put his head up a hatchway. I felt lonely and depressed sitting up on deck. It continued to drizzle all through the night, and the mournful grey glimmer of the obscured moon added to the solitude and sadness; my nerves were strung up beyond the point of sea-sickness.

During that solitary watch as the *Thessalia* rolled on eastward across the ninety miles of sea to Syra, in spite of having had only a few hours of anxious and uncomfortable sleep on a table throughout the last five previous nights I remained awake. Suddenly my depression vanished. I was beginning to wonder if we could sway the Cyclades over to the Provisional Government. Such a counter-stroke would dispose of the Greek Government's contention that the only support for Venizelos was in Crete, the islands of Asia Minor, and Salonika—the New Greece of the two Balkan wars—whereas the Old Greece of the War of Independence and the statesmanlike cession of the Ionian Islands by Great Britain in 1864 was solidly against him. Yes, somehow the Cyclades must be persuaded to adhere to the Provisional Government and accept a measure of administrative control by us. That would mean sending me more officers from home and allowing me to recommend for commissions various Levantine Britons out here. Our occupation of the Cyclades would be a mortal blow to the Athens government; it might not be too agreeable to the French. Only three islands were likely to be really difficult—Naxos, Tenos and Syra itself. This was due to the high proportion of Catholics from Venetian days who, once under the patronage of France, were now under the patronage of Austria and so pro-German and Royalist in sentiment. Sir Francis had asked the Vice-Admiral at Mudros to send a ship to Syra; he had replied that Venizelist troops would be coming from Mytilene. That might mean we should have to remain on board the *Thessalia* until they arrived. I began to worry again in the dim dark moonlight until in the first grey of dawn we dropped anchor off Syra. I saw the twin hills, one Catholic and one Orthodox, each covered with houses and crowned by a church, and then to my relief I made out the shape of a cruiser and knew that the Vice-Admiral had thought better of his refusal to send a ship to Syra.

While I was being rowed off to report to the Captain of H.M.S. *Edgar* soon after seven o'clock I prayed he would appreciate what I was hoping to do and give me his support. My prayer was answered. Captain Clifton-Brown[1] proved a genial and receptive man who, like nearly everybody else in the Aegean Squadron, had the welfare of the Provisional Government at heart and was not afraid of initiative.

"Buzfuz thinks I have too much initiative. I was Senior Naval Officer Suda Bay, and now he's sending me to Thasos as far away as possible."

Buzfuz was his name for Sir Cecil Thursby, the Vice-Admiral at Mudros.

I knew that it was vital for the adherence of the Cyclades to be accomplished without bloodshed. The Greek Government would take

[1] The late Vice-Admiral F. Clifton-Brown, C.B.

advantage of the slightest active resistance to use the influence they possessed in high quarters in London to obtain a veto on any further participation by the Aegean Squadron in swinging the Cyclades over to the Provisional Government, and that would give the French an excuse to control the Cyclades with the help of their naval forces.

The first move that suggested itself was an interview with the leading Liberals in Syra. They were summoned on board the *Thessalia* and, at a council of war held in the saloon, it was decided to arrest and deport at once the leading Royalists on the island. These were invited on board the *Edgar* where they were made as comfortable as possible until they could be taken to Salonika.

That was all right so far, but the Venizelist troops and a hundred Cretan gendarmes from Mytilene could not reach Syra for nearly a week; although we had secured the leading Royalists so easily I knew there would be no chance of a peacful occupation of Syra so long as the active and influential personality of that stout-hearted Royalist Colonel Deleres was still at large. I decided that a *coup de main* quickly executed was the only way of avoiding further trouble. Naxos, where the Colonel lived, was the largest island in the Cyclades and the least friendly to the Entente. I asked Captain Clifton-Brown to put a drifter at our disposal and picked fifteen reliable men to surprise Naxos three hours away to the south-east. The moon, though heavily obscured, was about full and would light the party on their way. All was still in Naxos when they arrived. The first thing I had done was to take over the headquarters of the Eastern Telegraph Company in Syra. Not a breath of news from Syra had reached any other island or the mainland itself.

Our men walked quickly up the narrow white streets in the drenched moonshine, hearing no sound except the barking of the many dogs. They soon forced the door of the Colonel's house; four of them ran up to his bedroom, wrapped him in his own blankets and carried him down to the drifter. The operation had been so successful that it was decided to spend a few more minutes in wrapping up the Demarch or Mayor in his blankets and carrying him away as a companion for the Colonel. By 2.30 a.m. the drifter was steaming back to Syra.

The next day I formally notified the Chief of Police and Harbour Master that a British Control had been established over the Cyclades.

One or two shots had been fired and there had been some disturbances on the Catholic hill. So I called on the Catholic Bishop and after genuflecting and kissing his ring, warned him that I should hold him responsible for the behaviour of his flock and that, if they misbehaved themselves, I should be reluctantly compelled to send him to Malta at once. I decided to let the Archbishop on the Orthodox hill call on me; I had been told he would certainly influence his flock to remain quiet until he saw which way the wind was blowing.

I had forbidden publication of the Royalist newspaper in Syra and affixed seals to the printing press. In Athens every Liberal newspaper had been stopped and I now handed over the printing press at Syra to the sub-editor of the *Patris*, who began to republish the great Liberal organ as a small but lively sheet.

All seemed to be going well when I was visited by a deputation led by Dr Alivisatos, a prominent Athenian physician who had taken refuge in Syra, to tell me that the Chief of Police had expressed his determination to resist the landing of the Venizelist troops. Dr Alivisatos went on to say they were relying on me to paralyse all opposition before the troops landed. I asked how I was to effect without bloodshed what could not be effected by Venizelist troops.

"You will find a way. We all have confidence in you."

There was a murmur of assent from the deputation, and with bows they withdrew.

We did manage by a ruse to disarm thirty-six of the police with their four officers; they were shut up in the kitchen of the former Austrian Consulate when the Venizelist troops landed after a rough passage from Mytilene; their faces were all pea-green, that of Colonel Kalemenopoulos being the greenest of the lot. However, he quickly recovered when his feet were on terra firma again, and I asked him to come along at once and deal with the forty police locked up in our kitchen. He said he thought they would be in a more receptive mood by the afternoon. I fancy the Colonel thought he would be in a more receptive mood himself by then. When he came along at five o'clock he looked a very different creature from the pea-green, unshaven, bedraggled Colonel I had welcomed in a drench of rain on the quay that morning.

After delivering a preliminary oration on patriotism Colonel Kalemenopoulos spoke to each of the police in turn and offered them the opportunity of taking the oath of fealty to the Provisional Government. It was like a game of Oranges and Lemons. Those who declared for the Provisional Government were embraced and sent upstairs to the drawing-room; those who declined were kept in the kitchen. Three of the officers remained faithful to the Government in Athens; one went over to the Provisional Government. Of the men about half elected for one side and half for the other. Those who adhered were incorporated in the troops of occupation.

In the great square of Syra, a beautiful piazza paved with marble, the adherence of the island to the Provisional Government of National Defence was solemnly proclaimed.

I was pretty well worn out at the end of that first week, and when I sat down after lunch at my desk in the former Austrian Consulate to dictate a report of the way we had handled our move to Syra I suddenly put down my head and fell fast asleep. When I woke I was furious to find it was past eight o'clock in the evening. Still, that sleep with my head on a desk did me good.

In the middle of December the British Legation and the whole of its staff moved to the transport *Abbasieh* moored at Keratsini in Salamis. One of the Secretaries wrote to say that the only thing which cheered up their cramped boredom were my reports of every island except one in the Cyclades adhering to the Provisional Government, and of my installing control, "There has been nothing like it since the West Indies in the eighteenth century," he wrote. Little did he think that the British Legation and its staff would be bored and cramped in that transport for another three months. The only island over which I failed to gain control was Milos; the French were as unwilling to let that pass out of their control as they would have been to part with the Venus of Milo in the Louvre.

The publication in the Greek White Book of telegrams from the King and Queen of the Hellenes to the German Emperor dispatched during those weeks of December and January suggest that if the Germans could have finished off Rumania in time to concentrate on Macedonia Old Greece must have gone to war with the Allies. For that possibility I had to make preparations in the way of arranging the necessary Intelligence. John Hope-Johnstone had arrived by now from Corfu with a kitbag containing a few clothes, one top-boot, several works on higher mathematics, the two volumes of Doughty's *Arabia Deserta*, a pair of bright yellow Moorish slippers, a camera and a flute. He was ten days older than myself, and among the friends with whom I've enjoyed good conversation I bracket Hope-Johnstone with Norman Douglas at the top. H-J was a King's College, Cambridge man with perfect taste in all the arts and an encyclopaedic store of information, but with such an overwhelming indolence that he could not make the effort to write even a brief letter. Yet should I call him indolent? When war broke out he was more than half-way on a journey by foot to Baghdad and in spite of having to wear very strong glasses nothing escaped him. He enlisted at the beginning of the war, somehow cheating the military authorities over his eyesight; then his myopia was discovered by his having saluted a drum he had mistaken for the regimental sergeant-major. He was expelled from the ranks and given a commission for General Service. Somehow he had drifted into C's organization and had been sent out to Corfu, whence by a stroke of good fortune for me he was transferred to Syra. I put him to preside over A, Intelligence about the enemy.

Sometime early in January a telegram from London asked for full details of Greek rolling-stock, railway-lines and any amount besides—information that would have been child's play to accumulate during the last twelve months but would now involve sending agents into Old Greece and getting them out again. In addition to some fifty questions that telegram went on to say that in the event of hostilities breaking out with the Government of King Constantine it was proposed to land two British Divisions at Itea in the Gulf of Corinth and march them up to attack Lamia in the hope of catching the King's army between these Divisions and the forces of General Sarrail. At the end I was told to comment on the proposed strategy.

After going over a large map H-J and I decided there was only one comment to make, which was to invite Military Intelligence to study a school history of Ancient Greece and read what happened to the Persians at Thermopylae, through which pass, twelve feet wide and nine hundred feet high for a stretch, it was proposed to march two British Divisions. Machine-guns on the ledges of those cliffs would have been much more deadly against an invading force coming from the south than Leonidas and his Three Hundred against the Persians coming from the north. H-J and I worked for hours over a more practical route for the two Divisions and telegraphed the result.

Two days later a snorter came from London:

To be decyphered by Captain Compton Mackenzie personally.
Following from the Chief of the Imperial General Staff.
Your business is to answer questions and not propose military operations of far-reaching importance. If anything like this occurs again you will be immediately recalled.

In spite of this thunderbolt from the C.I.G.S. we had a good laugh out of it because the group of figures representing "*following from*" arrived corrupt, and when decyphered read as "*Limehouse from the Chief of the Imperial General Staff*".

We were still laughing over this when I received a personal telegram from C telling me not to worry about the message from C.I.G.S., as there had been a mistake; I never found out what the mistake was. In October of 1917 I was dining with Theodore Cook in Oakley Street and one of the guests was Sir William Robertson. I occasionally caught him looking at me from the other side of the dinner-table with a puzzled expression. He must have been wondering if I could really be somebody who had once advised him to read a school history of Ancient Greece.

When the *Edgar* left for Thasos Commander Usborne[1] became Senior Naval Officer Syra in the minelayer *Latona*. I was glad to have during

[1] The late Vice-Admiral Cecil Usborne, C.B., C.M.G.

those first two or three difficult weeks a S.N.O. whose naval future was so obviously safe that he had the courage for some initiative. In 1931 he became D.I.D., or as I believe they call him nowadays, D.N.I.

At the end of December Sir Francis telegraphed that Vice-Admiral Thursby was coming to see me about the future of our organization and warned me to remember that he was very much an Admiral and that I was not even a pukka Captain R.M.L.I. I was in the middle of a bad go of neuritis when the Admiral arrived, but our translator Tsitsopoulos, who had been doctor of the port of Smyrna, managed to assuage the worst of the pain. By now Knoblock, Hope-Johnstone and I were living up at the former Turkish Consulate; I slept in the old harem. The Admiral was good enough to come up there and sat for two hours beside my bed. When he left I was able to telegraph to Sir Francis Elliot that he was in complete accord with my future plan for control of the islands and had pledged himself to help in every way he could.

On top of the difficulty I had during this year of 1916 to get the money to run my show in Athens I was in a jam with my own finances. Indeed, I should have had to give up Casa Solitaria as an impossible luxury on the pay of a Lieutenant R.M. if William Brady had not decided to make a film of *Carnival*, in which his daughter Alice was to appear. As he started without letting Pinker[1] or myself know what he was proposing to do Pinker was able to get £500 from him and this saved the situation for me, the Italian exchange by this time being very favourable. Pinker now arranged with the *Cosmopolitan* magazine for a series of ten short stories at 500 dollars, but I could not find the time to start on them. Then I told Pinker of a possible serial about a cabaret girl in Athens who was supposed to be English but who in fact had no passport; I would write a serial about her if Harper's approved of the idea. So contracts were made with them and with Martin Secker by which I was to get such a handsome advance that somehow or other I wrote the serial almost, one might say, in odd half-hours. This was the work entitled *No Papers* which was destroyed during the looting of my house when I had just finished it and was about to get it typed. I had every hope of being fully compensated by the Greek Government, but compensation always takes time and by the beginning of 1917 I was again hard pressed for money. Edward Knoblock generously came to my rescue with a loan of £400.

Faith went back to Capri in the spring of 1916. Norman Douglas had arrived in May with a bit of *South Wind* written, and according to a letter of hers to my mother of July 18th: *I have typed 35 chapters of Norman Douglas's book. It's some book.*

In September my father-in-law died in his 83rd year. His mind was

[1] My literary agent at that time.

clear and he remained an indomitable correspondent of delightful letters until the end. Indeed, his last letter to Faith arrived on the day a telegram had come to say he was dying. He had a stroke and never recovered consciousness, dying peacefully two days later. No man deserved more a kindly passage to eternity.

My own father had had an operation for cancer of the throat and his vocal cords had been removed. When I saw him during that leave in October, his voice was a whisper.

When I went back to Athens at the beginning of November Faith stayed on at Georgian House, Bury Street, for a while. This was lucky for Norman Douglas, who had been run in and charged with picking up two boys that July in the Natural History Museum. I had failed as already told to get him out to Greece or Albania. I have fortunately never been in a position to test the loyalty of my friends, but the experience of friends of mine in difficulty has often made me think that between rats and human beings is a distinction without a difference. At this moment practically all Douglas's friends avoided him, but two of them did stand bail for him; Joseph Conrad refused to do this.

Faith volunteered to give evidence for him, and her 1916 diary was shown in support of her testimony that Douglas had arrived in Capri on May 12th, had not left the island until August 15th, and had lunched with Faith at Casa Solitaria on July 7th. The Magistrate decided that it was a case of mistaken identity, and the charge against him was dropped.

Faith was back in Capri by my thirty-fourth birthday.

THIRTY-FOUR YEARS OLD: 1917

I HAVE written at length about the first ten months of my thirty-fifth year in *Aegean Memories*, which as I set out to record them in this fifth Octave is still in print. Those months at Syra were a long struggle to keep together the organization which now, thanks to the support of C, appeared too enviably large to leave in the hands of a mere captain. The details of that struggle I shall not repeat. One excerpt I shall allow myself and one story I shall tell which has not hitherto been told.

At the end of December, when we were rounding off our occupation of the Cyclades, S.N.O. Suda Bay had sent a signal to S.N.O. Syra that if there was any proposal to occupy the island of Cerigo such a project should be abandoned because arrangements had already been made at Suda Bay to occupy Cerigo with an expeditionary force of twelve Marines led by Lieutenant J. C. Lawson. Lawson was a Cambridge don who would write a book called *Tales of Aegean Intrigue*, full of academic facetiousness and hearsay that reflected small credit on his qualities as an Intelligence officer, although he did perform one piece of complicated paper detective work with tenacity and skill. He had come to see me once at the Annexe and we were mutually antipathetic; other people may have found him less of a priggish bore than I did.

I had urged S.N.O. Suda Bay through S.N.O. Syra that such an expedition should be done quickly, for I anticipated that the Greek Government would plead as a condition for accepting the latest Allied ultimatum that no more islands should go over to the Provisional Government. The ultimatum was accepted with that very condition on January 10th; Cerigo was not occupied until January 12th.

Sir Francis Elliot telegraphed to me that Cerigo must be given back at once to fulfil the conditions on which the Greek Government had accepted the ultimatum. This was communicated to S.N.O. Suda Bay. The next thing was a frantic telegram from the Venizelists of Cerigo, who were in a large majority, begging me to prevent their being handed back to the Royalists on account of the revenge that would certainly be taken upon them for having adhered to the Provisional Government. I begged Sir Francis to persuade Mr Balfour, who had succeeded Sir Edward Grey as Secretary of State for Foreign Affairs, to except Cerigo from the pledge, pointing out that the fears of the Venizelist Cerigiotes were amply justified. Sir Francis replied that Mr Balfour could not make an exception, and that the Greek Government attached great importance to the re-occupation of Cerigo, because they considered it in the hands of the insurgents a threat to their army in the Peloponnese; one of the demands of the ultimatum had been the moving of the Greek army out of Northern Greece.

The next step to secure a repeal for Cerigo was to suggest sending one of my officers to investigate on the spot and make a report, which would at any rate gain time. The twelve Marines were still there, but we could get no information out of Lawson, who had gone back to Suda Bay and evidently supposed that the fuss about Cerigo was a plot by Syra to wrest an island from S.N.O. Suda Bay. I sent Arthur Whittall, aged nineteen, to Cerigo. He was a charming young man with immense tact and perfect Greek.

Sometime in February I received his report on the situation. It appeared that in the enthusiasm of welcoming the Suda Bay expedition some of the more passionate Venizelists had thrown one of their opponents over the cliff; the prospect of being themselves thrown over a cliff when the island was handed back to the Royalists irked them.

Then Arthur Whittall made a grand discovery in the shape of a number of British subjects on the island, old men who in their far-distant youth had been at Ballarat in the gold-rush and while in Australia had taken out British papers. When news reached the Foreign Office that handing back the island to the Greek Government might mean the massacre of British subjects Mr Balfour was worried and asked Sir Francis Elliot for a suggestion. By this time Arthur Whittall had informed me that the whole island was determined, if it could not adhere to the Provisional Government, to become a part of the British Empire, which, as its inhabitants pointed out, it once had been. Cerigo, although many miles away, had been included in the British occupation of the Ionian Islands and had been voluntarily ceded to Greece by Lord Palmerston's Government. Evidence of the British occupation of Cerigo remained in the splendid roads all over the island.

I hardly expected that Mr Balfour would receive Cerigo back into the British Empire, but the suggestion that he should do so gained valuable time. When this was refused I suggested that although we had pledged ourselves that no more islands should adhere to the Provisional Government after a certain date, we had not pledged ourselves that no island should be allowed to declare itself a free and independent State. This proposal was put up to Venizelos, who saw no objection, provided the island was administered by ourselves. To this happy compromise Mr Balfour agreed; British statesmen can rarely if ever resist a compromise.

Arthur Whittall, who had been administering the island affairs with outstanding success, was at this moment grabbed from me by the Commercial Department of the Legation, and I had to replace him. The only officer available at the moment was Wilfred Macartney, who was a year younger than Arthur Whittall. He had already done good work in Zea and Amorgos and having the impudence of a schoolboy he might beard S.N.O. Suda Bay successfully. Lawson, furious when Macartney arrived to demand transport to Cerigo, asked why another officer from Syra was interfering in Cerigo.

"You'd better enquire from Mr Balfour," said Macartney importantly. "I have my orders. If you cannot see your way to assist me in carrying them out I shall ask S.N.O. Suda Bay to signal S.N.O. Syra that I am being obstructed by an Intelligence officer who draws his funds through Captain Mackenzie."

Next morning Macartney got his trawler, and reached Cerigo. Arthur Whittall had organized all the submarine look-outs in his own efficient way; there was little left for Macartney to do except play rounders with the Marines until word came that the island would not be handed back to the Athenian Government and was at liberty to declare its independence. There was much cheering and firing of muskets into the air. A Constitution was drafted. The free and independent Republic of Cerigo was declared and a Presidential election was held immediately. I received a telegram from Macartney to say that King George V had been elected President; without referring to Mr Balfour I took it upon myself to say that this was impossible. So another election was held, and this time Venizelos was elected President. Again I had to reply that this was impossible; it would be the equivalent of adhering to the Provisional Government, which was forbidden. So a third election was held, and this time it was myself who had the honour of being elected President. It would have been fun to be President of Cerigo, but I was too fond of Buzfuz to threaten him with apoplexy by such news; I declined the honour and a local worthy was elected.

Under the benevolent spectacled eyes of the eighteen-year-old adviser a Cabinet was formed; Ministers were appointed; the Army and the Police were organized. The President summoned his Cabinet and informed them that the time had come to take two grave decisions. The first was to outlaw King Constantine for life; the second was to declare war on the Central Powers. Macartney, poking about the island, had discovered in the old Venetian castle a quantity of hand-made paper stamped in orange with the Lion of St Mark which had been lying there for about a century and a half. On this official paper of the Republic of Venice, after a mass meeting of the inhabitants, war was declared upon Germany, Austria, Bulgaria and Turkey. I doubt if it ever reached them; it was the kind of communication a censor on either side would have enjoyed stopping.

Soon after Cerigo had helped to make the world safe for democracy

Macartney returned to Syra and the island remained a free and independent Republic until the abdication of King Constantine in June 1917, when it gave its allegiance to King Alexander. Macartney brought me back a packet of the Venetian paper, both used and unused. Reading through the archives written one hundred and fifty years earlier in ink which had kept most of its pristine blackness, I found that they recorded a system of administration curiously like our own Military Control Office in Syra; they were as much complicated as our own archives by the rivalries and jealousies of officialdom. With this discovery came a pang for the handiwork of the past. What chance could our archives in Syra, typewritten on the miserable paper of 1917 with ribbons almost as feeble as those of today, have of lasting for a century and a half in the cellar of a ruined Venetian castle?

What a deliciously absurd idyll that was! No real violence marred it; even the Royalist who was thrown over the cliff was only bruised. Who would have thought when Macartney came beaming back from Cytherea's isle that a little more than a decade hence he would be sentenced to ten years' penal servitude by a Lord Chief Justice who tried to emulate Judge Jeffries by the way he dealt with an offence for which six months would have been excessive punishment. At the time Mr Baldwin and his Government were trying to frighten electors with the red bogyman and that preposterous sentence on Macartney was intended to hide from the electorate the pitiably comic fiasco of the Arcos raid. Alas not so long ago we have had disturbing examples of the willingness of the judiciary to help Whitehall convince the public that it is not Redhall.

I had pointed out to C soon after we reached Syra that it would be impossible to carry on in our new quarters without the help of a sea-going craft. He had tried his best to secure us a craft from England, but it had proved impossible and finally he authorized me to charter any vessel I thought suitable. The *Aulis*, pronounced Avlis, had originally been the private yacht of Prince George of Greece, but for the last ten years she had been running as a ferry boat between Poros and the mainland. Her length was 140 feet, her draught 8 feet, her tonnage 200 gross, her speed 10 knots, and she had accommodation for 5 officers. She had a Greek crew and a Greek skipper, well spoken of. Pneumatikos was his name, and his appearance did not belie his name; he was one of the fattest men I have ever seen, and would have been a superb advertisement for Michelin tyres. The charter was arranged, and on March 20th the *Aulis* sailed into Syra and was moored at the quayside immediately under the windows of our port office; we had very soon grown too big for the old Austrian Consulate. We all trooped down like children to inspect this wonderful new toy. She had a roomy saloon aft, and a piano which, though it retained only four notes that sounded, was evidently a relic of former royalty, and as such respected as a mascot. Forward there was another saloon in which we would dine when roving the blue Aegean sea. There was an owner's cabin pointed out to me by Tucker with the air of a Vanderbilt. Unfortunately it turned out to be bug-ridden and I always had to sleep in the saloon. Here I pictured myself writing long reports on the perfect concord of Port Control, Passport Control, Naval Intelligence, Counter-espionage and Near East politics, at peace with everybody except the Central Powers. There was a small deckhouse looking aft which we planned should be an armoury, where, as we hoped, we should be given the lethal weapons to add the last perfection to this entrancing toy.

I find a confidential telegram to C with the date March 31st:

Rachmi Bey[1] is apparently trying to re-open negotiations. I expect to be in touch with him shortly. Man left for Smyrna yesterday. There is reason to believe he will consider the betrayal of Smyrna and Minister wishes me to telegraph you to-morrow how this scheme would be considered by the authorities. He is writing to Lord Hardinge on the subject. It will be necessary for someone armed with authority to negotiate to see Rachmi either at Smyrna or at some point nearer the coast. This I myself should enjoy trying to do. In that case I should have to make him an offer both of cash and of protection, and as a pledge of good faith bring him the two Turks whose release from Malta he tried to negotiate in October.

A rumour of Rachmi Bey's intentions had reached Athens the previous January and in one of the telegrams printed in the Greek White Book John Theotokis, the Queen's Chamberlain, told his brother Nicolas, the Greek Minister in Berlin, they had received information that the Vali of Smyrna had been bribed by the Entente to surrender the city of Smyrna after a pretended rising.

I had been in communication with the Vali, who had suggested two million pounds as a reasonable reward. Our people thought this much too expensive; in that March I had heard Rachmi Bey wanted to re-open the discussion and presumed that his ideas about the money had become less grand.

The two Turks alluded to in the telegram above were Sami Bey and another naval officer whose name I have forgotten; they had been taken prisoner when a Turkish destroyer was sunk off Chios in October 1914 and both of them were great friends of Enver Pasha, the leader of the Young Turks and now the most important figure in Turkey.

I wrote personally to Lord Methuen in Malta to ask if he would send

[1] The Vali (Governor) of Smyrna.

G

the two Turks to Syra in connection with an Intelligence problem and he immediately agreed, telling me to let him know when I wanted them and that they would be sent in a sloop.

Toward the end of April I went to Samos in the hope of getting in touch with one of the Vali's envoys on the Anatolian coast across the strait of Mycale. I was sitting on the shore beside the only column left of the Heraeum, the great temple that was once one of the seven wonders of the world, when I was approached by a Greek. In broken English he offered for a suitable reward to bring the new German Intelligence officer who had arrived to look after the coast south of Smyrna down to the shore opposite, where with half a dozen men I could easily capture him.

After moonset with muffled oars we rowed across the Strait. We waited in an olive grove until the first grey of dawn, but there was no sign of our German or of the fellow who had proposed the plan. I was badly had, but so was my quarry. The Greek, who had drawn on me for 200 drachmas in advance of another 300 if I captured the German, had made the same offer to him. The two boats must have passed one another in the darkness, both of them with muffled oars.

The Vali was worried by the activities of this new German officer and was afraid to send an envoy to meet me. However, at intervals throughout the early summer the negotiations went on.

Then a dreadful thing happened. The one or two agents we still had in Turkey used to communicate by letter post with a Levantine Englishman who had stayed on in Smyrna when Turkey went to war and had a team of Greek runners who used to take his information to the coast, where we picked it up. One evening the Turkish censor in Broussa knocked the ash off the end of a cigarette as he was reading through the mail and falling upon one of the letters it lighted up the secret ink. Twenty-four hours later eight of our Greek runners had been hanged and H— himself had been condemned to death. I could get no help from the Foreign Office, the Admiralty or the War Office in my efforts to save his life. "Mr H—— knew the risk he was running," was the reply from Whitehall.

I then telegraphed to Lord Methuen, who sent along the two Turks in whatever flower it was the sloop was called after. I asked the commander to let me have his two passengers on board the *Aulis* and promised him he should have them back in a couple of days. Then I handed him over to enjoy a good time at the country clubs which the rich Venizelist refugees had started.

I went to Captain Cochrane, the S.N.O. who commanded the light cruiser *Skirmisher*, and asked leave for *Aulis* to proceed to Mytilene that evening on an important Intelligence mission.

"But if, sir," I added, "S.N.O. Mytilene asks you where *Aulis* is, will you say she is on her way back to Syra?"

Cochrane looked at me sharply.

"And where will she be?"

"I told you, sir, on her way back to Syra."

"Very well. I won't ask any more questions."

I went back to *Aulis* where Tucker was waiting for me. I told him I wanted two sacks with a big stone at the bottom of each one. Tucker stared at me.

"Are you joking, Captain Z?" he asked.

"Hurry up, Tucker. We must get away as soon as possible and I want you to come with me."

Tucker brought the two sacks and soon afterwards we were through the Syra boom, our course set for Mytilene.

After an hour I sent for Pneumatikos.

"Tell him to set the course for Smyrna, Tucker."

"For Smyrna?" he stammered.

"Tell the Captain."

Pneumatikos was immensely fat and Tucker was pretty plump but both looked a little bit thinner at that moment.

"Captain Pneumatikos says 'What about the mines?' The entrance to Smyrna harbour is mined."

"What depth do we draw?"

"Eight feet, Captain Z."

"And what depth are the mines at?"

"Twelve to fourteen feet."

"So what are you worrying about?"

"Yes, but one of them might be higher," Tucker protested.

"Well, that'll just be too bad."

"But they'll fire on us."

"No, they won't. They'll see a small yacht flying the blue ensign armed with a maxim in the bows and a Japanese three-pounder aft. They will also see on either side of the maxim a couple of sacks with two red fezes sticking out of them. Curiosity is bound to win, my dear Tucker. We'll leave the two birds where they are for the present. We won't put them in the sacks until we're pretty close to Smyrna."

There was a lot of Greek exchanged between Pneumatikos and Tucker, but at last I was relieved to hear the Captain say with a sigh πόλυ κάλο (very good), and I knew he was going to carry out my orders.

There was a tremendous bustle as we approached the harbour. Flags going up and down in frantic excitement . . . figures in khaki uniform rushing about with field glasses . . . but as I had prophesied not a shot was fired.

I left Tucker on board when we dropped anchor and was rowed ashore in the cutter. With my sword clanking at my side and followed by the youth of Smyrna I found my way to the residence of the Vali and sent in my card. His Excellency received me at once. The conversation was in French. I told him I had come to re-open negotiations for the surrender of Smyrna and asked him if he would not consider a million pounds a reasonable reward for the carrying through of his undertaking successfully.

"You would have a wonderful time on a million pounds in England, Excellency," I assured him. "And now there's another thing. I understand that Mr H— is under sentence of death. You must see that sentence is not carried out."

"Mr H— is a great friend," said the Vali. "I would do anything to save his life, but I am already under suspicion from Enver and Talaat and if I help Mr H— they will make that an excuse to get rid of me."

I asked the Vali if we might go where we could have a view of the harbour. Then I pointed to those two red fezes in the sacks.

"You see those two figures, Excellency? There is a big stone in each of those sacks. They are the two friends of Enver Pasha whose release I was going to secure as a pledge of our good faith when I was in communication with you as long ago as last October and again all through last March and April. I gave orders when I left the yacht that if I was not back in an hour and a half that Sami Bey and —— were to be dropped overboard. Surely you will be able to satisfy Enver and Talaat that you were bound to save Mr H—'s life in order to save theirs?"

The Vali thanked me warmly for giving him an excuse to save H—, who really was a friend of his; and he was not shot. I did not feel justified in telling this story in *Aegean Memories* in case Rachmi Bey was still alive. However, I did tell it as fiction in *The South Wind of Love*.

The late Admiral Sir Sydney Freeman, who succeeded Admiral Thursby at Mudros, met me at a party some time in the 'forties and asked me if the story was true.

"More or less," I told him.

"Yes, I heard something about it at the time," he said. "I suppose the two Turkish officers chattered when they got back to Malta."

"They may have, Admiral. I did make an effort to get them exchanged, only to receive a telegram from London reprimanding me for negotiating directly with the Turkish authorities."

True to the time-honoured British policy of hunting with the hounds and running with the hare the British Government had decided to recognize the Provisional Government by sending Lord Granville to Salonika as Diplomatic Agent. This finished any chance of that reconciliation between King Constantine and Venizelos on which Sir Francis Elliot had set his heart. When the French brought Venizelos back to Athens in June and King Constantine abdicated Sir Francis went home on leave; obviously he would not be coming back and in fact after his leave ended he remained in London as head of the Foreign Trade Department at the Foreign Office. *Greek Memories* was dedicated to him in 1932 in affectionate admiration, but when at last it was possible for *Aegean Memories* to appear the proofs did not reach me in time to show them to him. I had intended to do this in case he wished to delete anything from his letters to me, which he had given me permission to print. To my grief and disappointment he died two months before his 89th birthday when I had expected to take the proofs with me to show him in Oxford.

No British diplomat had so difficult a post in the First World War as Sir Francis Elliot and none enjoyed so steadily the melancholy pleasure of seeing his advice proved right by the troubles that followed from neglect of it. If he had been an ambitious man he might have become embittered by the failure to recognize his work. The Foreign Office had wanted to give him a G.C.M.G. after the success of the June Note in 1916; King George V, who had got into his head that King Constantine was a Royal martyr, grumbled about such recognition of a man who he did not think had acted as *his* Ambassador. So the G.C.M.G. was not awarded until Sir Francis Elliot left Athens. Above everything he asked for truth, and that gave him a sardonic charity toward human nature which was like a finely-hammered suit of armour. He was not a man to whom intimacy came easily. He kept always about him the shyness and reserve we associate with youth; he had been one of William Cory's favourite pupils at Eton, and on the walls of his study at the Athens Legation hung the oars he had won as bow of victorious Balliol eights. Perhaps that eternal youthfulness was the key to his character. He was thirty-two years older than myself, but I used to assume as a matter of course that he would understand and sympathize with my wildest projects. And he always did, even if sometimes he had to rule them out as practical politics. To few men in my long life have I owed as much.

I knew when Sir Francis Elliot left Athens that our organization would be faced with a harder struggle than ever for survival. The new Counsellor, Dayrell Crackanthorpe, was to remain as Chargé d'Affaires; he might have handled affairs in the moon more successfully. I have told the squalid story of intrigue in *Aegean Memories* and nobody has been able to contradict a word of it.

The final spur to achieve my recall was a visit I paid to Venizelos in

August. The Legation believed that my appearance in Athens would immediately provoke a riot, or at any rate they pretended to believe this because I was credited by these newcomers with a basilisk charm to which high-ranking officers and officials succumbed.

The new Greek Government wanted to give me the Order of Merit. It was argued in Athens that inasmuch as I was the only non-Hellene to whom it was to be awarded it might give the impression that Great Britain had launched the Triumvirate on their revolutionary movement. I was pressed to ask for leave from home to wear it, but I knew I should be refused and thought it would be more dignified not to afford them an opportunity of refusing.

At that interview I urged Venizelos not to give way an inch in the matter of Controls, and pointed out to him that the multiplication of generals in Athens served no purpose except to provide jobs for creatures incapable of being useful either in the field or behind the lines elsewhere. I warned him that General Phillips was pulling strings at this moment in the hope of being sent out to Athens again, and suggested that he should personally object to such an appointment. I warned him that probably I should be unable to hold out much longer in the Aegean, but assured him that so long as I directed the Aegean Intelligence Service it would be identified with his ideas.

On August 11th came this solemn rebuke:

With reference to your recent visit to Athens and your interview with Mr Venizelos, His Majesty's Chargé d'Affaires informs me he was unaware of your being in Athens. I consider that it was most improper:

   (*i*) *For you to have gone there without having first acquainted His Majesty's Chargé d'Affaires.*

   (*ii*) *To have visited a high Government official without going through the usual diplomatic channels.*

In future whenever you or any of your staff find it necessary to go to Athens in pursuance of your duties, you are first to obtain permission from His Majesty's diplomatic representative.

Cecil E. Thursby,
Vice-Admiral

The lightning which this thunder accompanied was practically a complete surrender to my scheme of control, which I knew would receive the support of Venizelos. Soon after this the Vice-Admiral was recalled. I felt sure that the Foreign Office, the War Office and the Admiralty had got together at last and that news of my recall would come very soon.

Toward the end of August one of my officers came back from Athens with news that the gossip everywhere was that I was going to be recalled; on August 28th came the telegram from London:

Regret inform you you are recalled from your post and are to return immediately.
Please inform Vice-Admiral.

The Vice-Admiral had gone and his successor Sir Sydney Freeman had not yet arrived at Mudros so that it was ten days before I received formal permission to sail in the *Aulis* to Naupaktos, where a French torpedo-boat was to pick me up and take me to Taranto.

Those last days in Syra were a continual strain. Every officer attached to my service asked to be recalled and I had a job to prevent even those who knew local conditions and spoke Greek. After I left, all the others except poor Francis Storrs, who was condemned to stay in Athens with Myres, managed to get recalled.

My Greek employees were in a state of despair—clerks, translators, porters, coastguards and the rest; Tsitsopoulos burst into tears every time I spoke to him. Dozens of the Syra people called at the old Turkish Consulate to express their regret.

Murray Molesworth, a young Gordon Highlander who had been severely wounded in France and whom C had sent out to me in February, secured leave in order to travel home with me. I was grateful for this with the luggage I had—three packing-cases full of the papers necessary to write an authentic account of the years 1916 and 1917. The Italian Minister and Military Attaché had both sent special letters asking for my luggage to be accorded diplomatic immunity in Italy; it was my intention to leave everything in Capri on my way home. Tucker and I destroyed a quantity of papers before I left; I saw no reason to hand over to Myres, who had been put in charge of counter-espionage, and what I knew would be his incompetent Athens Bureau papers compromising dozens of people. Crackanthorpe complained to the F.O. and Myres complained to M.I.5, but Sir Francis insisted that in destroying certain material I had acted with absolute propriety, and greed for the fruits of my work was rebuked.

We were due to sail at midnight, but there was such a press of people to bid me good-bye that I asked leave from the S.N.O. to postpone sailing until one o'clock so that nobody's hand should be left unshaken. The *Aulis* was moored stern on to the quay just opposite the office. I had bequeathed my bed to Tsitsopoulos; he, who had tended me through many days and nights of pain during the last two years, had wept away at least a stone of his bulk during the last ten days. The parting with him was bad enough, but the parting with Lisa on that tempestuous autumn night was poignant. She had busied herself with my packing during the last few days but had not said a word about my going away. When I went aboard she came down to make sure my bed in the saloon was properly made. I had left Lisa my big wardrobe of which she was so proud and the rest of my furniture. I put my arms round her to kiss her good-bye and she seemed hardly heavier than a flower as she drooped in the rain of her own tears.

"Jamais plus," she sobbed. "Vous jamais plus. Lisa jamais plus vous voir."

To the last she spoke that absurd broken French to express her conviction that she should never see me again.

I had to leave Lisa sobbing in the saloon; there were so many others to whom I had to say good-bye before we sailed. The last I saw of her was on the gusty mole standing by Tsitsopoulos and waving a small lace handkerchief as the yacht swept by westward into the gale. The mole was crowded with people, and the wind seemed to catch the farewells in English, Greek, French and Italian and toss them into oblivion.

In spite of the gale I soon fell asleep in emotional exhaustion. About five in the morning a heavy sea smashed the skylight of the saloon and I was drenched. I remember splashing my way to the lavatory, because the cold water immediately made me feel sick; I remember Molesworth splashing to my aid and both of us shivering and vomiting into the bath, unable to stand steady enough for a more suitable utensil. I had to go and sleep in the owner's cabin; it must have been too rough even for the bugs, or I was too exhausted to notice them, for I slept on and did not wake until we were gliding between the embankments of the Corinth Canal about nine o'clock of a lovely morning.

I had been warned that a number of my supporters planned to greet *Aulis* at the Piraeus; feeling that enemies would say I had staged a demonstration I had cancelled the call there.

Syra seemed already far away as we sailed westward along the Gulf of Corinth on that Sunday morning; the Hellas I was leaving was not the Hellas of faction and fighting, of controls and zones, of reports and telegrams, of double-chinned generals and leather-bottomed jacks-in-office. I was leaving the Hellas of my childhood when Volo was Iolcos by the sea; when the infant Perseus, not the infant Macartney, was pulled ashore at Seriphos; when a sea-monster attacked Andromeda, not a submarine imagined by the ever-credulous Myres; when Ariadne was in Naxos, not one of our port-control officers. And then I began to remember what a marvellous adventure those months in Syra had been for all of us. I do not believe that any other set of young men had such a wonderful time in the First World War; we were bound to create envy all over the Mediterranean.

At three o'clock in the afternoon the yacht dropped anchor off

Naupaktos in the Strait of Lepanto, where we were to be picked up by the French torpedo-boat. Molesworth and I were rowed ashore and sat in the grass of water-meadows on the eastward side of the castellated harbour. The *Aulis* turned round and dipped the blue ensign astern; Larkin waved from the bridge; nine months hence he would be killed in France, serving with the Tank Corps. I see now *Aulis*, in which we had had so much excitement and laughter, growing smaller and smaller, and the wake of her like the smudge of a finger down a cloudy mirror slowly clouded over again yard by yard. At last she is a speck up the Gulf, and at last she is not even a speck.

The *torpilleur* was so long in arriving that we began to wonder if our French hosts had forgotten about us. Then suddenly she appeared and presently we were steaming fast to Patras, whence we were to escort two French battleships to Taranto.

The difference between French and British naval officers was that a French officer expected to enjoy my company because I was a novelist, whereas a British officer hoped my company might be endurable in spite of my being a novelist. The Captain of the *torpilleur* was as usual a much older man than one would have found in command of a British ship of the same class. Yet he insisted on my sleeping in his cabin, and when I protested against being such a nuisance said that he should be up all night. We dined before sailing; anxious to show my appreciation of the hospitality, I ate as much of the excellent food and drank as much of the excellent claret as I could. The calm of Patras harbour induced a false security, for as the sun went down the wind was rising fast.

What a night! It would have been bad enough if the torpedo-boat had made a direct crossing; but her duty as escort of the two battleships involved her in making circles round them all the way. The straits of Otranto can manage a sea when the wind is blowing hard from the south that will inspire respect from any craft; to make circles all night on such a night round and round a couple of battleships is to compete in horror with Dante's infernal circles.

To add to sea-sickness, my leg, which had been mildly painful for a week, decided to test my ability to stand the most acute agony it could contrive. The heat of the cabin was of hell, and gradually through the night fine cinders gathered to a depth of at least a quarter of an inch all over it. I was flung out of my bunk half a dozen times when I was trying to make for the Captain's private water-closet in a nausea that compared with the pain was almost agreeable. I had a bottle of aspirin which for all its use as an analgesic might have been a bottle of saccharine. I can affirm that it was the worst night I have spent in eighty years.

Molesworth in a hammock had been sick but he had not had to fight with the sciatic nerve at the top of its form. In my wretchedness when I limped ashore at Taranto in the morning I left my sword behind in the Captain's cabin. I looked with disgust at the two battleships round which we had been tearing all night long like a terrier round a couple of elephants. What a night! Rolling in a beam sea to port, bucking to a following sea, rolling in a beam sea to starboard, pitching into a head sea, rolling in a beam sea once again, and all of it in a temperature of about 100°, fire cinders permeating the stale air.

The Italian customs at Naples paid strict attention to the letters of Count Bosdari and Colonel Vitale and my three packing-cases of papers reached Capri intact. After a couple of nights I had to go on to Rome, but was able to promise everybody that I should be back in about a month for a much longer stay.

C had telegraphed before we left Syra that I was to see Sir Samuel Hoare[1] on my way through Rome and communicate to him any knowledge I possessed about Italian plans in the Aegean, Anatolia and the Yemen.

Lieutenant-Colonel Sir Samuel Hoare had arrived in Rome at the end of July as head of a British Military Mission. When I called at 143A Via Quattro Fontane the first person I met was my old friend Henry Lygon, who by now was a Major with the (too often appropriately) green tabs of an Intelligence officer.

Sir Samuel Hoare was extremely agreeable and invited me to lunch with him at the Grand Hotel where he and his wife were staying; Lady Maud was a sister of Henry Lygon.

That afternoon Henry said he wanted to have a talk with me and we drove along the Appian Way. As the ancient vehicle jogged slowly past the tombs Henry all but wept upon my shoulder.

"When I was sent out here, Monty, it was with the idea that I should be the head of this new Mission and now Sammy has got the job. He's my brother-in-law and I've always been fond of him, but this job was meant for me and now Sammy has managed to collar it for himself because he likes Rome."

"But, Henry, I had a formal notification at the end of July that he was taking over here."

"Yes, but he was supposed to stay only for a short time and then leave the show to me. If he hadn't taken this fancy to Rome he would be gone by now. Sammy's a very clever fellow at getting what he wants, and he decided he wanted Rome. Of course, he's a Quaker."

"I thought he was a High Churchman."

"So he is, but he's a Quaker at heart, and when Quakers want something they always manage to convince themselves that it's what God wants. My being his brother-in-law wasn't going to stand in

[1] The late Lord Templewood.

his way. And he's managed to get me sent to Albania with Aubrey Herbert."[1]

I wanted to laugh, but Henry was almost weeping; so I managed to hold my mirth. The notion of Henry Lygon and Aubrey Herbert on a joint mission to Albania was to anybody who knew them both as well as I did an almost farcical situation. It would have been impossible to choose a more ill-assorted pair. Whatever Aubrey might effect in his way with the Albanians he so dearly loved would be nullified by Henry; whatever Henry might effect in his way would be at once annihilated by Aubrey. I never could persuade either of them to tell me the story of that Albanian partnership, the details of which will remain for ever unknown.

I tried in vain to console Henry with a tirade against the worthlessness of office and the inevitability of intrigue among officials; he felt too bitterly his supersession by a brother-in-law to heed what I said. That drive with Henry Lygon is still vivid in my mind's eye. I still see the Campagna spread on one side of us, soft and opaline in the September weather. "Rome's ghost since her decease." I still hear the clip-clop of the horse's hooves upon the Appian Way. Neither the sight nor the sound could be recaptured in the blaring Rome of to-day.

I discussed Italy's future in the Mediterranean with Hoare, who took in my information cautiously, as if indeed it was as indigestible as the Italian food he was forbidden to eat. He and Lady Maud gave me food which after Syra seemed the most delicious I ever tasted, but the Chief of the Military Mission was allowed scarcely more than spinach himself. As I look back at this transit of Rome it seems to consist entirely of delicious meals and champagne with Sir Samuel and Lady Maud at the Grand Hotel at which I did all the eating and drinking. From time to time I would suggest to Hoare that it might be useful for me to see the Italian Director of Military Intelligence and the Italian Director of Naval Intelligence as I had done on my way through Rome last autumn, but somehow Hoare always found an excuse for being unable to arrange an appointment with either.

Molesworth and I left Rome on September 17th and stayed at the Ritz for a night in Paris. I went round to visit Clive Bigham at the Bureau Inter-Alliés, who told me he had arranged a dinner that night at the Ritz. Mrs Phipps, the wife of Eric Phipps,[2] the First Secretary, liked my books and wanted to meet me. Besides them he had asked the Ambassador's son, Vere Bertie,[3] and his wife, and the Military Attaché, Colonel Le Roy Lewis and his wife. Molesworth was taken charge of by

[1] The late Hon. Aubrey Herbert, M.P.
[2] The late Rt. Hon. Sir Eric Phipps, G.C.M.G.
[3] Viscount Bertie of Thame.

somebody at the Bureau Inter-Alliés to be given as dashing an evening as was obtainable in Paris at that date.

The dinner was held in that recess in a corner of the dining-room which may no longer exist in the Ritz of to-day.

Clive Bigham encouraged me to tell stories about Athens in 1916, and being one of the most voluble raconteurs of our period I told tales until well after midnight, having a most appreciative audience. I should say that, inasmuch as all telegrams to Athens from the Foreign Office were repeated to Paris in 1916, I might have been talking in the Chancery at Athens to Erskine and Sells. This I mention because there will be a sequel to this dinner presently.

I suppose I ought not to say it was an exceptionally delightful evening, seeing that I did most of the talking, but it *was* a delightful evening; twenty-one years later Sir Eric Phipps, then British Ambassador in Paris, would recall it to me when the Saintsbury Club was being sublimely entertained by the Club de Cent, the élite of the world's gourmets.

The next day Molesworth and I left Paris to cross by Le Havre on a dirty night of equinoctial weather. Before we were out of the port one of the ship's officers told me I was the senior officer on board (a Captain of Marines afloat takes precedence over a Captain in the Army) and asked me to superintend the boat-drill. I declined firmly. I said that during a crossing such as we seemed likely to have I intended to remain in my bunk, and that if we were hit by a torpedo I thought the quickest and least uncomfortable way of being drowned would be in my bunk.

When I reported to C at 2 Whitehall Court his first question was: "What have you been doing to Sammy Hoare?"

"Why, nothing that I know of, sir. He was very kind to me in Rome. He gave me lots of good food and champagne at the Grand Hotel. I wasn't aware of any cloud."

"Well, he doesn't like you," said C in that slurred voice of his, the hint of a smile playing round the finely cut bow of a mouth. "Look at this," he went on, tossing a telegram across his desk. "The War Office sent it over."

I read:

If there is any suggestion of appointing Captain Compton Mackenzie to be Military Control Officer in Rome I feel it is my duty to insist that such an appointment would be unfavourably viewed by the Italian Government on account of his conspicuous activities on behalf of M. Venizelos.

"Was there any question of my being appointed to Rome, sir?" I asked.

"None whatever," said C. "Did you give Sammy Hoare the idea that you'd like a job in Rome?"

"It never entered my head. I suppose that was why Hoare kept on making difficulties about my seeing the Italian D.M.I. and D.N.I., whom as you know I saw last autumn. I ought to have taken that card I used to hang round my neck sometimes in Syra."

"What card was that?"

"A card inscribed: TALK FREELY. I DO NOT WANT YOUR JOB."

And then C told me some of the tale of his own fight with people in the War Office anxious to pull his organization to pieces.

I found the job C had in mind for me after I had had a rest was Tripoli, with Tunis and Libya thrown in.

"It wants somebody who can handle the French and the Italians."

The next day C called me up on the telephone at the old bow-windowed Savile in Piccadilly where I was staying for my time in London.

"Come round at once. There's a terrific strafe from the Foreign Office," he said.

When I got to his room C pushed across the table a note from Ronald Campbell,[1] Lord Hardinge's private secretary. It was to say Lord Hardinge had heard with pained astonishment that when Captain Compton Mackenzie passed through Paris the other day he had visited Maxim's at night and in the presence of a number of people of all kinds and classes had talked with the greatest indiscretion of diplomatic secrets. The letter went on to say that should anything like this occur again the Foreign Office would lose the confidence it had hitherto reposed in Captain Compton Mackenzie.

"It's a very nice strafe, I think," said C with a touch of complacency. "You notice that bit about having confidence in you. I like that."

The dear old boy was so gratified to learn the Foreign Office had had confidence in one of his men that by this time the letter was beginning to assume the characteristics of a testimonial rather than of a strafe.

"Yes, I think it's the nicest strafe I ever read," he went on, gazing with pride at the note in Campbell's neat handwriting.

"Oh yes, it's a pleasant enough strafe," I agreed. "The only trouble is that there's no truth in it. I never went near Maxim's when I was in Paris."

Then I told C of the dinner Clive Bigham had given and how the guests were all connected with the Embassy.

"You mean you didn't go on to Maxim's after this dinner?"

"No, no, sir. I went straight up to bed."

"I'll write to Campbell to tell Lord Hardinge that any indiscretion

[1] The late Rt. Hon. Sir Ronald Campbell, G.C.M.G.

must have come from his own diplomatic people. Who were at this dinner?"

I named the guests.

"He'll have to strafe them now," the old boy chuckled. "I'll tell him you were fully entitled to suppose you were talking to a privileged audience. But I shan't make much of a fuss because I must say I really do like this strafe. I consider it's a great compliment."

"All the same, it will probably mean a black mark against me at the F.O."

"You've got a warning mark against you in the War Office already," said C. "I happened to catch sight of a list of names and against yours was noted *This officer has too much initiative, but should make an ideal Number Two.*"

Perhaps that judgment on myself stuck in C's mind; about a fortnight later, when the Tripoli scheme was still hanging fire, he sent for me to say he had decided what to do with me.

"I'm going to have you as my Number Two here as soon as you've had a rest in Italy."

I must have looked a little doubtful about the success of such an appointment.

"You realize what that would mean?" he pressed.

"It would mean one row after another," I assured him.

"Yes, but I don't intend to let them get me out," he declared. "I'll go through the war, and I'll stick on for a couple of years after it's over, and when I go you'll step into my place."

"But I don't want to be head of the Secret Service, sir. As soon as the war's over I want to get back to my own writing job."

"Damn it, mine's a pretty good job," snapped the old boy, nettled by my lack of excitement at the prospect of stepping into his shoes. "It's much more fun in peace-time than in war-time, I can assure you."

"Well, sir, if you want me to be your Number Two here for the rest of the war, I'll enjoy it, but not after the war. Freedom will have become an obsession by then."

Two or three days later he rang me again at the Savile to come round to Whitehall Court.

"You know my proposal to make you my Number Two here?" he said. "What do you think has happened? A round robin from all the staff here asking to be transferred if you are appointed."

I laughed.

"They were far-sighted and prudent, sir. I should certainly have done my best to get most of them transferred as soon as possible unless they learnt to do their job better than they have been doing it for the last two years."

"Yes, but this round robin knocks out my plan to have you here."

"That was the intention, sir."

"Wholesale resignations might smash me at this time when the War Office are trying to get control of my show," he muttered. "I'm annoyed about it; I should have liked to have you here."

"Don't you bother about me, sir."

"I suppose you think I let you down in Syra?" C asked with a hint of challenge in the out-thrust chin.

I had known ever since I returned that this had been at the back of the old boy's mind, but we had talked hardly at all of matters in the Aegean.

"Not at all, sir. Your splendid backing made it more and more of an enviable job to divide up among greedy generals. I started with £300 a month in September 1915; in September 1917 we were drawing £12,500 a month. No wonder it was felt I had too much initiative."

"Well, we'll see presently what happens about this Tripoli business," said C.

I picked a bad time to come back to London after a long absence; it was the week when German aircraft displayed their greatest activity. I recall dining with Knoblock one night in those exquisite Albany rooms of his, in which there was not a single article of furniture that was not Regency, when a dud bomb broke the glass in Burlington House. Then there was the morning of the daylight raid. I was again in Knoblock's rooms, the windows of which looked down Vigo Street. We went out on a balcony to stare up at the Gothas which shimmered far up like paper windmills. They were flying eastward over Regent Street. After a glance at them I went back indoors and sat on Knoblock's high purple-covered Regency sofa while he stood on the balcony, his head cocked over like a duck eyeing a hawk. I told him rather irritably he would be safer from flying shrapnel fragments inside.

When an air-raid was threatened maroons went off and young men on bicycles used to ride along the streets with placards on their backs, TAKE COVER. One night I was walking along a deserted Piccadilly past the Ritz when a bomb fell just inside the entrance to Green Park. I was top of the class at the Savile that evening for near escapes from bombs.

The dud shells of our air-defences were almost more of a menace than the enemy's bombs. One evening when I was at the cinema in Bear Street, which was between Leicester Square and Charing Cross Road, the commissionaire came along to ask me if I would come out and speak to some boys outside. I went with him and found about a dozen kids from Seven Dials hacking away to extract a dud shell which had buried itself in the road.

"They won't pay any attention to me, sir," the commissionaire explained.

"But why should they listen to me?"

"They'll see you're somebody high up in the police, sir."

I had vaguely wondered when I entered the cinema why I had been shown to a seat with much ceremony, not having grasped the effect of a Marine's blue uniform. Even the kids from Seven Dials were overawed and agreed to desist from trying to blow up themselves and the cinema by detonating the shell with one of their tools.

On the other hand, if London considered my uniform strange, it cheered up a bluejacket who was carrying a full cargo of liquor up Bond Street. I had noticed him from the opposite pavement, ignoring with bibulous determination the military officers he passed; suddenly he caught sight of me.

"This is something I recognize," I could imagine he was saying to himself as he plunged swaying across the road in order to give me the most obsequious salute he could contrive. "But I'm not going to bloody well salute any of those imitation buggers in khaki," he was muttering to himself as he passed on, peering blearily for another uniform worthy of his acknowledgement.

Hope-Johnstone and I enjoyed a good jest that October. I told him to let out to various people under a vow of secrecy that I was already writing an account of what had happened in Greece during the last two years. I was supposed to be reading this book to him chapter by chapter. H-J was to come chuckling into various clubs and when asked the joke he was to say: "I've been reading the latest chapter of Mackenzie's book. He's just reached General Thingumabob, and, really, I think his portrait of Thingumabob is the funniest thing I've read for years." Hope-Johnstone did his deadly work so skilfully that he caused the kind of panic in high places Harriet Wilson's *Memories* caused once upon a time.

One day C rang me up to come round to Whitehall Court at once because the D.I.D. wanted to interview me.

"What the devil's all this about some book you're writing?" he asked. "The D.I.D.'s boiling."

"Admiral Hall's sleuths are on the wrong scent, sir."

"Well, you'll have to come across to the Admiralty and tell him that yourself."

So we went down to C's car and drove round to the open space behind the Horse Guards, where the car was parked. Then, from the back, C and I entered the ganglion of the British Empire, the old boy stumping ahead of me along the corridors until we reached the D.I.D.'s ante-room. Serecold, his pleasant secretary, with an herbaceous border of ribbons, led us into the presence.

I had heard a great deal about "Blinker" Hall from many people; what I had not heard was that facially he was so like my own Chief. His nose was beakier; his chin had a more pronounced cutwater. Nevertheless, when I looked at the two men I could have fancied that each was a caricature of the other.

Admiral Hall came to the point at once.

"Is this true that you're writing a book about your experiences?"

Before I had time to reply he went on.

"Do you know you would be liable to a court-martial? You're still in uniform, remember. And don't think you can write a book in this country and get it published in America."

"I'm afraid your information is not accurate, sir. I am not writing a book. I dare say when the war's over . . ."

"That's another matter," he broke in. "I'm talking about while the war lasts. I hear you've already written at least half a dozen chapters."

He stopped to fix me with a horn-rimmed horny eye. I felt like a nut about to be cracked by a toucan.

"I'm afraid, sir, I haven't yet written a word, and I have not the slightest intention of writing anything about Greece for a long time to come. I seldom uncork experience till it has been kept in the cellar about ten years."

I doubt if Admiral Hall believed me. I had a feeling he thought he had frightened me out of persevering with this mythical work. One day he would be frightened out of publishing his own reminiscences which were withdrawn after being announced for publication.

A day or two after this interview I met walking along by Queen Anne's Gate Eric Holt-Wilson of M.I.5, who told me that "Blinker" Hall had once demanded the arrest of all the postmasters between Scapa Flow and London because his bag to Admiral Jellicoe had been tampered with on the way up.

"And then it was discovered the D.I.D. had forgotten to seal his own letters before he put them in the bag," Holt-Wilson murmured with a compassionate smile.

When I heard that Sir Reginald Hall had been appointed head adviser to the Conservative Party I anticipated some bad advice: I was not wrong. They lost the election in 1924 which he had assured Stanley Baldwin was a certainty for them.

The possibility of my going out to Tripoli to work up an organization to deal chiefly with the communications of enemy submarines along the North African coast was continually under debate during October. Apparently we had no Intelligence organization between Morocco and Egypt. It was proposed I should operate in Tunis and Algeria as well; in

H

Libya the Senussi tribesmen were being particularly helpful to the Germans. I pointed out that the first necessity would be a craft to get about in. Could I have the *Aulis*?

This was held to be an extravagance. Why could I not rely on trawlers or an occasional sloop or destroyer when I wanted to move from one place to another? I asked what length of coastline they fancied I was to work along.

"About three or four hundred miles, I suppose," said somebody.

"About two thousand miles," I exclaimed. "I do wish you'd use a large-scale map for these dreams of the future."

Apropos of large-scale maps, the largest I ever saw was in Montagu House, the meeting ground of the War Cabinet. Here Mark Sykes[1] took me to an upper chamber and showed me a map of the Near and Middle East after the war; it came down like a theatre-curtain on its roller when he pulled a cord. I remember noticing that the French were at Erzerum, but whether this was provided for by the famous Sykes-Picot agreement which pooled the Near East I have forgotten.

"If we get another flood," I observed, "it's just the place for French battleships. They all look like arks. I hope the two brutes we escorted to Taranto will get stuck on the top of Mount Ararat for keeps."

Only two years later that lovable man Mark Sykes would die at forty; he was a heavy loss to his country.

Montagu House became the Ministry of Labour. Was there ever a large-scale map in that upper chamber of the Welfare State?

I recall a jolly evening that October in Ivor Novello's high-up Aldwych flat with my sister Fay and Phyllis Monkman, and Violet Loraine at the piano singing:

> The gypsy warned me, the gypsy warned me,
> She said to me, "my child,
> He's a bad lad, a very bad lad,"
> But I only looked and smiled.

But the night of that October to which I look back with the greatest sense of its richness in time was a Sunday night at Magdalene College, Cambridge, with Stephen Gaselee,[2] who was Pepys Librarian but working temporarily as a Clerk in the Foreign Office, of which he would one day become Librarian. His other guests were Ronald Storrs[3] and Bruce Richmond.[4]

[1] The late Sir Mark Sykes, Bt.
[2] The late Sir Stephen Gaselee, K.C.M.G., D.Litt.
[3] The late Sir Ronald Storrs, K.C.M.G., LL.D.
[4] The late Sir Bruce Richmond, D.Litt.

Storrs was for the moment in the Secretariat of the War Cabinet, having lately returned from Baghdad, and in December he was to become Military Governor of Jerusalem; Bruce Richmond was Editor of the *Times Literary Supplement*.

I remember arriving at the College lodge in a dusky autumnal mist and being greeted as I passed through by a terrific stamping on the flagstones by a saluting sergeant. Although most of the College had been handed over to the military, that was the last I saw of the war for twenty-four hours.

We dined with our host in the Combination Room, with plenty of silver and candles, seated at what may have been the High Table transferred from the College Hall, which no doubt had been handed over to some O.T.C. Mess.

I wish I had kept at the time a list of what we drank, because, apart altogether from the quality of the wines, the quantity was truly remarkable. Nevertheless, at about seven o'clock in the morning Storrs and I were capable of drinking two brimming pint glasses of old Scotch ale, the last drop of liquor of any kind left in Gaselee's room, whose Carian guests, instead of talking the sun down the sky, had talked him up. Storrs certainly talked most; Gaselee and I were about level; Richmond was comparatively taciturn.

For many years it had been Gaselee's habit to wear scarlet socks whether with ceremonious black or tweed dittos; from that night all but fifty years ago I hear the voice of Ronald Storrs crying, "Cardinal! Cardinal! Do you remember?" before reeling off the ode of Horace or lyric of Anacreon that seemed to catch the fugitive moment and imprison it in immortal verse.

I thought of Francis Storrs left behind in Syra and now in Athens poring over his archives for the benefit of Commander Myres, whom he disliked and of whose judgment of living men he had an even lower opinion than I had, however shrewd his judgment may have been in archaeology. Francis had been of very great help to me in Syra and I wished he was with us to quote Horace in competition with Ronald, though Francis would have been half asleep long before that exuberant elder brother of his would be thinking the night had just begun. And what a night it was! It was a night woven out of Persia and Arabia, out of Egypt and Mesopotamia, out of Lydia and Caria, out of Lesbos, Samos, Athens, Halicarnassos, out of Cumae, Neapolis and Rome. And of that night not one word of wisdom or folly do I retain in my memory, nothing indeed except the glow of good wine and brandy, and Stephen Gaselee's scarlet socks and the voice of Ronald Storrs crying "Cardinal! Cardinal! Do you remember?" and Bruce Richmond quiet in a comfortable armchair, over the back of which were the skins of Stephen

Gaselee's two Siamese cats, of whose popularity he was one of the pioneers.

Next afternoon I wandered round Pembroke College with Storrs and called on Quiller-Couch, who, alas, was in bed with a violently acute lumbago and sweating with pain. We went back to London that evening in order to be in time for the war again on Monday morning.

I was disappointed I did not have a chance of a talk with Q, to whose early encouragement I owed so much. However, I had a memorable evening with Edmund Gosse, who wrote to me on October 7th from 17 Hanover Terrace, Regents Park:

My Dear Compton Mackenzie,

Our son goes off to India to-night; so that we shall be rejoiced to see you at 7.45 to-morrow (Monday). You will find us "desolate, but all undaunted", and we are looking forward with immense pleasure to welcoming you, and hearing of all your adventures.

I only wish our beloved Henry James were with us still. He followed your career with the warmest anticipation, and we were talking about you the very day before he had his fatal attack.

Always your sincerely,
Edmund Gosse

Gosse had married a daughter of Epps' Cocoa, which used to be advertised as "Grateful and Comforting". Sylvia Gosse and her sister were always affectionately known as Grateful and Comforting. I fancy both were at dinner that night. The only other guest was Evan Charteris, who had not yet had a shot at whitewashing the Butcher Cumberland—for which he had the advantage of consulting the diary of Lord Elcho in the possession of the Wemyss family and never yet published in full.

The *pièce de résistance* at dinner that night was the largest cauliflower I have ever seen, which occupied the table as proudly as a roast turkey. "You see," said dear Gosse, "we are doing our bit at home."

This allusion was to the growing food shortage and Gosse was anxious to impress on me that at 17 Hanover Terrace no attempt was being made to deprive the troops by self-indulgence over food at home. After dinner he took me into his little book-lined study and gave me an inscribed copy of *Father and Son*.

"You know, my dear boy," he said, "you have caught my fancy more than anybody since our dear Louis died."

It is fashionable nowadays for critics unable to write a sentence of good English prose to sneer at Edmund Gosse; it is equally the fashion to sneer at Robert Louis Stevenson. Regrettably it was Frank Swinnerton who started the last fashion with a book about him published by Martin Secker.

As October wore along, without rival interests being able to compose their differences and decide whether or not they wanted me to go to North Africa, I grew tired of London. Sir Francis Elliot insisted that I ought to take a long leave at once for the sake of my health; I agreed and toward the end of the month I started for Italy.

In Paris I told Clive Bigham about the sequel to his dinner party at the Ritz.

"Oh, I know who that must have been," said Bigham. "That was Le Roy Lewis. Your name was suggested by the F.O. as a possible Assistant Military Attaché in Paris, and Le Roy Lewis was not in favour. No doubt he decided to make certain you wouldn't be appointed."

I had had an opportunity since I left Capri on that May morning in 1915 to learn a great deal more about place-hunting and self-seeking than most novelists are ever afforded; I had supposed I was no longer capable of being surprised by evidence of it. Nevertheless, I was surprised by what Clive Bigham told me about that guest of his at dinner.

Yet when I left the Gare de Lyon that night on my way back to Capri I lectured myself on what I felt might become a tendency to suppose I had a grievance. I reminded myself that office in any shape, diplomatic, military or political, was not my career. Promotion, decorations, and the rest of it were of no importance to me; the Legion of Honour was enough. Throughout those days in Greece I had never had to ask myself whether some action of mine would injure my career. I had no right as an amateur to criticize professionals for being afraid to do what I had done.

As I look back now to these years in Greece I realize that whatever I was able to achieve was achieved by my ability to become absorbed in the ruling passion of the moment. My Sunday school at Gunwalloe, my gardening at Rivière, my building up of that Intelligence show in Athens and Syra, and in due course my islands in the Channel, my preoccupation with the gramophone, my life in the Hebrides, my time with the old Indian Army and even now in my eighties the discovery of the Arcadia I have found in France, these have been some of the ruling passions of the moment. I have had to work very hard and I still have to work very hard to enjoy them. I move out of my thirty-fifth year to say this, but I am anxious that nobody reading this record of my life and times should suppose that I am not always aware of my own good fortune. I have had to mention pain a good deal, but it has not been done to excite sympathy. I believe that pain has been of immense value; I am sure that without the intervals of pain I have had for sixty years I should not be able to concentrate in the way I am still able to concentrate upon the work in hand.

When I reached Turin on a gusty evening I dined in the station restaurant; a man opposite me at the table was reading an Italian newspaper. Suddenly he crumpled it up and flung it on the floor.

"Caporetto is a great disaster," he exclaimed in Italian. "Why do these papers write lies? *Un desastro! Un desastro!*"

The magnitude of that disaster was beginning to transpire even through the false optimism of the Italian Press; by the time I reached Capri the very existence of Italy seemed in the balance. I think it is true to say that during that desperate autumn a new Italy was born on the line of the Piave. It had been well for the future of Europe if the British and French delegates at Versailles had realized as much instead of listening so credulously to the silly and boastful legend that Italy had only been saved in 1917 by the soldiers of Great Britain and France.

I was a little worried by what seemed Faith's almost unreasonably bitter remarks about the British and Americans in Capri, and told her I thought it was time she forgot about those quarrels in 1916.

In the first volume of her reminiscences *As Much As I Dare* she wrote of these quarrels over her failure to regard Kitchener's death as a mortal blow to Great Britain. She realized that his work was done and that his death, when it came, far from being a mortal blow, was in fact an advantage. No doubt my letters had blamed Kitchener for the failure of Gallipoli and no doubt I had written about that mine which sank the *Hampshire* as a blessing in disguise. However, she was not equipped to argue with the state of mind that the propaganda of war, begets. On one of my transits through Rome I ran into Gilbert Frankau and asked him what he was doing there. By a *lapsus linguae* he told me he was there for purposes of propagation.

"A much better word for it, Gilbert. The propagation of weeds in the human mind," I told him.

Soon after I returned to Capri I had a letter from Algar Thorold in Rome to say he had been put in charge of the Propaganda Mission in Italy. Thorold was the son of a former Bishop of Winchester, a strange personality who, as I remember, finally became a Buddhist monk in Ceylon. He said he was writing to me at the suggestion of the Ambassador to ask if I would take the responsibility for Naples and the South of Italy. The work would include "*the distribution of propaganda literature, the organization of lectures, photographic exhibitions, information service, etc. and need not be, materially speaking, of a very fatiguing nature. What is required is the brain on the spot. . . . I understand that you are, for the moment, released from Public Service. . . . It would, of course, involve residence in Naples. The post would be paid, though not, I fear, at a very high rate, as the Government still considers propaganda a somewhat secondary war expense.*"

I wrote at once to say I was only in Capri on leave, and that in any case it was imperative for me to devote all my time to writing a book. My finances were indeed in a sorry condition. Somehow I must write a novel before my leave expired. But what should its subject be? As if in answer to the question, on the last day of October a telegram came from London through the Consul-General in Naples to ask why I had visaed the passport of a certain Trixie Ellwood who was believed to be a German national. I telegraphed back that as far as I knew she was a British subject; any further arguments about that poor girl were closed by her death.

My memory went back to Athens in the autumn of 1915. An agent of mine of whom I have written at length in my war memories as a comic figure of the first order said to me:

"Skipper, two English girls have arrived from Constantinople via Salonique. Bertha Proctor and Trixie Ellwood. Trixie is really a Hun. She's singing at the Trianon."

I went to the open air Café Concert in Patissia called Le Petit Trianon. At the top of the bill I read

Trixie
La Belle Anglaise
et
L'Enfant Gatée d'Athènes

A girl in a short fluffy skirt came prancing on to the stage amid loud applause and a banging of iron tables. She had long slim legs, a baby face, and pale golden hair; her voice as she sang some English song of a bygone Gaiety success was breathless as a child's.

I gave orders that my agents were not to waste their time trying to solve Trixie's nationality; there was more important work for them to do.

Soon after this I received a note from Miss Bertha Proctor asking me to protect her against persecution. I interviewed a buxom Lancashire woman of about forty who in spite of years of cabaret life on the Continent still spoke with the Burnley accent of her youth.

"Look, I've come to ask if it's by your orders that these bloody detectives I don't think have been buggering up all my trunks and all Trixie's trunks, looking for something they'll never bloody well find. They've found nowt, lad, and that's evidence we're nowt but what we say we are. Eh, it's damn disgusting, and that's a fact."

Hardly had Miss Proctor flounced out of the room than one of the

junior members of the British Naval Mission with the temporary rank
of Engineer-Lieutenant-Commander arrived to complain of the way
my blackguards were persecuting poor Trixie.

"Look here, see the girl yourself. Ask her any questions you like.
You'll find she's perfectly harmless."

So I had gone to the Pension d'Artistes and had talked to Trixie.
Whether or not she really was English I could not find out but I realized
the one ambition of that little lost soul was to be English and I
threatened to sack any of my agents who bothered her again.

The young Englishman fell deeply in love with Trixie, who stayed on
in Athens when Bertha Proctor went back to England.

In 1916 the young Englishman was ordered home and came to see
me in a perturbed state.

"Look here, I love this girl. I can't marry her because my people at
home wouldn't stand for it. But I can't leave her here. God knows what
will happen to her. Can't you get her a British passport and give her
your visa?"

This I had done, and then I suppose some jealous rival denounced
her to M.I.5. However, by the time M.I.5 started to investigate her
nationality Trixie had escaped to that ideal England of which she had
so long dreamed.

Her story had fascinated me when I heard it first and it was from the
tale of herself and Bertha Proctor that I had put together the novel
called *No Papers*, the manuscript of which had been destroyed when my
house was wrecked.

I was hoping to get one day the compensation I had claimed from the
Greek Government after the Commission under the chairmanship of an
English County Court judge had finished their task of examining the
many claims for damages in that December of 1916. That might take
another year or more and I needed money now. The telegram about
Trixie set me thinking and I decided to make her a subordinate character in a novel called *Sylvia Scarlett*; it was Stevenson's unwritten novel
which he intended to call *Sophia Scarlett* which had given me the name
when Sylvia herself appeared as a subordinate character in *Sinister
Street*.

On November 3rd, St Sylvia's day, I sat down to write it in the hope
of finishing it by the first week in February; it would be hard going to
write about 300,000 words in just over three months, but somehow it
must be done.

While I was in Syra Hope-Johnstone had done two things for me; he
had made me read *War and Peace* and the novel which inspired Tolstoy
to write *War and Peace*, the *Chartreuse de Parme*. When at the beginning of
July I was very ill with dysentery, a swollen internal gland and a

violent go of neuritis in a temperature of 110° I had decided, after
dragging myself in agony 365 times along the passage in four days and
nights to oblige the dysentery, that it was no longer worth while to cling
on to life. I told H-J I had decided to die.

"But you haven't read *War and Peace* yet," he protested.

"It's too late now, H-J. I can't keep alive in this infernal heat and
pain merely to read a long book like *War and Peace*."

Hope-Johnstone was firm and Constance Garnett's translation of
War and Peace bound in mauve was placed on my chest. I read the first
few pages and decided I would stay alive until to-morrow to see what
happened next. It was lucky that Prince Pierre's endless talk did not
occur at the beginning or I might have closed *War and Peace* prematurely. However, I became absorbed, so much absorbed that I read on,
and some days later, at the end of *War and Peace*, I rose from my bed,
weighing just under eight stone and looking almost transparent but
resolved to live and continue the war with greedy generals and insecure
diplomats.

War and Peace may have given me back the will to live, out of the life
Tolstoy poured into that great book, but the *Chartreuse de Parme* gave me
the assurance that life was worth writing about as well as living. I had
tried to read the *Chartreuse de Parme* when I was an undergraduate and
had been bored by it. Nobody should read this best of all novels until he
possesses the worldly experience to appreciate it. It is not even intel-
ligible to the unversed mind. No novel ever written was so essentially
the fruit of worldly knowledge. Few women care passionately for it, but
the woman who does care for it may be herself a Sanseverina. It is the
only novel I have read in which I could identify myself with the principal character and imagine that I would have behaved exactly like
him in various circumstances; it is the only novel I have read in which I
have been able to fall in love with two of the characters, as Fabrice fell
in love with the Duchess Sanseverina and Clelia Conti.

When I picked up my pen to write *Sylvia Scarlett* I realized that the
hundreds of telegrams I had written during the last two years had
emptied the honey from what the *Encyclopaedia Britannica* calls my melli-
fluous style. Telegram after telegram at nearly two shillings a word had
made every adjective an unwarrantable extravagance. I was comforted
by the thought that Stendhal had taken the Napoleonic Code as a
model for his style; I was captivated by Stendhal's way of making his
characters express so much of themselves in direct speech.

There was another reason to prune the decorations with which my
work was now associated and that was the shortage of paper. I was
compelled to write the first part of *Sylvia Scarlett* on the manuscript of
Guy and Pauline turned upside down. This meant that there was no space

to rewrite a sentence on the other side of the paper, the other side of the paper being completely occupied by the sentences of *Guy and Pauline* upside down; some of those revised sentences were on the pages on which *Sylvia Scarlett* was being written, and an infernal nuisance they were.

I did not go out during those stormy November weeks, and Faith always made some excuse for not inviting any of the British and American colony to Casa Solitaria. Instead she used to welcome the visits of Bianca and Isabella Caracciolo and their cousin Bianca Binyon. I had not met any of them before and was delighted by the two girls, still in their 'teens, without a word of English.

Many years before two painters, who were friends, came to Capri. One was Edward Binyon, a cousin of the poet, the other was Prince Caracciolo di Luperano, a descendant of that Caracciolo who was a victim of Nelson's deplorable action in that deplorable Neapolitan episode. He and Binyon married sisters, two beautiful Capresi *contadine*. A *contadina* is not some kind of a countess, but a country girl. Binyon died in 1875. His daughter Bianca lived with her mother after being educated in England, and his son Bertram, a fine tenor, used to visit his mother and sister every year. Prince Caracciolo remained in Capri for the rest of his life and produced a large family. Donna Giulia, the eldest daughter, spoke English, French and German perfectly; she ran a small circulating library and was great friends with the British and American colony; her two youngest sisters avoided them. Faith had made friends with them when she was out of humour with her English friends.

Halfway through that blusterous and chill November the visits of the two girls suddenly stopped. Faith kept going into Capri every afternoon, and then one night after dinner a note was brought to Casa Solitaria. Faith took it in and came back into the *salone* with a face of despair. She sat down and the note dropped to the floor. It was a single sentence written by Bianca Binyon:

> *Nini sta gravissimo*
> *Bianca*

Nini Caracciolo, whom I had never seen, was the youngest son of the Prince; in his very early twenties he had been laid low with rheumatic fever from which his heart was not strong enough to recover. He died that night.

Faith was in an emotional collapse and kept on saying "My fault! All my fault!"

Next morning our neighbour Brooks came along and from him I heard something of the story. Nini Caracciolo had shown promise of being a better painter than his father one day; Faith had just taken up sculpture. Their common interest had been the first bond; that bond had been strengthened by love. All through the summer that love-affair had been providing a rich topic for Capri when the war had emptied the island of the usual crowds of visitors that used to provide it with scandals galore. My return had made the young man go wandering about the cliffs through the savage weather in a state of despair. Hence the rheumatic fever. Faith had tried to persuade him to be sensible but he had been set on unhappiness.

"You say everybody in Capri knew about Faith and young Caracciolo?"

"I'm—um-um—afraid so—um-um-um—Capri gossip you know."

"I'd better go to his funeral," I said. "That ought to stop Capri gossip."

Brooks was deeply relieved. He had come down this morning to make that very suggestion.

My presence at the funeral successfully silenced the gossips who had been speculating what I should do when I heard about young Caracciolo. I knew that something must be done to occupy Faith's mind as my own mind was occupied with the problem of writing an inevitably very long novel against time. So I asked her to tackle the task of typing it, which would enable me to revise the book as I was writing it. And this by a tremendous effort of will she succeeded in doing.

So that stormy Autumn passed into a stormy January throughout every day of which I sat in a silk smoking-suit the elbows of which were in holes by Christmas. I never went out. When Faith had finished typing what I had written the previous day she would play the piano scores of Verdi's operas which I had acquired. I never became a musical snob or a musical prig and thank God I enjoy Verdi as much to-day as I did fifty years ago. Pauline, who as a kitten had been such a joy when I was writing *Guy and Pauline*, was as much of a joy now when I was writing *Sylvia Scarlett* on the other side of it. She had no kittens of her own that autumn and used to sleep with me, back to back, her head upon the pillow beside me.

Ten days after I started on *Sylvia Scarlett* I received a letter from Sir Francis Elliot:

I called on C yesterday to talk about your affairs. He was very sympathetic and said he would do his best and get you four months' leave on the ground of health, leaving the question of your future employment for later consideration. . . . I think you may feel fairly confident of four months' peace and quiet. It appears that there has been a complete reorganization of C's Department and co-ordination of it with the D.M.I.'s Department, the result being that some of C's best men have been taken away from him.

At the end of the month I heard from C:

I have taken some time to reply to your letter because we have been extremely busy over a threatened re-construction. I think it is quite a good idea your taking long leave and getting yourself thoroughly fit once more. As regards pay, the rule is that you have six weeks' full pay sick leave and after that your pay is supposed to stop. If you like, however, I will do my best to have a special case made, for I think we may say with perfect honesty that your being run down is due to your trying work. . . .

The Tripoli scheme was turned down just after you left, but Egypt has now informed us that they intend to do the work themselves. So you see if we have done no other good we have stirred them up a bit! . . . This new reconstruction will turn the office upside down, but that is all. I think it will work just as well in an inverted position, and like the Cardinal's curse "nobody will be one penny the worse" (or better). In the meantime, and while the decisions of the great have not yet crystallized into concrete pronouncements, we are all rather irritable. . . .

What is to be the title of the new book?

Is there any danger of Capri coming within the Hindenburg line?

Day after day I worked at *Sylvia Scarlett*. It was to be divided into three books—*Sylvia and Philip, Sylvia and Arthur, Sylvia and Michael*, and each book was to consist of seven chapters. My average day of writing and revising was twelve hours.

By five days after my thirty-fifth birthday I had written 280,000 words in eighty days. Then I cracked. The remaining 20,000 words would take nearly two hundred days.

What had added a spur to that cracking pace had been a note from C which reached me on New Year's Day:

I find that in giving you leave, I exceeded my powers. I understand, however, that your health entirely prevents you from working here in London, and that you require further rest to make you fit.

Will you please write me a letter stating this, that I may put it in as a reason for granting you leave until the end of February.

THIRTY-FIVE YEARS OLD: 1918

BY the end of January I realized that there was no chance of finishing *Sylvia Scarlett* and told Martin Secker. He was rather relieved, because the paper famine and price would have made it impossible to publish a novel of some 300,000 words. It was decided to publish the first two parts in August, and the third part (with two and a half chapters still to write) in the spring of 1919. So in August *The Early Life and Adventures of Sylvia Scarlett* appeared, printed on a foul flaccid greenish paper. The available paper ran to a first impression of 12,000 copies, which were sold within a week or two; the book was then out of print for over a year.

The reception of *The Early Adventures* was mixed. Those who had enjoyed the book were more than generous in their praise, but many of the old brigade were shocked by the apparent contempt for all the conventions which even as late as this still exercised their power. The book was handicapped by being incomplete. Yet to judge by the fatuity of most of the reviews of *Sylvia and Michael* when it came out in the spring of 1919 I doubt if it would have made much difference. All except a very few critics were completely bewildered. *Sylvia and Michael* was the first expression in fiction of the weariness and disgust inspired by the war, and in 1919 most of the critics had been left behind by the march of time; they still thought war should inspire lofty and romantic notions in the mind of a novelist. Moreover, they were suspicious of a writer who had failed to live up to the label they had affixed to him. The fact that Sylvia herself had already appeared in *Sinister Street* added to the puzzle of my changed style. The mood in which I wrote some of *Sylvia and Michael* had become the fashion ten years later when *Gallipoli Memories* was rebuked for making the circumstance of war often agreeable and amusing. I have been reading through the notices of *The Early Adventures of Sylvia Scarlett* and *Sylvia and Michael* and I have been tempted to print some of the opinions of contemporary writers still alive. With the amused tolerance that overtakes an octogenarian I refrain.

The trouble with British critics was, and with a very few notable exceptions still is, their lack of any width of experience. Even if they do travel abroad they travel about covered by a sort of plastic insularity which is transparent enough to let them observe other lands but is impervious enough to prevent any kind of communication with the people of those lands. I have had the good fortune to be assured by Frenchmen,

Italians, Greeks, Poles, Jews, Hebrideans, yes, and even by Irishmen that I have not blundered in my efforts to bring them to life on the printed page. Relying as I do so much on dialogue, I fancy that only readers with a dramatic sense enjoy my novels; they must be able as it were to play all the parts themselves, and so grasp their life. I am not interested in creating characters of such psychological complicacy that pages of patient analysis of human motive are required to present them on the printed page. The writer who does this seldom convinces me that his characters ever existed outside his own imagination and I am not interested in reading about abstractions to which my own imagination is unable to give flesh and blood.

I have been led away from that spring of 1918 by turning over the pages of that old press-cutting album.

So long as I was able to keep Faith preoccupied with typing during the day what I had written the day before and with playing those piano scores of Verdi's operas to me while I was at work in the evening, she was too tired not to sleep at night. When I cracked at the end of January and was having one violent attack of pain after another she went back to reproaching herself with having been the cause of Nini Caracciolo's death and between the pain and the sickness after the morphia administered by Dr Gennaro, I was in no condition to draw her out of these moods of morbid depression.

To counteract any possibility of my becoming a morphia addict Dr Gennaro used a form of it called Atoximecon which made the patient three times as sick as ordinary morphia for the next twenty-four hours.

A sad amount of nonsense is talked about addiction. One is either a natural addict, in which case whatever the drug, be it morphine, chloral or cocaine, it may be in danger of causing addiction, or one is not a natural addict. What is true of drugs is equally true of alcohol. I could not possibly become a drug addict or an alcoholic. I always indulge doctors, and if Dr Gennaro felt that the sanctity of the Hippocratic oath was being guarded by giving me Atoximecon I did not feel I had any right to argue with him.

One day Dr Axel Munthe came down from Anacapri and prescribed arsenic as a possible prophylactic against the sciatic neuritis which kept laying me out. I did not believe for a moment that arsenic would have the slightest effect, but I agreed to try it. I need hardly add that arsenic had no more effect as a prophylactic than ordinary water. What was much more valuable than Munthe's advice about my neuritis was his advice about Faith, with whom he had become great friends during my absence from Capri. He does not figure in that gallery of Capri portraits I painted in *Vestal Fire* because Faith made me promise not to include that great personality. She feared I might present him to the world as a comic figure.

I have met many of the greatest romancers or, to use the more accurate Italian word, *improvisatori* of our period and I must give the first place to Axel Munthe. Lawrence of Arabia, Ford Madox Ford, Frank Harris, Dion Clayton Calthrop, Peter Cheyney, Halliday Sutherland, Sir Henry McMahon, and many another whose fame was confined to a circle of private friends, had great gifts of improvization but none of them within my observation had quite the spontaneity of Munthe's fairy stories. The immense popularity of *San Michele*, which was written at Capri during this very year of 1918, is a tribute to Axel Munthe's skill. He was no longer living in that strange mixture of Scandinavian Gothic and Imperial Rome that was called the Villa San Michele.

Faith wrote of him when we were up at Caterola in the spring of 1914:

"Sometimes from the terrace of the little house I would see over the top of the wall an untidy whitish hat sailing swiftly along. I would wait hopefully for its wearer to appear in our gateway, for his alert descent of the steps that led to the terrace. He who never took a *carozza*, but walked from his far-off tower in Anacapri down the Phoenician steps into Capri would sometimes come still further, swinging up the paved Tiberio footpath to visit us.

"With his grizzled beard, his tall youthful figure and his spectacled eyes which for all their blindness were never deceived, Dr Axel Munthe was the most interesting and exciting figure on an island that was full of personalities. His apparent remoteness from the preoccupations of common humanity was deceptive, for no one had a livelier finger on the pulse of local gossip than he. There was little he did not know about all of us.

"And yet, in his Saracen tower Materita, his seclusion seemed absolute. The world surely could not penetrate those massive walls and that forbidding gateway? The illusion of exclusiveness fascinated the many guests to Materita. A visit to Capri was not really perfect without an invitation to the tower, and to be shown over Villa San Michele by the owner himself was an honour which sent the visitor driving back to his hotel with a warm sense of superiority. San Michele with its matchless view and dim green-lit interior is about a mile away from Materita."

There are many stories I could tell of Munthe's power of improvisation, but let my favourite stand for the rest. Faith used to play his accompaniments when he was singing Brahms *lieder* with not much voice but making the very best of it with perfect diction and expression. On one occasion his Ave Maria peal at Materita was ringing the Angelus at six o'clock.

"What a beautiful note that third bell has, Dr Munthe," said Faith. Munthe listened as if he was hearing that bell for the first time.

"You are quite right, Mrs Mackenzie. I had never noticed what a beautiful note that bell has. You have a wonderful ear. I had not realized how beautiful. *Most* beautiful."

A fortnight later Faith was again at tea in Materita. Staying with him was a Baroness whose name and nationality I withhold. Presently she arrived in the *salone*, cool and collected and beautifully dressed.

"I hope you are not feeling too tired, Baroness, after that hot walk from the *foresteria*?"

Munthe's guest-house was nearly a kilometre away from Materita.

"No, no, Dr Munthe. I'm not at all tired."

This was not surprising because the Baroness had walked no farther than along the corridor from her room to the *salone*.

In due course Ave Maria sounded from the Materita peal.

"Do you notice what a beautiful note that third bell has, Baroness?" Munthe asked.

"Yes, indeed, Dr Munthe," said the Baroness with a suitable expression of rapture at the lovely sound. "Oh, yes, *most* beautiful."

"I will tell you an interesting story about that bell," he announced. "A few months ago I was in Florence and one afternoon from the window of my hotel I heard at Ave Maria time one bell more beautiful than any of the many bells sounding through the city. I said to myself I must have this bell for my Ave Maria peal at Materita, and for three days I set out to find from where that bell was ringing. I would get up at six; I would listen at midday; and again at six o'clock in the afternoon. Then I would go to this church and to that church, to this religious house and to that religious house, but nowhere could I find that bell. And then at last on the fourth day of my search I found the bell was ringing from a small nunnery in Lung' Arno. I was very excited. I knocked at the door, and presently through the grille I could see the eyes of one of the *suori* looking at me. 'Open, please,' I said. 'I am the physician to Her Majesty the Queen of Sweden and I must speak urgently to the Reverend Mother Superior.' Well, to cut my long story short I have been able to persuade the Mother Superior to let me buy that bell for my Ave Maria at Materita, and that is why you heard that beautiful bell, Baroness, when Ave Maria rang at six o'clock."

"Oh, what a wonderful story, Dr Munthe," the Baroness sighed rapturously.

And indeed we can agree with her when we recall that only a fortnight earlier Axel Munthe had noticed the full beauty of that bell for the first time.

One day about halfway through March, Munthe arrived at Casa

Casa Solitaria

Herm

Solitaria when Faith was out. Pauline had just produced three kittens and I begged him to keep his Aberdeen terrier outside.

"Ah, he is perfectly all right. He can look after himself," said Munthe. A moment later we heard a yelp and the Aberdeen came in with a bloodied nose; Pauline had struck.

"You were right," said the dog's master, "I should have taken your advice. And now, my friend, I am going to give *you* some advice. It is about Mrs Mackenzie. She is heartsick."

With this preliminary that remarkable man went on to give a remarkably accurate appreciation of the state of affairs at Casa Solitaria. I shall preserve the essence of what was a conversation between us of over two hours in a single piece of direct speech in the Stendhalian method as if Count Mosca were talking to Fabrice. Perhaps in writing about this time I instinctively go back to those packed anxious hours when I was writing *Sylvia Scarlett*.

"Mrs Mackenzie has had two very difficult years. When she married an artist younger than herself she knew that she was taking a risk and she decided that her own artistic aspirations must be laid aside. She knew that she might have been a pianist of the first rank but she recognized that either through indolence or lack of self-confidence she had thrown away her music. Therefore she resolved to sacrifice all her own aspirations as an artist in order to help yours. So long as you were struggling to make a name for yourself she was happy, but when you enjoyed such a fantastic success so young she began to feel she was less necessary and to turn again to the idea of self-expression. Then you began to be tormented by these recurrent fits of pain for which perhaps this arsenic may be a prophylactic, perhaps not; I have no confidence; it is merely an experiment. Mrs Mackenzie could then feel that she was necessary to you. Yet even your pain robbed her of something. It made you the centre of attention and in defence of her own personality she was often being ill herself. We really know nothing yet about hysteria. No, do not protest. You think of hysteria as an excitable manifestation of some foolish girl. You are quite ignorant of the depth of such a malady. Mrs Mackenzie has talked to me once about her mother and I have warned her that she might someday have to struggle to avoid such a surrender.

"When you went to the Dardanelles Mrs Mackenzie felt that she must somehow do war work, as it was called. She became exasperated by the solemnity with which so many other women regarded their own war work. She lacked any ability to believe that she was of the least real use and, feeling exasperated as much with herself as with numbers of fussy women, she came back to Capri. Here she felt she was able to be of real use by typing out a great deal of Douglas's book *South Wind*, but

I

then she fell out with the women here who were not doing any war work but talking a great deal of nonsense about the war. She confided in me about the way she was being called pro-German because she wasn't prepared to cut one or two German women here married to Italians. She found a refuge from irritation in the company of the two youngest Caracciolo girls and thus became friends with their youngest brother. Early last summer she thought her friend Mrs Le Butt was, as you say, making eyes at young Caracciolo. There was a bitter quarrel and Mrs Le Butt went back to England. Then Mrs Mackenzie faced the fact that she was in love. It became common gossip and Mrs Mackenzie, knowing this, resented being criticized by women whose stupidity over her supposed pro-German sentiments had made her despise them. So, if I may put it so, she felt she must defy them. I am sure you have enough imagination to understand how easy it is for a woman getting close to forty to grasp at her fleeting youth. She felt again that she was being useful to a young artist and she could not reject that happiness. Yet all the time she knew Capri was watching that love-affair and wondering what would happen when you came back from Greece, where I hear you were regarded by half the country with as much veneration as something between the Archangel Michael and Byron and by the other half as something between Robespierre and the Devil himself.

"Well, you came back and before you came Mrs Mackenzie told young Caracciolo that their romance was over. He went wandering about in his unhappiness and was struck down with rheumatic fever. His heart was weak. He died. Mrs Mackenzie believed that weak heart of his was a broken heart and that she was responsible for his death. That was six months ago. Lately she has been having lessons again from that Dutch sculptress at Anacapri and she has begun to search in sculpture to express the creative longing in herself which was at rest while she was able to feel it was granted expression by young Caracciolo's need for her. But, I tell you, she is still heartsick.

"And now what about the future? I realize, knowing how much you owe to your wife, that you have always felt what might be called a sense of emotional responsibility for her. In other words, though I do not suppose that a man like you has been faithful, I think in whatever love-affairs you may have involved yourself that you have never had the slightest temptation to break up your marriage, because it would never have entered your head that your wife could fall in love with somebody else. What are you going to do now?

"There are three courses open to you. You can both of you pretend to yourselves that last summer never existed and go on as a conventional marriage. In that event I will prophesy that sooner or later you will find yourselves involved in divorce. Now, I know you well enough to be sure that such a divorce will make you feel guilty because, even if you no longer feel an emotional responsibility for your wife, you will feel that she once gave you a great deal and that without her you might never have reached the position you have. Will you be able to leave her in her mid-forties to make a life for herself and start trying to fulfil the aspirations she once had to be a creative artist herself?

"Your second course is to break up your marriage now. But how will you excuse yourself to yourself, or for that matter to others, if after apparently letting everybody suppose that you didn't believe it was a serious love-affair you make it an occasion for divorce?

"But there is a third course. Why don't you both admit that marriage in the conventional sense is no longer possible? Why don't you give freedom to each of you to live his or her own life and yet agree to live together in friendship as man and wife? You have no children. Neither of you is handicapped by any responsibility except to the other.

"And now for an immediate piece of advice. It is essential that Mrs Mackenzie should be cured of all this morbid self-reproach for being as she thinks responsible for young Caracciolo's death. Persuade her to invite the two younger Caracciolo girls to pick up again the friendship she enjoyed with them until the death of their brother. Whatever evil tongues may say, I am sure that they would be glad if that friendship were renewed."

That friendship was renewed; the company of Bianca and Isabella Caracciolo remains for me a precious souvenir of those Capri years. It was an invaluable anodyne for Faith and gradually her self-reproaches became less frequent. Moreover, her sculpture absorbed her more and more completely. As for myself, although the violent pain which had been almost continuous until half way through March would allow me by the end of that year freedom from it for sometimes as much as a fortnight, throughout that spring and summer I could not count on more than a week of such freedom, and those last chapters of *Sylvia and Michael* were not finished until the beginning of July.

The news of the great German offensive in March made Faith terribly anxious for her brother Christopher. A letter from him written on March 14th did not reach Capri till the end of the month.

We are at present undergoing the ordeal by gas every night which is far from pleasant. So far I haven't been caught, but it's a pitiable thing to see the victims afterwards. I'm living almost permanently in a wonderful dug-out made by Australians with the historic 39 steps, and we are waiting patiently for the Boche to make up his mind to attack us—poor devils. . . . Logan Pearsall Smith has sent me a book of modern poems to read and tells about the excitement of an aeroplane bomb falling in his quiet Chelsea street and the counting of broken window-panes,

as a gauge of patriotism. He had 56 broken but one old lady claims 67 and is sus-
pected by her neighbours of having broken some herself. Give my love to Monty.
Our Intelligence officer is a great admirer of his.

On April 3rd Christopher wrote:

I would be writing to you anyway to enquire about Monty's health and also to
inform you that I am safely out of a most appalling week of rearguard fighting—
I think the most uncomfortable time I've had out here—and my beloved General
was killed by my side, so I am more than lonely now. . . . We have fetched up now
at a fine modern château and the gramophone (a Decca portable) is going again
this evening after a fortnight's silence, and with a log fire and panelled walls all
seeming serene, but my goodness, we have been through it. Our new General is a
splendid giant, called Edmund Ironside, friend of the Furzes and so on, only 38
but with nearly 20 years' service in the Gunners with intervals in the Intelligence
and a qualified interpreter in 11 languages. You would love him; he's rather a
Seton Merriman hero in his cosmopolitan omniscience but he's certainly a great
character.

In June Christopher Stone would be awarded the D.S.O. for gallantry during those nerve-wracking March days.

Some time in that early spring Abbot Ford, late of Downside, the
titular Abbot of Glastonbury, came to Capri. He was an engaging
figure of a man and arrived in a week of fine weather without a greatcoat. When he was leaving for Rome, where I think he was working
with Cardinal Gasquet, I lent him my Spanish cloak, which he wore
with an air. He was a little on the defensive over the treatment accorded
to the monks of Buckfast Abbey, most of whom were German Bene-
dictines, and went so far as to say he had pressed for their internment; I
was amused by this echo of mediaeval monastic rivalry.

No face in Capri was more welcome when I returned than that of the
gardener Mimi Ruggiero, who had seen me off to Gallipoli from Naples.
I hear him now as I walk with him along the curved terrace in the cliff
below Casa Solitaria; we were congratulating ourselves on the way the
young cypresses had all survived two stormy winters and on the way
that *Iris Susiana* brought from Cornwall had increased. I could almost
recall the actual Italian of his words.

"It is curious, *signore*, but you are quite different from the other
inglesi here. You understand what I am thinking and most of the
inglesi here hardly understand what I am saying."

Some twenty-five years later a Barra crofter would say to me of a
broadcast I had given about the Islands:

"What I was saying to myself, a Chompton, when you were talking.
'How does *he* know what *I* am thinking?' "

Eric Linklater was present at the time, and in his most sonorous bass observed:

"Well, you'll never get a greater compliment than that."

When critics complain that I only present characters from without I can always recall those two remarks.

Mimi Ruggiero had done a great job on Ventrosa in directing the gnome-like *contadini*, father and son, who for two years had been cutting that path up the two-thousand feet of the mountain's southerly face through myrtle, rosemary and lentisks, up from the beach which could only be reached by boat from the Piccola Marina, up over the Green Grotto to a large land grotto at the base of a sheer precipice from the summit. Here during that summer it was Mimi's delight to spend a night as remote from the buzz of Capri as one of the shepherds of Theocritus. From the grotto he cut a path up beyond the precipice, at the top of which a gate had been made to secure his eclogue from false quantities in the shape of inquisitive tourists. The path up to that gate was rosy on either side with cyclamens (*C. neapolitaneum*), and on the slope of Monte Solaro beyond it was a large patch of *Crocus Imperati*, purple and golden heralds of the spring on a sunny day in January.

Above the Green Grotto was a profusion of butterfly orchises, but the most remarkable floral vision was a cascade of *Lithospermum rosmarinifolium* falling a full three hundred feet. None of the other *lithospermums*, in spite of one of the garden varieties being called "Heavenly Blue", can compare as a blue with *rosmarinifolium*. In British rock-gardens it is grown with difficulty and the feeble specimens I see remind me of some beautiful wild thing caged. Here and there in that blue cascade a white or lavender sport would try to assert itself, but they were far too few to interrupt the beauty of that cascade.

The dullness of the long straight ascent up the northerly side of Monte Solaro from Anacapri was rewarded when one turned left at the top to enter a fairly wide valley sown with whatever crops would provide fodder. At the head of this valley was a four-roomed cottage with a couple of stone-pines beside it and behind it the land rose fairly steeply to the highest point of the mountain, from which one looked down that 500-ft. limestone precipice into the *macchia* of Ventrosa. Above the precipice on the south side of Monte Solaro looking down on Capri was the little fourteenth-century church of Santa Maria di Citrella, on the walls of which were several small models of ships offered by mariners in gratitude to Our Lady of Citrella who had come to their aid in storm and tempest. Mass was said here only once a year. That was at dawn on September 8th, the feast of the Nativity of the Blessed Virgin. This feast was a survival of the Bacchanalia, the end of the vintage being celebrated at Citrella for Anacapri and at the top of Tiberio for Capri. The previous night was a night of revelry, with song and dance and much drinking of wine.

Except on that one day of the year the peace of Citrella was profound and I have spent many hours there, gazing at the long line of the Parthenopean shore and dreaming the past of Rome to life. Mimi and I thought it would be fun to grow tulips in that valley, and when he found a proprietor who was willing to sell us about a couple of acres I was able to buy that land with some of the money earned by *Sylvia Scarlett*.

Faith became more and more absorbed by her sculpture and in April suddenly said to me one morning, after being interrupted in it by having to type out the page or two of *Sylvia and Michael* I had struggled through on the previous day, "I think it's time you had a secretary."

I realized that the moment had come to talk about our future together, and it was during that talk that the pattern of our life together was laid down for the next forty-two years. Both of us made a pact of friendship on that day, and the pact was not broken. We should celebrate our golden wedding in 1955.

By coincidence almost immediately after that pact we heard that Nellie Baker, who after doing secretarial work in one of the hush-hush Government offices for a couple of years, had fancied the life of a convent, no longer fancied it and had left the sisterhood the headquarters of which were close to Tyburn. She seemed the obvious person to take up secretarial work again for me. She arrived in Capri about the middle of May and a few days later was at work compiling a catalogue of all the characters in my books. At this date I was still supposing that I should carry on with my Comédie Humaine to be called The Theatre of Youth. At the same time I was pondering a long novel about the Great War under the general title of *The Chronicles of Argos*, the first volume of which was to be called *The Dark and the Fair*. And I was still trying to finish *Sylvia and Michael*, and cursing that breakdown in January which had upset the gathering volume of *Sylvia Scarlett*. Nellie slept in Faith's room at first but presently moved into the little *foresteria* which our landlord Edwin Cerio had built on the cliff above Casa Solitaria; it was called Romita.

During the winter and early spring Capri had been abandoned to depression, but as the year wore on the resistance of the Italian army to the Austrians was all the time becoming tougher and tougher; with summer the Neapolitans arrived for their newly discovered pleasure resort so close to Naples, and Capri soon seemed as gay as it had ever been. A little disquieting was the news that representatives of a group of Milanese profiteers had been enquiring into the possibility of buying up all the Capri hotels. No changes were made in this year, but the Isle of Capree had already cast its shadow before.

Lady Sybil Scott with her daughter, Iris Cutting, came from the Villa Medici in Florence to stay at the Villa Quattro Venti, well named, which belonged to the American artist, Elihu Vedder. Her husband Geoffrey Scott could spare only a week from his work at our Embassy in Rome. It was he who wrote that brilliant book on architecture which was published on the fatal Fourth of August 1914, as it were stillborn; at this date it had not yet come to life again. Later he would write the *Portrait of Zélide*, and die prematurely. Faith when she met him said he was exactly like a Lubbock; when Lady Sybil married for the third time she married Percy Lubbock. Iris Cutting, whose father was American, was a truly remarkable girl of 15 for whom I confidently prophesied a name in literature one day. I was right, as the books of the Marchesa Origo testify to-day.

Herbert Trench came to stay at the Quattro Venti, a poet of repute and a distinguished if solemn personality who had been the director of Lord Howard de Walden's experiment at the Haymarket before the war. I had not forgotten Max Beerbohm's trick with *Apollo and the Seaman* and I was more amused by it than ever when I met Trench himself. Reggie Turner arrived in Capri about the same time as Herbert Trench and warned me against letting myself be caught up by Trench's theory of spirals. "He believes he has discovered in them the secret of the origin of life," he told me.

Soon after this I found myself walking up to Anacapri with Trench, and just as we were going to turn round to walk along into the little town Trench began to explain his theory of spirals. At that point the cliff drops sheer down into the bay of Naples for about 800 feet, only a yard or two from the side of the road. Trench kept making spiral gestures to expound his theory of life's origin and with each gesture he backed nearer to the edge of the cliff.

"If you don't look out, Trench," I warned him, "your spiral origin of life will become the spiral origin of your own death."

Trench peered round over his shoulder at the sea below; he gave a sad reproachful smile. "I know exactly what I am doing," he said, and I am bound to admit that in spite of those spirals he did not fall over the cliff and disturb a couple of dolphins in the sea below.

On one occasion Trench came to lunch with us at Casa Solitaria. When Carolina announced that lunch was served, we went into the dining-room in time to see Pauline dragging a large crayfish by its feelers backwards over the porcelain tiles, followed by her three kittens, Freeman, Hardy and Willis. The crayfish was rescued and as soon as we sat down at table Trench started to tell me of a play he had written about Napoleon. He would cut himself a morsel and raise it to his mouth, but he would be so much absorbed by his play that the morsel would remain on the fork for some minutes at a stretch. Carolina looked at him anxiously, and presently explained to him that the crayfish had not been harmed by the cat.

Trench waved aside the interruption and went on.

"I read the play to Sybil and Iris last night and at the end they were like that." He made a gesture of admiration and wonder, unable for a moment to find words to express it. It was on this occasion that he went on, his voice lowered into a reverential murmur, "You won't misunderstand me, my dear fellow, when I say it is genius."

The next day Lady Sybil and Iris were lunching with us at Casa Solitaria.

"Oh, my dears," said Lady Sybil, "Herbert Trench read his Napoleon play to Iris and me yesterday. It went on for hours and at the end of it we were both of us like that," but the gesture Lady Sybil made was not of admiration and wonder but of utter exhaustion.

Reggie Turner's arrival added to the gaiety of that summer. He was now about fifty, and as witty as ever; with enough money to live comfortably in Florence, his middle age seemed to promise a happy old age. He had an amusing story of Hugh Walpole, who had given Reggie Turner's address on letters when he was coming to Florence.

"But he didn't give my name, and one day I heard a commotion going on in the block of flats where I lived. The postman had knocked at every door on his way up and from below I could hear indignant denials. "*Non c'è nessuno Oog Vollapolé qui.*" At last the postman reached my door and I was able to assure him I would see that Oog Vollapolé received his letters safely."

A new arrival at Capri was a young Dutchman called Van Decker, who had plenty of money and gave some wild parties in the Villa he had rented. Word went round Capri that at one of them he had danced a *pas seul* wearing nothing but a little bunch of roses.

The Parroco, who by now was a Monsignore, wrote to me to use my influence as a Catholic to discourage such painful orgies. I had been laid up when this party happened and so could tell the Parroco that I was sure the stories he had heard were much exaggerated. In fact in this case rumour was true; Van Decker *had* danced that *pas seul*, wearing only a small bunch of roses. What would happen everywhere in Europe in the search for pleasure after those intolerable years of war was anticipated in Capri. The anxious days of that last desperate German offensive had left behind a feeling of optimism about the ultimate result of the war. On May 31st Christopher was writing to Faith:

I forgot when I wrote to you last but I think you had practically all my news about our extremely unpleasant walk back from Bapaume and the loss of General Barker. I stayed on at the Brigade with his successor General Ironside and then drifted to Divisional Headquarters and became what is called a lay learner but was soon rather bored with that work and now I'm A.D.C. to the General. An amusing end, if it is the end, to my military career but I was really getting tired of soldiering and had lost interest in people and things. General Pereira is most delightful; he's a devout R.C. and was in the Coldstream . . . we are in a very important part of the line. I suppose we shall have some more fighting soon. . . . This weather ought to do Monty no end of good. You are both quite strangers nowadays. I can't fancy him wasted with illness and you a probably grey-haired sculptor . . . we are full of French and Americans here and you needn't worry about the news at all. Foch has the matter well in hand. Do you read the "Winning Post"?[1] "What make is your new car?" "I can't remember the name." "Is it a Panhard?" "No, I don't think so, but I'm sure it starts with P." "Oh then it must be a Ford. All the others start with petrol."

That impression of confidence in Foch reflected the general relief that at last the British High Command was to be definitely subordinate to a French Commander-in-chief in whom they all had confidence. Lloyd George's success in bringing this about in the teeth of opposition by the British High Command, supported by King George V, may be called the peak of his achievement as Prime Minister.

More and more British officers were taking their leave from the Italian front in Capri. I wish I could add that they presented an agreeable view of the British officer, but too many seemed to suppose that the way to enjoy Capri was to sit and get drunk in Morgano's Café, and not merely drunk but boringly drunk. I had a telegram from London asking me to enquire into the whereabouts of some officer missing after his leave. I fear I made no effort to do so; I did not think that questioning those other officers on leave would be either profitable or pleasant.

Two large Russians arrived in Capri some time in June—Nadegin and Mariascess. They had been working at the Russian Embassy in Rome when the Tsarist officials had been replaced by Menshevik nominees. Now the Bolsheviks had taken over the Embassy and the two of them had to decide upon their future. Nadegin had a beautiful barytone voice, Mariascess an equally fine bass. Nadegin had spent a couple of years in Siberia, having been sent there when a student after the mild revolutionary demonstration of 1905. He was a figure from Chekhov, and Faith, who had just become a devotee of Chekhov, was fascinated by him; between them a friendship was born that summer which would

---

[1] Robert Sievier's weekly that was trying to go one better than the old *Sporting Times* or Pink 'Un.

last until he died a couple of years before herself. I called the two Russians Bim and Boum after two figures in a popular Italian play for marionettes; Nicholas Nadegin would remain Bim to the end of his days. Boum proposed to Nellie Baker and I had to announce their engagement, in which I had no belief as a likely preliminary to marriage. Boum left Capri at the end of the summer and became a professional singer, fading out of Nellie's life as abruptly as he had come into it.

I have written so intimately in *Extraordinary Women* of those two years when Capri became Lesbos for a while that I feel disinclined to spoil my story by writing about them all over again in a prosaic autobiography. I wrote of "Rosalba":

"On that fine May morning in the last year of the war her short accordion-pleated skirt made the long skirted bourgeoises of Lucerne shudder and crick their necks to stare after her rifle-green jacket and waistcoat, her double collar and her black satin tie with the coral pin, her long jade cigarette holder and slim ebony stick, and that rippling hair lustrous and hatless."

That is how I first remember Mimi Franchetti, a daughter of the Italian composer of operas, when I saw her in the Krupp suite of the Quisisana Hotel the day after she arrived in Capri from Switzerland. Every one of the characters in *Extraordinary Women* is an exact portrait with a single exception; Rory Freemantle is a composite creation of my own.

I have felt the same reluctance to portray in prosaic day to day shape the characters of *Vestal Fire*. In this book almost every figure is a portrait, and the earlier events were related to me in detail by John Ellingham Brooks, to whom *Vestal Fire* was dedicated. By now the two old ladies at the Villa Torricella were already brooding miserably over the failure of Count Fersen-Adelswärd to live up to the ideal they had made of him. Fersen himself was deep in opium dreams at the Villa Lysis, round which the thickets of casuarinas and the acacia called mimosa were growing denser all the time, much deplored by Mimi Ruggiero, who was not allowed to cut so much as a twig. My only memory of Fersen in that year of 1918 is of meeting him one evening in the spring as he was turning into the Via Tragara and of his plucking something hastily from his buttonhole, not quickly enough, however, for me not to see that it was the ribbon of the Legion of Honour, which he had awarded to himself in some opium dream.

On July 23rd my father died after months of dreadful pain. For three years before his final illness he had been unable to speak above a whisper and he was not to be spared the last miseries which cancer of the throat inflicts upon its victims. I believe myself that one of the causes of cancer may be frustration, and that the cancer develops from an effort by the cells of the body to perform a kind of rejuvenation to compensate for the failure of the mind to achieve what it had hoped to achieve. I have told in my first Octave about my father's engagement to Adelaide Neilson and of her dying in his arms in Paris a month before they were to be married. The result of that shock had been the loss of his hair. Still in his twenties the handsomest actor on the British stage, who had returned from a triumphant tour in the United States as Adelaide Neilson's leading man, was denied any hope of playing modern parts in London. He recognized that he must always wear a wig and he wisely decided to concentrate upon the white wigs of old English comedy. He started the Compton Comedy Company in February 1881 and at first included four or five of Shakespeare's comedies in his repertory. For the first two years of its existence he was responsible for the Stratford festival. Then, against my mother's earnest advice, he took out of his repertory all but one of Shakespeare's plays, *The Comedy of Errors*, to be succeeded at Stratford by F. R. Benson, who had started his Shakespearian company two years after the Compton Comedy Company.

By 1890 Edward Compton was the most popular actor in the provinces, particularly loved in Scotland, Ireland and the north of England. He made a large annual income and having inherited from a long line of Puritan ancestors a horror of extravagance he accumulated enough money to go into partnership with Milton Bode in acquiring provincial theatres and sending out touring companies of successful musical comedies.

Nevertheless, in spite of his financial success he always regarded himself as an unlucky man. His heart yearned for a London success and from time to time he leased London theatres. His greatest hope had been Henry James's play *The American*; when this failed in 1891 he did not attempt another London season until 1907. Nobody was allowed to be aware of the frustration. He was gay in company, a splendid raconteur, and in spite of his own frustration he was completely devoid of jealousy. Gratefully I have inherited from him ignorance of what jealousy means. I have also inherited from my father the ability to make friends immediately with simple people; I do not believe he ever had an argument with a cab-driver, a scene-shifter or a porter in his life. I can add to that inheritance a sense of obligation to that public which for well over a hundred years would remain faithful first to my grandfather, then to my father, and finally to myself. My father regarded the profession of acting with a reverence I was never able to accord it; he would not enter a music-hall until he was over 45 because he regarded music-halls as the vulgarization of a noble profession. When he entered into partnership Milton Bode used to make him go to music-halls from time to time in order to see the performance of some comedian or girl for the pantomime he and Bode would be putting on next Christmas.

My father and I were never really intimate after I was three years old. He always regarded me as a mysterious creature and his own share of the responsibility for my existence was to him equally mysterious.

Three days after my father's death an Australian naval surgeon arrived at Casa Solitaria at eight o'clock one morning to say he had orders to take me to Taranto for a Medical Board. Dr Gennaro's medical report which I had submitted a month earlier by order of the Adjutant-General of the Royal Marines had evidently failed to satisfy the authorities that my health warranted such an extension of leave as I was enjoying.

We took that charming Australian, whose name I have annoyingly forgotten, to Morgano's. Here, to quote Faith,[1] "He was set upon by about a dozen ladies who all declared that moving Monty from Capri was not to be thought of; he was in the middle of a book; he was constantly ill; moreover, he could not possibly be spared. Few medical officers can have suffered such determined opposition to what was their plain duty."

After lunch that afternoon I packed; the Australian officer dined with us and we were to meet early next morning at the funicular to catch the boat to Naples. Half-way through dinner I felt that warning stab in the heel which always precedes by a couple of hours the worst kind of attack I have. I said nothing because I was afraid our guest might suppose I was deliberately trying to evade that journey to Taranto. He left at about half-past ten and within another half-hour I was in agony. Faith and Nellie wanted to bring the surgeon back, but I would not let them and insisted on the Atoximecon. The pain was not relieved. I had another injection. Still no relief. Then in the small hours I had a third, but the pain was as ferocious as ever and I was retching continuously.

At five in the morning Nellie went along to the hotel where the surgeon was staying and he came back with her to Casa Solitaria. He looked at me.

"How on earth were you ever passed fit for active service?" he asked.

I told him I had never had a medical test; I had as it were floated away directly from Capri to the Dardanelles.

"Well, you won't do any more active service in this war," he said.

Then he gave me what must have been the strongest injection of morphia I had ever had, and presently I was unconscious.

The Australian surgeon said he was catching the boat to Naples alone and should send a telegram to the Admiralty to say I was not fit

[1] *More Than I should.*

to travel. He should also tell the medical board in Taranto that I should be invalided out at once.

I heard no more about medical boards, but I was not invalided out and remained in Capri on full pay, being demobilized as a New Year's gift on the last day of the year.

At the end of August came the first notice of *The Early Adventures of Sylvia Scarlett*; it was in the *Daily Chronicle* and could hardly have been stupider. At the same time as the notices began to come in for *The Early Adventures* the first proofs of *Sylvia and Michael* arrived. The *Nation* notice, a full-page lecture presumably by Edward Garnett, among other things rebuked me for being facetious about the *avant garde* of painting. That it was Sylvia herself who was being funny about the Ovists who were wiping out the Cubists by maintaining that ovals not cubes were the key to reality the *Nation* did not seem to grasp. In any case Sylvia was not so far out. Two years later A. G. Gardiner, the late editor of the *Daily News*, was in Berlin and reported to the *Nation* that perhaps the most interesting of the younger painters were the Ovists.

During August and September I was reading through the papers I had brought from Greece and constructing the war novel in seven volumes I proposed to write. *The Dark and the Fair* was to be preceded by two earlier volumes, and the whole work was to be called *The Labyrinth*. It would be divided into *Alien Corn, The Apple of Discord, The Dark and the Fair, The Topless Towers, The Molehill, The Mountain, The Olives of Home*.

All through October I was searching for the names of my characters. I have always spent a great deal of time over choosing my names and even after sixty years of it I can still be surprised by a new name to make a note of. Then at the end of that October I decided it was too soon to write a novel about the war. Experience which had not been "cooled a long age" might produce *rapportage* instead of genuine creative work. I began to feel glad that *No Papers* had been destroyed in Athens. True, to some extent I had used my war experience in *Sylvia and Michael*; some of Sylvia's experiences in Russia had been related to me by a French cabaret girl I had known in Athens. In the end I decided to put *The Labyrinth* aside. Nine years later when experience had been laid down long enough in the cellar of my imagination I felt, after finishing *Extraordinary Women*, that the time had come for this *magnum opus* to be started. Then I realized that Tolstoy had used his experience in the Crimea to write *War and Peace* but had taken his story back to the Napoleonic wars. He had moved his story from the less to the greater; if I were to move my story back to the Crimea I should be moving it from the greater to the less. I had been held up in the middle of *Extraordinary Women* by the difficulty of handling all those variations of the theme. During that hold-up I had started *Gallipoli Memories*. I said to myself that it was absurd to suppose I could write a great novel about the Great War on the scale I planned; I should be much wiser to take advantage of my memory and of the papers I had preserved to finish *Gallipoli Memories* and carry on with *First Athenian Memories*, *Second Athenian Memories* and *Aegean Memories*. I was in a position to write the truth about Greece in 1916 and 1917 and it was my duty to preserve that truth.

So *Alien Corn* and the rest of them were abandoned; the only title I really minded losing was *The Olives of Home* which I had found in the *Peace* of Aristophanes.

I suppose it was wandering about in *The Labyrinth* that made me decide to have a shot at a purely comic novel. Anyway, on November 1st I sat down to begin *Poor Relations*, the first chapter of which was gloriously interrupted three days later by our beloved Carolina arriving with the news that the war was over. I can see her now standing in the door of my bedroom with the coffee and hear her voice:

"*Signorino, signorino, la guerra è finita.*"

Whenever she was really excited she always took the years away from me by calling me "signorino", which I may explain means "young sir".

Apparently the bells of Capri had been ringing all night for the joyful news, but away in Casa Solitaria we had not heard them.

There was to be a High Mass and a solemn Te Deum in the Duomo, to which I went with Bianca and Isabella Caracciolo. I was in uniform for the occasion and in the packed church I had one of those fainting fits by which I am occasionally seized in restaurants for lack of fresh air. The girls and their cousin Bianca Binyon supported me down the aisle and on the steps outside I passed out. I received much sympathy when I came to from the three or four beggars who were allowed to give the faithful an opportunity before and after Mass of paying in something to their charitable account in purgatory. Most British tourists do not realize that the beggars they see by the church doors of Spain and Italy believe that they are giving as much as they get when they receive alms.

Presently I was able to walk along to Morgano's and join in the reception of the exciting news about the Austrian collapse and be invited by Vernon Andrews to a *brindisi* he was giving that night to the island notables. A portrait of Vernon Andrews was painted by me in *Vestal Fire*, where he is called Nigel Dawson. I quote:

"Nigel Dawson was a tall, slim, good-looking young man of about twenty-five whose chief of many vanities was a desire to be taken for eighteen in which he often succeeded. His mother, left a rich widow in America, had brought him to Europe when he was twelve, and he had thrived in the cosmopolitan culture with which she had provided him at the hands of various tutors."

Vernon Andrews was shamelessly homosexual; at the same time he was generous and hospitable, and everybody liked him. Morgano's Café was packed for the *brindisi*, for which Vernon had provided champagne galore. "Drinks and speeches, tears and raptures, toasts and panegyrics culminated in a short Italian speech by Monty," wrote Faith.[1]

I recall from that speech my salute to the Italian flag: "Rossa col sangue dei combattenti eroici, verde colla terra sacra della nostra Italia irredenta, e bianca colla. . ." I forget how I phrased it in Italian but I know that the white of the flag signified the impossibility of suspecting the purity of the motives which had led Italy to enter the war, the red symbolizing the blood of the heroic fighters who had given their lives for the green of unredeemed Italy now at last gloriously redeemed.

I doubt if d'Annunzio would have been moved by my eloquence in the tongue of which he was master, but it had a great effect on the bearded councillors of the *municipio* by a dozen of whom I was embraced and kissed on both cheeks. No doubt the champagne and joyful emotion contributed, but it was probably those beards that made me faint again.

I was led outside to sit and recover in the air of that small vine-hung terrace above the *strada*. Then came the question of whether I was sufficiently recovered to stand the long walk back to Casa Solitaria. Ann Heiskell suggested that the Villa Discopoli on the Via Tragara would be walk enough and that I could sleep in Diana's bed for the night.

Ann and Morgan Heiskell had become close friends of ours from the day we met them first on our arrival in Capri in the spring of 1913. Morgan Heiskell was now in some job with the American Army. He was a good painter and a superlative photographer. His father and mother from the Middle West were living in a small villa in Capri, old Mr Heiskell being able to make Morgan a handsome allowance. Ann was a West Virginian from Wheeling who had been at Vassar. She was a great beauty and moreover of extremely individual beauty; to this day if I read or hear something about Vassar I always think it must be the best college for a girl either in England or America, so completely was Ann devoid of any ability to deceive herself about life.

Diana, of whose bed I was to deprive her that night, was just six and a younger brother for her had been born in 1915; this younger brother Andrew was always called Bobbie in his childhood. Six years hence I should dedicate my children's book *Santa Claus in Summer* to Diana and Bobbie and it remains my own favourite book. No letters give me more

[1] *More Than I Should.*

pleasure than those I still sometimes receive from mothers and even grandmothers to tell me that *Santa Claus in Summer* was their favourite book as children. It appealed only to little girls, I fancy; I never received a letter from a father or a grandfather to say it was his favourite reading.

So back at the Villa Discopoli that night Diana was taken out of her bed for me to sleep in it. It was a very successful bed; I slept until half-past twelve next morning without stirring.

We had hardly recovered from the emotion of Vittoria Veneto than we heard the news of the Armistice, and we felt we really could rejoice; the war really was over at last. Next day the Capri band arrived at Solitaria to play *God Save the King*.

I was reasonably well for the rest of the month and made good progress with *Poor Relations*.

Now instead of casualties we were reading of the deaths of friends from the Spanish influenza that swept away so many who had survived the trenches. One death that much affected me was that of Francis Storrs, who died on Armistice Day; he had been such an invaluable support in Syra and had almost literally worked himself to death there. Then he had to put up with weary months in Athens under Myres before he was given a job in London.

Sometime early in December Julian Huxley came to Capri. I hear now the very tone of his voice when we were walking along the cliff path between the Punta Tragara and Casa Solitaria as he tells me he wants me to meet a Belgian girl Maria Nys who was staying at the Quisisana.

"She is the fiancée of my brother Aldous—the poet," he added, lowering his voice respectfully.

Maria Nys was self-consciously "intellectual"; she kept on asking me "intellectual" questions and making "intellectual" observations which my lack of "modernity" prevented me from appreciating, whether she made them in English or French; it was not a successful meeting.

I recall too from that visit of Julian Huxley my saying to him what a sad disillusionment life in Italy had meant for me over E. M. Forster's first novel *Where Angels Fear to Tread*. I had been completely carried away with admiration when I had read it first nearly ten years earlier. Now, I had just read it again and found it a completely artificial drama of Italian life imagined by a cloistered introspective temperament. For me his Italians had all turned into academic caricatures without flesh and blood. The terms "introvert" and "extravert" had not yet come into fashion to provide facile literary jargon for budding intellectuals who usually cannot spell "extravert" correctly. I do not remember whether Julian Huxley agreed or disagreed with me. In my thirties and forties I was disillusioned by so many books I had read with passionate enthusiasm in my 'teens and twenties that I decided to risk no more

C.M. dictating to James Eastwood with Hamlet

Faith with Bob

C.M. on the quayside at Herm, Jethou beyond.

disillusionment; now in my eighties I am able to believe that some of my early loves in books could still enchant me.

We had several deaths in Capri from the "Spanish 'flu", and I was suspected of succumbing, but it was a false alarm.

Our great anxiety in that December was the illness of Pauline, who became very ill. We sat up with her for four nights, keeping her strength going with sips of brandy and milk, and in the end that dearly loved cat recovered, but it was a very close thing.

One of our diversions that winter was "Bye-bye", or to give him his proper name, Prince Rufo. He was a small, spritely octogenarian with a pointed white beard and a lineage as long as an Orsino or Colonna. He had little money and had accepted a job as secretary to a Neapolitan *pescecane*, or war profiteer, "shark" as they were called in Italy. This particular profiteer was a reincarnation of the immortal Trimalchio drawn by Petronius. At the beginning of the war he had been the *facchino* or porter of a small fireworks factory in Naples, of which he had somehow become the owner, and of which he proceeded to make a factory of explosives; by the time the war was over he was almost literally rolling in money, a large fat man with a retinue of parasitic flatterers. While the finishing touches were being put to the new *palazzo* at Posilippo he had built he was staying in Capri; he had already acquired the other two essentials for a Neapolitan *pescecane*—a larger solitaire diamond than most of his rivals and a secretary. He felt that in engaging a prince of ancient lineage as his secretary he had made the secretaries employed by other *pescecani* look small fry.

In spite of the food problem, which was acute, Trimalchio the Second was able to give banquets in Capri that seemed almost as luxurious as those of his predecessor in the days of Nero. I hear that vulgar monster calling from the head of the table *"Principe! Principe!* Do this, do that! Get this, get that! Show this, show that." One thing I remember Bye-bye had to show was a drawing some young artist had done of Trimalchio in which he was made to appear almost handsome. On being shown it by Bye-bye each parasite flattered in turn and declared it to be a marvellous likeness of their host. I once asked Bye-bye how he could put up with his preposterous employer.

"He pays me so well," said Prince Rufo, "that I can afford to laugh at myself."

And sometimes on a halcyon December day Bye-bye would laugh with us at Casa Solitaria, where that thick nasal voice calling "Principe! Principe!" was inaudible.

There is a widely spread belief among reviewers and no doubt among other people that the writing of a "funny" book is a form of self-indulgence and almost a complete holiday from serious work. In fact,

K

the writing of a "funny" novel involves more technical accomplishment than the writing of any other kind of novel, so far as my experience goes. I know that P. G. Wodehouse would agree with me. How many "funny" novels written during the last fifty years have survived more than a month or two? Very very few, which suggests that it may not be so easy as all that to write a "funny" novel. *Poor Relations* was my first attempt, and I found it heavy going during that November and December.

I was filled with gloom by Lloyd George's message on the eve of the General Election when the Coalition programme was announced to be the trial of the Kaiser, the punishment of those responsible for atrocities, the expulsion of all enemy aliens, an effort to keep Britain for the British, and a land for heroes to live in. The only intention I warmly welcomed was the promise to wring the last mark out of Germany in indemnities; I lacked the foresight and economic wisdom of Keynes.

When the result of that General Election was declared, with a majority of 262 for Unionists and pseudo-Liberals, I was gloomier than ever. For me the Coalition represented the fruits of that intrigue in June 1915 which had cost us Gallipoli and so lengthened the war. The only comfort I could derive from the result of the Election was the way Sinn Fèin had swept the Irish poll.

News came just before my thirty-sixth birthday of a splendid offer from Cassell's. Six books at £1,500 advance for each and a £4,000 option on four of the six for possible serialization. I knew this would be a blow to Martin Secker, but in my financial state I could not refuse such an offer. However, I did stipulate that Secker must have two more books after *Sylvia and Michael*, and to that Cassell's agreed.

THIRTY-SIX YEARS OLD: 1919

THE first three or four months of the new year were full of arguments
between Martin Secker and myself over his failure to print enough
copies of the *Early Adventures of Sylvia Scarlett* and running the risk of not
having the reprint ready even in time for the publication of *Sylvia and
Michael*, the bone-headed reviews of which in many papers were an
exasperating reminder of the stupidity from which I had suffered in
Greece for two years. They reminded me of an incident a year ago in
Syra after a German U-boat had been sunk in Taranto harbour and its
papers were found by divers. I received an urgent telegram from
London ordering me to remove a convent of French nuns from Tenos
because they were in communication with the enemy. Inasmuch as
these nuns had always been of the greatest help to us I demanded proof
of this accusation. In due course a copy of the Taranto papers was sent;
in them was a warning to the captain of the U-boat to keep away from
Tenos because the French nuns there were in communication with the
enemy. The brain that analysed those papers could not grasp that to
the Germans *we* were the enemy. In politics and in criticism we were
becoming more and more exposed to the substitution of verbal association for thought; to that Intelligence officer the only enemy was
Germany.

The boneheadedness of some reviewers unable to associate disillusionment with war was an irritation which quickly passed away and
I waited to hear what the American publishers, Harper's, thought of
the first six chapters of *Poor Relations*, which had been sent to them by
Pinker. Another epistolary argument was begun.

"Tommy" Wells of Harper's wrote to Pinker:

*These chapters are no more like Mackenzie than they are like any one of a
number of second-grade English and American writers. . . . The writing is
commonplace and the reading is dull. . . . Everybody here who has read these
chapters agrees with my judgment of the story. . . . The critics will flay the author
and the public won't buy the book. Nobody can expect them to . . . Mackenzie ought
to be persuaded to chuck this manuscript into the drawer of a desk and forget it. . . .
I haven't lowered one bit in my regard for what he has written up to date and I hope
to see him go ahead to still greater things. But he cannot expect success with a book
like "Poor Relations". He doesn't deserve it.*

I wrote to Pinker:

If I had paid too much attention to the opinions of editors and publishers I shouldn't be where I am now. However, I certainly don't propose to hold Harper's to the contract. . . . It is regrettable that the American public don't like me as much as the British public, but that is not my fault. I can't be expected to alter my whole style of writing to exchange a certain success in the U.K. for a doubtful success in America. What Wells says about "Poor Relations" as a serial I obviously cannot contest. What he says about "Poor Relations" as work is frankly rot. I am amazed by his awe of the critics. I have never in modern days heard of anyone connected with literature being frightened either by British or American critics. It takes me back into the good old days of yore when people were frightened of dragons. If Wells thinks the American public won't buy the book, very well then let us try somebody else. It is perfectly certain that the British public will buy the book.

To Thomas E. Wells I wrote:

What is really the trouble is that I am not a success in America: the critics accord me a good deal of attention whether to blame or praise, but the great mass of the public regard me as in England they regard, let us say, D. H. Lawrence. . . . I naturally don't like the idea of your losing over my books . . . so far as "Sylvia" is concerned by my letting you have the two books on a single advance you will probably not lose actually, at any rate I hope not. "Plashers Mead" ("Guy and Pauline") presumably cannot come to life again, though in Great Britain the book did over 15,000 at six shillings at the worst period of the war on publication and is still selling very decently. "Sylvia" in Britain was sold out a week after publication last August and though Secker could not manage to get a reprint till March he expects to sell at least 25,000 by the end of this year. "Sylvia and Michael" has been published at eight shillings net and thereby incurred a good deal of Bolshevism from the libraries, Smith's as usual leading the attempt to squash any book that will deprive them of a farthing of their preposterous rate of profit. Nevertheless, the book has broken down the opposition and Secker tells me he anticipates 25,000 with that also by the end of the year.

Now comes the question of "Poor Relations". You don't like the idea of it as a serial and of course I am not going to force it on you. In your letter to Pinker, however, you went further by saying it was second-class work. . . . If you think the book has no chance in America you obviously kill its chance before it appears. Suppose I let you have it without any advance on the same royalty basis as before however reasonable I show myself thereby, I have no guarantee that my reasonableness will be appreciated. If I insist on an advance that you consider exorbitant and make your acceptance of my terms a condition for renewing our contract you will probably prefer not to renew that contract. . . . I am pretty confident that "Poor Relations" will do at least 25,000 in Britain, and I shall find myself in the ludicrous position of having no American publisher for it unless I leave Harper's and go elsewhere. I hate changing publishers, but I hate still more being published under protest. . . .

Wells wrote to me:

If all authors could and would write letters like yours there would never be the slightest possibility of a misunderstanding between them. . . . I am delighted to know you are having such success in England and we are all puzzled as to just why we cannot duplicate this success in the United States. I believe we can, if we keep at it.

Now as to the question of "Poor Relations" . . . I am sure it is not a serial and I frankly feel that it is not of a quality with your other work, and that it has less appeal to a big public than any book that you have written. But we don't claim to be always right and I hope you may prove we are quite wrong. If you decide to let us have the book on the same royalty terms as the others but without any preliminary advance, we will put every effort into making it a success. And please take this letter as a guarantee that your reasonableness is tremendously appreciated . . . we have every wish to continue as your publishers. . . . I wish we could have our talk about those next twenty novels you propose to write, for I am sure that we could get together on some plan by which we might gain a wider audience for you in this big country of ours.

I may have inherited from my American grandfather an ability to realize that a publisher is as much entitled to his share as the author he backs, just as an impresario is as much entitled to his share as the actor he backs. The only interest I have had in money was the ability it gave me to spend it on whatever at the moment was adding something to my interest in life. I have been lucky enough never to have had to worry over what book I was going to write next; the only question has been which book. I had expressed to "Tommy" Wells a wish that we could meet so that I could tell him about the next twenty books I planned; all my life I have had at least twenty possible books at the back of my mind. Even now at 81 as I write these words I have over twenty novels, with their titles, as possibilities in the future. Never for a moment having been anxious about the endurance of my vitality, I have never tried to save money because I have always supposed that when it was required I should only have to write another book to earn it. It has never entered my head to invest money in stocks and shares. I was in a very sticky financial position when I sat down in November 1917 to write *Sylvia Scarlett*, but it only served as a spur to intensive work; I had no qualms about the future. It is natural for people to suppose that a novel which takes ten years to write must be a better novel than one which takes ten weeks. Fertility among writers is steadily diminishing and the fertile writer must expect to be regarded with suspicion by his less fertile *confrères*. Apart from my fertility, critics began to be annoyed by my versatility. One remains jack-of-all-trades and master of none until old age, when versatility is accorded admiration. I look back and think of the way Winston Churchill's versatility was sneered at until his great moment came in 1940, after which that versatility became one of the wonders of the world.

Somerset Maugham was a fertile enough writer to be able always to feel secure about his future. Nevertheless, he was never carefree about money because he had an ambition to leave more money than any author had ever left. Extravagace in other people pained him. It may have been in the summer of next year at Capri that he said to me seriously:

"You're very extravagant, Monty. You should try to save money."

"My dear Willie, how on earth can I save money after somehow keeping up a villa in Capri on the pay of a Captain of Marines without being able to write a book for nearly three years? I have had to pay off lots of debts and if one has paid off lots of debts one has a right to enjoy extravagance."

I can see his very expression and hear the very tone of his voice as he replies:

"I've saved one hundred and eighty-six thousand p-pounds."

Success did not come to Maugham in a big way until 1910; that was certainly a monetary achievement.

I had the usual interruptions of pain while I was writing *Poor Relations*, and it was not finished until the last day of April. I inscribed:

> "This theme in C Major with variations to the romantic and mysterious Captain C by one who was privileged to serve under him during more than two years of war."

The book was published at the beginning of October and its circulation in Great Britain and the Colonies was over 30,000 before the year was out. The flaying "Tommy" Wells prophesied I should receive from the critics on both sides of the Atlantic did not happen. There was not a single bad notice from a British or American paper. I had supposed that all my previous novels showed evidence of plenty of comic invention. Yet apparently my ability to write a novel in which humour predominated came as a surprise, and I was constantly being congratulated by reviewers upon revealing a hitherto unsuspected gift; the American critics were less surprised, but in spite of the warmth of their judicious praise *Poor Relations* remained a *succès d'estime* without making much impression on the great American public; over that "Tommy" Wells was right.

During that winter and early spring of 1919 more and more Russians were coming to Capri. Before the war the Russians had all been revolutionaries: now they were all either exiles for life or not yet sure what their future was to be. Nadegin had decided that he would never see Russia again while the Bolsheviks were in power. He wrote poetry which other Russians assured us was really good, even great poetry. One day he would publish a collection of his poems and inscribe the little volume to Faith and myself. However, poetry did not offer the prospect of a livelihood and for that he counted upon his magnificent barytone voice.

A Russian sculptor arrived, from whom Faith took lessons. Michele Katz had come to Italy with a travelling scholarship from the Academy of Fine Arts at Petrograd. I commissioned him to do a bust of Faith in rose marble which was exhibited at the Royal Academy in 1920 and also at Glasgow and other cities. Then it was stored in London when Faith went back to Capri and mysteriously vanished; it was never found, although her name was on the plinth. Katz was sufficiently encouraging to keep Faith completely wrapped up in her sculpture. Later in the summer he did a fine head of myself which was cast in bronze. What interested me when I was sitting for him was that from day to day the clay head resembled in turn the various aunts on my mother's side and my mother herself. Yet when it was finished I could not detect a likeness to anybody except myself. Much to the disapproval of Nadegin, Michele Katz went back to Russia and did some work for the Bolshevik Government. Later he found the régime too cramping for an artist and went to Sweden, where he was naturalized. I do not know if any of his work may be seen there to-day. He was certainly a sculptor of the highest promise.

Two young Russians called Florenski also arrived, and gave some gay parties before they too disgusted Nadegin by returning to the U.S.S.R., where one of them became an important official.

At the same time as Nadegin was giving well-attended concerts in Capri Renata Borgatti gave small concerts in her studio at the Punta Tragara, which was pulled down at the end of the year to make way for the *palazzo* being erected by somebody who had made money out of the war.

Faith wrote of her when she first came to Capri in 1917:

"A young girl of the hockey type, with the face and figure of a woman, the eyes of a boy, the voice of a man, the strength of an orchestra and a velvet touch. She often came to Casa Solitaria and played Wagner like an orchestra, every now and then singing in her deep, hoarse, masculine voice. She knew the operas by heart because her father was the greatest Italian Wagnerian tenor, and she had worked with him . . . in 1919 Renata was back in Capri, with short hair, more power in her remarkable hands, and some of the Spanish masters at her finger-tips. I don't

suppose her fortnightly concerts paid, because she charged scarcely anything and her audiences were small, though spellbound. When I go to
hear her twenty years later, and see her subdued by the awful and
inevitable atmosphere of the London concert hall, which is heavy with
the sighs of generations of overworked and satiated musical critics, I
long to cry:

" 'Ah, but you should have heard her at Punta Tragara, playing
music because she loved it, with divine irresponsibility and some wrong
notes, because she never practised enough. You should have seen that
silhouette swaying to the music in the candlelight which flickered
because outside the wind was booming from the south-west. You can't
tell, unless you hear her like that, what an artist Borgatti is!' "

I painted her portrait as Cléo Gazay in *Extraordinary Women* and take
out a few lines:

"Picture her then with straight nose and the jutting brows that hold
music within them, with a finely carved chin out-thrust less for a sign of
obstinacy than for some austere determination of her mind. Her feet are
large like a man's, and her clothes are flung around her without any
regard to the fashion of the moment. They are not really so much
clothes as curtains hung up to exclude the night or let in the day as
desired. . . . She had suffered, as women of her temperament are condemned to suffer, from passions which were not returned, which could
not be returned, because the masculine side of her nature was so
dominant that she sought women as she found them without waiting for
those who were temperamentally akin to herself. . . . Her grey eyes were
half the time clouded with the preoccupation of why she had been made
as she was."

In the middle of March Faith and I came back from a party to find
the kitchen door knocked in and Faith's room rifled of her jewellery. On
her dressing-table was a photograph of herself upside down. The only
other things taken were a cheese and a bottle of absinthe which had
been presented to Faith by Mimi Franchetti. The police investigation
ended in the marshal of the *carabinieri* informing me that without any
doubt the outrage had been committed by Signorina Borgatti and that
the jewellery taken had all been flung into the sea.

"But, *maresciallo*, the cheese? Was that flung over the cliff?" I protested.

That burly officer shrugged his shoulders.

"Who knows? It could have been eaten, *signore*."

"And the bottle of absinthe?"

"It could have been drunk."

"But you have no evidence that Signorina Borgatti showed any sign
of intoxication."

He shrugged his massive shoulders again.

"It could have been flung into the sea out of spite, for this is clearly a case of *dispetto*."

Faith was naturally loth to believe in this theory and insisted that the robbery must have been committed by one of the Milanese workmen who were already laying the foundations for transforming Capri into the Isle of Capree. She was so depressed about the whole business that she went to Naples to consult a local sibyl who told her that the robbery had been committed by a woman.

"That's merely a matter of thought transference," I urged. "Your head was full of the possibility that Renata *might* have done this. Anyway, we can't possibly let her be accused of it by the *carabinieri*."

In the first week of April I persuaded the *pretore*, Avvocato Galatà, to order the police to drop the matter, which remained officially a mystery.

"And for goodness' sake forget about it," I begged Faith. "So long as these ridiculous women are indulging in these ridiculous love-affairs we shall have these exhibitions of tormented and disordered nerves. If Borgatti did it, that bottle of absinthe Franchetti gave you after Bim's very successul concert may have filled her with green-eyed jealousy and she surrendered to the emotion of the moment. I wish Bim wouldn't encourage you to go on wandering about in his complicated Russian mazes of the mind."

I have myself an aversion from building up a situation; in the process the simple explanation is usually lost. Psychological embroidery had for some time now taken the place of simple incident in telling a story, and I realized already that, if I were going to continue along the path I had chosen for myself as a writer, I should have to withdraw from any attempt to compete. I wanted to live as well as to write. It was the endless talk of whether Renata Borgatti had done it and if she had done it why she had done it that first may have begun to make me contemplate going off to the South Seas. I was still eighteen months away from any clear decision about my future, but the need for some profound change in my manner of life was beginning to prod me gently.

My recreation in those days of early spring was going for long walks with Diana Heiskell. The relief of a child's mind amidst the endless imbroglios and pasticcios of Capri was immense. She had a birthday at the end of March so I suppose she must have been on the edge of seven. We explored various grottos together, including the scramble up to the Grotto Maraviglioso from a boat; it was marvellous indeed, with stalactites and stalagmites that took us to fairyland. Most vividly of all I recall a walk to the Grotto of Mithras, just beyond which we came

upon a large patch of white violets, the only white violets we had seen in
Capri. We were able to pick a big bunch for each of us and feel at the
end of it that there were just as many white violets as ever. All my life I
have been blessed with the ability to enjoy the friendship of little girls on
equal terms, in which either I become as young as the little girl or she
becomes as old as myself. I do not know which it may be.

News came early in April from the Embassy in Rome that an open
cheque was waiting for me from the Greek Government for the sum of
£4,103, 6s. 10d. Erskine, who was still Counsellor, suggested that it
should be called for personally. I was laid out with one of my bouts and
asked Faith to go and deal with it. Erskine suggested that the wisest
thing to do would be to send this open cheque by way of the Embassy
bag to my bank in Oxford.

Ten days after I finished *Poor Relations* I started on *The Vanity Girl*, the
original title for which had been first *Marriage à la Mode* and then *The
Bird of Paradise*, both of which had to be rejected because they had been
used for earlier novels. This was the first book of my contract with
Cassell's and was to be serialized in one of their monthly magazines. At
this date Cassell's had been bought by the Berry Brothers when they
were building up their newspaper empire; Newman Flower[1] was
Literary Director of the famous publishing house in La Belle Sauvage,
that historic Court off Ludgate Hill which would be destroyed in the
German attempt to destroy the city of London during the Second
World War. My association with Cassell's would be one of unbroken
harmony for nearly twenty years. Dear Newman Flower himself is
a cherished memory of what a publisher ought to be.

Nellie Baker being now expert with her shorthand, I tried the experiment of dictating the new novel, but after the first few thousand
words I decided that the task of almost certainly rewriting what I had
dictated was even more arduous than writing it, and except for occasional articles, reviews, and correspondence I abandoned dictation. I
found that dictating a novel was like undressing in public: if I go blind
I shall have to dictate again, but in that case I shall not be worried by
the expression of resigned patience upon the countenance of my steno-
grapher when waiting for the epithet I am searching. When George
Moore started dictating his books his style became increasingly lucid,
easy and graceful; on the other hand the style of Henry James became
continuously more elaborate and complicated when he started to dictate those later novels of his. I never attempted to compose directly on a
typewriter in spite of my wretched handwriting, and so I have never
established that affectionate intimacy with their machines which so
many authors enjoy.

---

[1] The late Sir Newman Flower.

Interrupted by pain whenever the damnable *scirocco* poisoned the atmosphere, and by too many visitors, I finished *The Vanity Girl* at the beginning of August.

Lloyd Osbourne and his wife Ethel arrived in Anacapri. We became intimate friends immediately. As he sat there in the garden of the Café Lauro where I had enjoyed so many dinners (at any rate after I discovered that by wearing red socks instead of white I could discourage those infernal flies from biting my ankles) I found it hard to conjure from this largish man with a soft Californian accent the boy for whose entertainment *Treasure Island* had been written, or even the young man who collaborated with his step-father in those two masterpieces, *The Ebb Tide* and *The Wrong Box*. With Ethel he was very much the dutiful American husband, quietly obedient if asked to go and fetch a powder-puff or whatever it was she had left behind in the Hotel Paradiso where they were staying. With publishers and editors the mailed fist only was apparent; there was no sign of the velvet glove.

He never let a quotation from R.L.S. pass without extracting a fee. I recall his saying to me that I was foolish to spend any more money on acquiring land in Capri, which offered me no prospect of selling one day at a handsome profit. He had just bought some land in an unspoilt part of the Riviera where he was going to build a villa: Juan-les-Pins.

"Do you know it, Monty?" he asked in that gentle voice of his; we were immediately on Christian name terms in the swift American way. I admitted complete ignorance of Juan-les-Pins.

"Well, take my advice, dear boy, and let me find you the right piece of land there on which to build yourself a villa. It will get more valuable every year."

How right he was! But I was never tempted by the prospect of buying anything—land or book or picture—because it would one day be worth its weight and more than its weight in gold. The sight of limited editions wrapped in paper on a top shelf because one day the owner of them expects to make a profit depresses me. I had never bought a book for any reason except that I wanted to read it when I felt like reading it. I was one of the small number of original subscribers at something over £30 to *The Seven Pillars of Wisdom* because I wanted to read it, but I have to admit, with still a faint feeling of shame, that when I was offered £400 for it not long afterwards I did sell *The Seven Pillars*.

Another visitor to Capri was Charles Mendl,[1] who would soon become Press Attaché at the British Embassy in Paris. He was escorting a Mrs Wiltsee, of whom I recall nothing except her habit of bathing with her head in what looked like a paper bag to preserve her complexion.

[1] The late Sir Charles Mendl.

Charles Mendl had recently been gratified by the news of his brother's[1] having been made a K.B.E.

"I think it is quite something, don't you?" he asked a little anxiously.

In those days that ribbon of the wrong shade of purple and orange was not regarded with reverence. When the Queen Mother was made Dame Grand Cross of the Order the ribbon was changed to just the right shade of pink and grey. To-day the Most Excellent Order of the British Empire is recognized with respect in spite of the disappearance of the British Empire itself. When it was instituted, the Most Distinguished Order of St Michael and St George which was first awarded to officials of the Ionian Islands, both British and Greek, was regarded as a piece of soft soap which had fallen out of the Bath.

In a year or two Charles Mendl himself would be a Knight Bachelor. He was a great squire of dames in 1919, not yet married to Elsie de Woolf. He was diverted by my tales of the extraordinary women; one day he asked me about one of them.

"*Oui, oui*," I told him, "*elle est guignotte.*"

"Oh ho, my dear man, you're very much behind with your argot. Nobody calls a lesbian a *guignotte* nowadays. The word is *gousse.*"

"Oh, is it?" I exclaimed. "Well, I'm probably the only man alive who can tell you the origin of *gousse.*"

Mendl naturally looked incredulous.

"In 1915," I went on, "two French cabaret girls were working in a café at Bucharest. Flonia was a tall blonde *diseuse* of much accomplishment and also a woman of intelligence from Lille; Marthe was a cosy little brunette from Marseilles who sang familiar *café concert* songs. News came to Bucharest of the Salonika landing, and Flonia made up her mind that the place for them was the Tour Blanche at Salonique. They had difficulty in getting their passports visaed but at Costanza by the Danube's mouth the British Vice-Consul helped them on their way. Flonia soon tired of Salonique and felt that Athens would be a more congenial background; there they arrived safely in 1916. Flonia was of considerable help to my Z bureau in Athens; indeed with her help I was nearly successful in capturing the German mail, a story told in my book *The Three Couriers*. One day she said to me,

"*Dis, Mackenzie, qu'est-ce que c'est goossagal?*"

I explained what a goosegirl was and asked why she wanted to know. She then told me about the way the British consul at Costanza, "a very sympathetic type", had helped Marthe and herself on the way to Salonique.

"What are you two girls by profession?" he had enquired, pen in hand.

[1] The late Sir Sigismund Mendl, K.B.E.

"*Nous sommes des guignottes,*" Flonia had replied.

"What? Goosegirls?" he had exclaimed.

Flonia, who was not at all a goosegirl herself, had started the fashion in Athens of calling the girls who had little feminine affairs in the *pension d'artistes* "goossagals". That was soon contracted to "gousse". At the end of 1916 I extracted the French cabaret girls from the dangerous mess in Athens, and from Syra managed to get them safely shipped back to France.

"So that is the origin of *gousse,*" I told Charles Mendl.

And *gousse* is still the word to-day. It may be seen in any dictionary with (pop.) beside it; *guignotte* has been displaced and is hardly likely to come back into popular usage.

The only other contribution I ever made to the origin of a slang expression was that of "lally" the name for snuff used by female convicts up to the last war: I do not know if it survives. Lionel Brough, a popular comedian of the 'nineties, was affectionately known to the public as Lal Brough. Snuff became "Lal Brough" in rhyming slang and as so often happens the second word of rhyming slang was dropped; hence "lally".

I have the proud distinction of being quoted in the Oxford English Dictionary as the first authority for "nosy parker", J. B. Priestley being the second. From time to time credulous pedants write to one of the Sunday papers supposed to take more interest in literature than the others to ask if somebody will confirm the derivation of "nosy parker" from the efforts of Archbishop Parker in the time of Queen Elizabeth I to rout out suspicions of Popish sympathies among Anglican clergymen. The original "nosy parker", of course, was one who played Peeping Tom to love-making couples in Hyde Park.

I must stop before I go on to jeer at those who derive "All my eye and Betty Martin" from "*O mihi beate Martine*" or "bloody" from "by Our Lady", and other absurd philological speculations by goggling pedants.

We had many moonlit musical parties on the terrace of Casa Solitaria that summer. Sometimes, but rarely, Charles Thornton was persuaded to come down from Anacapri and play for us Brahms's piano music, which he did superbly. Thornton, whom I painted in *Vestal Fire* as Anthony Burlingham, was almost the most remarkable of our Capri fauna. He had been a subaltern in the Blues in the early 'eighties with a large income. In those days when the Guards messed in the Guards Club it was the custom to wear smoking-jackets of many colours. Thornton decided to be different by appearing one evening in a black smoking-jacket, which made such an impression that the contemporary dinner-jacket was born, the tuxedo of the U.S.A.

Thornton was homosexual and had gradually spent nearly all his

fortune on young men or on paying blackmail. Now at sixty he lived in
a cottage in Anacapri with a tyrannical housekeeper and a Bechstein
grand on which he used to play all day with intervals of attending to the
geraniums on his little terrace. He was never to be seen without a dark
blue cricketing-cap on his bald head; he even wore it in bed.

The composer Respighi and his wife were living up in Rosaio, which
they had rented from Edwin Cerio for the summer. He was a shy, delicate little man who could never be persuaded to come to parties. He
said he should like to set some of my verses to music, but I could not find
that volume of poems now twelve years old and out of print; so I missed
the chance that one or two of them might have been brought to life by
the man who gave us the fountains of Rome.

At the beginning of August the lesbian dovecotes were fluttered by
the arrival of Romaine Brooks. She had arrived as a girl in Capri from
Pennsylvania, determined to become a great painter but completely
impoverished. J. E. Brooks, who was one of the many homosexuals that
left England at the time of the Oscar Wilde case to find in Italy a haven,
was captivated by her boyishness and married her. Soon after this she
found herself the unexpected heiress of a coal-mining fortune and
decided that for her Paris was the heart of a painter's life. She and
Brooks agreed to separate and on condition that he remained in Capri
she agreed to allow him about £300 a year. On hearing that Romaine
was arriving, Brooks hastily evacuated the Villa Cercola for a *villino* and
she moved into that large studio for the summer. Faith found her "a
figure of intriguing importance, because for the first time I met a
woman complete in herself, isolated mentally and psychically from the
rest of her kind, independent in her judgments, accepting or rejecting as
she pleased movements, ideas, and people. The arrival of this striking
personality was a sensation. . . . Feverish bouquets of exhausted blooms
lay about the big studio; letters and invitations strewed her desk,
ignored for the most part, while she, wrapped in her cloak, would
wander down to the town as the evening cooled and sit in the darkest
corner of Morgano's Café terrace, maddeningly remote and provocative."

Mrs Brooks's portrait of d'Annunzio and a self-portrait hang in the
Luxembourg in Paris, and she said she should like to do a portrait of me.
She saw in me an opportunity to indulge the interest she was taking at
this date in studies in grey. Owing to work and illness I had been less in
the sun than others in Capri during that blazing summer. She was tired
of the summer tan. A young American woman who was the mistress of a
Parisian shirt-maker (not Edouard or Butler) came to Capri that
summer.

"When I saw her last she had the most lovely complexion," Romaine

Brooks sighed, "and now she's the colour of old chestnut wood. Ugh!"
Perhaps I failed to appear sufficiently impressed; at any rate the
painting was never made. I painted my own portrait of Romaine
Brooks as Olympia Leigh in *Extraordinary Women*. It was she who fired
Faith with a desire to go to Paris for a while on her way to London,
where she wanted to take a house. I gave her half my Greek indemnity,
and in October she set off. She wrote a vivid account of her stay in Paris
in *More Than I Should*. The only thing I envied her was the opportunity
she had of meeting James Joyce, whose *Ulysses* was reaching me every
month from Chicago in *The Little Review*.

Martin Secker had written in July that Francis Brett Young was
proposing to give up being a G.P. in Brixham and live entirely by
writing. He wanted to know how cheaply he would be able to live in
Capri and would be writing to me.

I find the draft of a letter I dictated to Nellie Baker, from which I
quote. He must have written on Secker's advice to enquire about Il
Rosaio.

*The Rosaio is a charming little place; but it only has one bedroom. We have
given it up for some time now, and Edwin Cerio, our landlord at Casa Solitaria,
will let it for 60 lire a month during the winter. You could get a room for your man
close at hand. The piano you would have to hire. Anacapri is not so warm as
Capri; it is over 1,000 feet above sea level.*

*I might be able to let you have our casetta on the Piccola Marina. It is actually on
the beach itself, and would probably be ten degrees warmer than Anacapri. The
casetta would be 50 lire a month which is what I pay myself. The present exchange
is very beneficial to us and I should think you can count on its being 35 lire to the
sovereign next October.*

*I think frankly it would be a mistake to fix on anything for six months without
seeing it yourself; the variety of Capri is so extraordinary for so small a place that
it is like deciding whether to live in Cornwall or the Canary Islands for the winter.
I don't think you can get a better place than Capri, but of course it is no good
pretending that we have unbroken fine weather in the winter. We don't.*

*You ask about fleas. My secretary to whom I am dictating this assures me that
fleas do not bother us in winter. I myself never have any bother with fleas; they find
me unpalatable. I am much relished by bugs but mercifully bugs are non-existent in
Capri. The only one I ever saw walked out of a book I had brought back from
Greece nine months afterwards. Bring with you enough gauze netting to make a
mosquito net; you can get the stuff more cheaply in England and it can be made up
here, not that there are many mosquitoes in winter but even one in a week maddens
me.*

*I am afraid this letter is vague, but let me know as soon as possible what you
decide. At present in Rosaio there is rather a distinguished Italian composer called*

Respighi whose wife is a very good singer. They are leaving at the beginning of October, and I'd like to let Cerio know as soon as possible whether you want Rosaio so that he doesn't let it to anybody else.

Francis and Jessica Brett Young arrived about a week before Faith left for Paris and London. Cerio wanted to make some alterations at Rosaio and the little house might not be ready for them till after Christmas. So I offered to lend them our *casetta* on the Piccola Marina, which consisted of two rooms built over a boathouse. We had furnished it only as a place for lunch and a siesta after bathing but Edwin Cerio produced enough furniture to give them a bedroom until Rosaio was ready, and there they were installed.

Francis Brett Young had published several novels and some of the best neo-Georgian poetry, besides composing one or two charming songs. He had served as a major in the R.A.M.C. in the East African campaign, of which he had written an admirable account in *Marching on Tanga*. So far he had not enjoyed a popular success and this was worrying him, particularly now that he had given up medical practice and was resolved to live by his pen.

I recall walking with him one day along the Via Tragara soon after the news of the great success of *Poor Relations* and discussing why my books were selling better than his. I suggested as a possible explanation of my good fortune that I had a lower sense of my responsibility to art than he had and therefore did not mind playing the clown occasionally, which he would naturally feel was beneath the dignity of anybody with such a lofty idea of his calling.

Francis stopped with a solemn gesture and said in a tone of grave astonishment:

"You are not suggesting are you that I have no sense of humour?"

"No, no, Francis, of course not," I quickly replied. "I should never dream of suggesting such a thing to anybody, least of all to you. I was suggesting that you would not sacrifice your principles merely to entertain the public."

This explanation did not satisfy Francis; he pointed out that the main object of a novel *was* to entertain the public.

"I express myself in my poems to satisfy myself, and to some extent in my music also. I am not seeking to preach a way of life in my novels any more than you are. What is the secret of your success?"

"I really don't know, Francis. Perhaps humour doesn't enter into it. I had always supposed the Comic Muse was continually asserting herself in all my previous books, but in nearly all the enthusiastic reviews I've been getting for *Poor Relations* the reviewer has expressed surprise at such an hitherto unsuspected quality in my work."

During this talk about Brett Young's failure so far to attract the public's purse as successfully as I had, I advised him to drop the Francis and call himself simply Brett Young. I reminded him that Arnold Bennett had never won popular success until he gave up calling himself Enoch Arnold Bennett, and added that I was sure I should never have won it if I had continued to call myself M. Compton Mackenzie after my volume of poems.

In the course of many years of unbroken friendship I only once again upset Francis Brett Young; it was after reading *The Crescent Moon*.

"I never realized that the moon was the other way round in the Southern Hemisphere, Francis."

"It isn't."

"Are you sure?"

"Of course I am."

"Then why do you make your savages salute the crescent moon rising when actually it is setting?"

An expression of what can only be called horror passed over the usually placid countenance of Francis.

"Good God," he exclaimed, passing a hand across his forehead. "How on earth could I have made such an appalling blunder? And not a single reviewer noticed it."

"That hardly surprises me," I commented.

There was nothing Francis could do about that crescent moon; the whole story depended on its rising in the evening. It was a fantastic mistake for a man whose observation of the natural scene was always so beautifully exact.

In that autumn I was beoming more and more earnestly set upon escaping from the oppressive post-war atmosphere to the South Seas for at least a couple of years, and early in December I put this advertisement in *The Times*, *The Morning Post*, *The Athenaeum* and *The New Statesman*:

> Novelist requires for long voyage expert shorthand typist, healthy, young, good sailor, not afraid of luggage or savages: small salary and all expenses paid. Write, stating age, experience, etc. Box 9275 The Times, London, E.C.4.

I received 57 letters in answer to this. Here are a few extracts:
From a woman of 28 in Scarborough:

> *My chief experience being that of a traveller I regret very much that I cannot apply as a typist, but if I had any chance for the vacancy of this post I could take a course to perfect myself in that capacity. I am a born traveller and come of travelling people. During the war I have been nursing in French hospitals where we had to deal with blacks from Central Africa.*

L

From a woman in West Norwood:

I am not afraid of luggage; not having met savages, I cannot say, but I have no racial antipathy.

From a widow of 29 in Baker Street:

As to the savages, I cannot say I have ever met any uncivilized ones but I imagine they cannot be much more alarming than the civilized savages one meets with quite frequently and I am not afraid of them.

From a girl in Leytonstone:

I am young, a good sailor, and not afraid of savages but I don't quite understnad about the luggage. Am I expected to pack it, carry it, or do without it? . . . I am prepared to run most risks for the sake of adventure. I am quiet, dull, capable of great endurance, honest, and often stupid, but with occasional flashes of very sound common sense, and able to meet any emergency. Aged 21.

From a man of 39 in Battersea:

I do not think the savages will worry me much. There are plenty of them at home. However, as there are certain risks I think that, in the event of a safe termination of the journey, it will not be an unreasonable condition, if your book proves a great success, that I shall receive a substantial bonus in addition to the small salary. If engaged, I shall require an immediate advance, being without funds.

From a woman of 24 in Liverpool:

I don't see why you shouldn't take a lady. I'm very slim and would cut my hair and dress as a boy the minute we left the ship if it was any help but I should think the effect of an English girl in khaki breeches, short tunic, and peaked cap, on a savage chief would be worth putting in your novel. . . . I suppose you'll think it wouldn't be proper. Tommy rot! My folks were horrified when I went in the Army but now they admit it has done me a world of good. . . . I have been reading that the "New Hebridesites" were cannibals but are now nearly all Wesleyans or Roman Catholics. What could be more respectable?

What impressed me was that three-quarters of those 57 letters were from women.

"There's no doubt about it, Francis," I said to Brett Young after showing him some of those letters. "The women are much less tired by the war than we are."

Martin Secker came out to Capri at the beginning of December, when we had long talks about the possibility of some arrangement by which he would buy the copyrights of all my books and I would invest the money in buying a third share of his business as a sleeping partner.

Before Faith left Capri that autumn Nellie Baker had had to return to England because she was going to have a baby by Vittorio, the second Caracciolo boy. However, Carolina's daughter Gelsomina slept at Casa Solitaria and so we were able to have our morning coffee before her mother arrived with the day's marketing.

Secker and Jessica Brett Young were always on rather prickly terms. He believed she was responsible for persuading Francis to leave him and go to Collins' for his next books. Secker was anxious to dissuade me from that expedition I was planning to the South Seas and eyed disapprovingly the orange volumes of the *Pacific Pilot* on my shelves and the books I had accumulated about the South Seas. I told him that I was contemplating a book upon the decline and fall of a civilization under the destructive influence of Wesleyan missionaries, with whom to-day I should have to include the Seventh Day Adventists; my conscience still pricks me sometimes for not having written that book.

Secker and I on a halcyon December day went to Ventrosa; I see him now reclining exhausted in a bush of rosemary after the long ascent and descent. I still see those two Cleopatra butterflies, cousins of the English brimstone, whose pale yellow wings deepen to orange at the leaf-like tips. The excitement of seeing those Cleopatras in December must have engraved itself upon my memory. I intervene from the present to say that just after writing those words I saw in my garden in France two Cleopatras again after over forty years had passed. I had not seen one since the summer of 1924 in Capri.

Martin, in the hope of luring me away from that South Seas plan, suggested that in one of the almost inaccessible gorges of Ventrosa I should keep Barbary apes.

"I'm sure you could get a pair from Gibraltar."

"We have quite enough Barbary apes on Capri in the shape of these Milanese profiteers who will ruin the island," I told him.

I recall, too, from that halcyon day telling Secker that I thought some arrangement should be reached among novelists by which they bound themselves not to kill even their subordinate characters under the windows of other novelists.

"In *Joan and Peter* H. G. Wells drowns the parents of his protagonists just underneath my bedroom window."

"You'd better get the Authors' Society to take it up instead of fussing about their contracts with publishers. . . ."

I cut in before Martin could enlarge upon that familiar grievance of his.

"Yes, yes. But what would Wells say if I shot my next heroine in his garden at Easton Glebe?"

Martin Secker's company was always a joy to me. I have known few people with such an overwhelming sense of the ridiculous. He would relate some story and be so much overcome by the absurdity of it that he would have to mop the tears in his eyes. I never heard him laugh loudly, but those tears communicated mirth more eloquently than any laughter.

Secker went back to England in the middle of December; soon after he left, a letter arrived from D. H. Lawrence, who was finding the climate of Picinisco, a beautiful mountain village in Southern Italy, too cold in December. In this letter, which is lost, he wrote that he had been driven from England by the melancholy of elms; he had never forgotten a remark I had made about them when I visited him in 1914 at that cottage in Buckinghamshire. I had told him then I had a cottage in Capri which I should always be glad to lend him if he ever decided to return to Italy. Was that cottage vacant now? If it was, might he and his wife take advantage of my offer to lend it to them?

I wrote back to say I had just lent the cottage to the Brett Youngs. At the same time I urged him to come to Capri, and promised that Brett Young and I would try to find him cheap and fairly comfortable accommodation. I think it was the Brett Youngs who found the two large well-furnished rooms and kitchen at the top of an old *palazzo* close to the *piazza*, with a view of the Bay of Naples northward and of the outspread Mediterranean to the south. The Lawrences arrived just after Christmas and were pleased with their quarters. The charcoal stove in the kitchen was a source of pleasure to Lawrence because he had mastered the art of cooking with charcoal and enjoyed a demonstration of his skill. There was a young Rumanian who with a rather ludicrous optimism had come to Capri for a while during his quest for the Absolute; Lawrence had made friends with him in Morgano's. He, too, was proud of his skill with a charcoal stove and used to compete with Lawrence. Francis and I once called when they were in the middle of an argument about Plotinus, both of them fanning away energetically at the *fornella* while they were arguing. Frieda Lawrence had retired to the bedroom; the kitchen and the sitting-room were full of the fumes of charcoal and neo-Platonism; Lawrence's red beard was black. Francis and I hurried to open the windows before we and the two philosophic cooks were asphyxiated.

Lawrence had read a book by John Barnet on the early Greek philosophers—Heraclitus, Parmenides, Anaxagoras and the rest, and when he noticed the book on my shelves told me how deeply he had been impressed by it. He took it away with him to re-read, and one day as Lawrence and I were walking up and down the *piazza* talking about those ancient Greek philosophers he suddenly stopped and began to argue that men must give up thinking with their minds.

"What we have to learn is to think here," he affirmed solemnly in that high-pitched voice of his with its slight Midland accent. As he said this he bent over to point a finger at his fly-buttons, to my embarrassment and the obvious surprise of other people strolling on the *piazza*.

"You'll be getting a jobation presently from the *guardia*," I said, and went on to tell him how the old *guardia* had one evening seen one of the English visitors being rather too familiar with a young Caprese. He approached from behind and tapped him on the shoulder.

"*Queste cose, signore, si fanno in casa privata*," he gurgled in a reproachful vinous voice.

The Englishman, whose name I withhold, was quite shameless and told us the story as a good joke.

Lawrence was as little amused by it as Queen Victoria would have been, for he was still much at the mercy of that puritanism which had infected the spirit of merrie England since the death of the last Plantagenet. Yet in spite of disapproving of my silk shirts and silk pyjamas and blue Harris tweed suit—worn according to him in one of his published letters to match my eyes—he liked me as much as I liked him.

"I have never known anybody Lorenzo has liked as much as he likes you," Frieda bubbled from the depths of her Teutonic bonhomie. "He thinks it is a splendid idea that you should go to the South Sea Islands together."

Lawrence and I used to talk about the South Seas by the hour. He writes in one of his letters of me as "playing the romantic" in Capri. Presumably that was the silk shirts; the only time I did play the romantic was with Lawrence himself when we were talking about going to the Pacific together.

I was writing to Pinker that February to ask him if he could get a contract out of Cassell's or Hutchinson's for a book about the South Seas. I had a first-class photographer (Morgan Heiskell).

D. H. Lawrence is also bitten with the idea of doing half the writing, and it is obvious that if D. H. Lawrence is to come with me I should have to find his expenses in advance. Therefore it would be foolish to embark on any kind of scheme without a good guarantee.

We used to have great afternoons at Casa Solitaria with Brooks thumping away on the Erard Grand and Lawrence and me singing *Sally in our Alley* and *Barbara Allen*. Francis, who had a perfect ear, used to sit looking slightly pained by the way Lawrence and I were singing in different keys. They were jolly times, but I used to regret the way Frieda was for ever encouraging her Lorenzo with boisterous laughter to pull people to pieces. No doubt this eternal "knocking" of everybody was the result of those wretched years in England she and Lawrence had spent during the war, when spy-mania was rampant and when, on top of her divorce, she was so much on the defensive as a German that attack was the only alternative. Yet that silly spying accusation at Zennor might not have happened if Lawrence had refrained from painting the roof of their cottage with bright stripes of colour, which convinced the local coastguards that he and his German wife were signalling to U-boats.

Nevertheless, I used to wish the Lawrences would sometimes say a good word for somebody. Catherine Carswell wrote in *Savage Pilgrimage* that Lawrence "had come to like Compton Mackenzie but not his island, nor his influence. . . . He was sick of this cat Cranford of Capri."

No doubt petty gossip was as rife in Capri as it is in any English village. Nevertheless, if Lawrence and Frieda had not themselves always encouraged that gossip they would not have taken it so seriously, and let it be added, contributed so much to it, Lawrence by searching for dark explanations of somebody's casual behaviour, Frieda by her own feminine enjoyment of it.

In a letter about New Year's Eve at Morgano's Lawrence wrote of my coming in and merely waving to them. "We were very much poor relations." The reason why I merely waved to the Lawrences was that I was extremely anxious to talk to somebody for ten minutes before somebody arrived; the explanation was as simple as that. Such egocentricity could sometimes verge upon the fantastic. One day when he and I were walking along the Via Tragara he stopped abruptly and proclaimed twice;

"There's not going to be another war."

Snatching my stick and striking the wall by the edge of the road he shouted at the top of his voice;

"*I* won't have another war."

That winter Lawrence was working on *Fantasia of the Unconscious* and I lent him the L. C. Smith typewriter of which only the red half of the ribbon was still usable. The original typescript of the book must therefore have been in red, which the author declared had been helpful; I never grasped why. On that typewriter Faith had typed *South Wind* and *Sylvia Scarlett*; Nellie Baker had typed *Sylvia and Michael*, and *Our Betters* for Somerset Maugham; now Lawrence had typed on it *Fantasia of the Unconscious*.

On my thirty-seventh birthday Lawrence brought that typewriter back to Casa Solitaria.

THIRTY-SEVEN YEARS OLD: 1920

I SEE now Lawrence coming down the steps of Casa Solitaria on that sunny morning, one arm holding the L. C. Smith typewriter on his head, the other carrying a bottle of Benedictine, my birthday present. Anybody but Lawrence would have hired,a *facchino* to bring that heavy typewriter from the piazza the mile and a half to Casa Solitaria, which included some steep steps down to the rough cliff path that led to our house. This was Lawrence when for an hour or two he was at peace with life; in such a mood he was Puck and Ariel in one. He eyed the world with delight and seemed a part of the Classic scene; on other occasions he would seem as remote from it as a noncomformist chapel on the Acropolis.

About now Mary Cannan arrived in Capri. She and Gilbert were divorced; her eyes waving from side to side as she talked, she would relate to Lawrence and me the intimate tale of her life, first with Barrie and then with Cannan. Now on the defensive herself, she always encouraged Lawrence and Frieda to discover and discuss the weaknesses of others. Gilbert himself, like half a dozen more British writers, was lecturing in America and occasionally a cutting would arrive in which he was telling imaginary stories about himself and some of us to interviewers. In a year or two he would be certified insane, and would spend the last thirty years of his life in a private asylum in Richmond, agreeably enough because he thought it was his own house.

I sent Lawrence the copies of *The Little Review* I was receiving from Chicago with the serialization of James Joyce's *Ulysses*. He was horrified by it. I see now a gloomy Lawrence walking along that cliff path to Casa Solitaria. He is wearing a covert coat, only the top button of which is fastened; he is carrying a string bag in which there is an orange and a banana and under his arm are the copies of *The Little Review* I had lent him.

"This *Ulysses* muck is more disgusting than Casanova," he proclaimed. "I *must* show that it can be done without muck."

Were Lady Chatterley and her lover conceived at that moment? That first reading of *Ulysses* set Lawrence off talking to me about sex for a couple of hours. What worried him particularly was his inability to attain consummation simultaneously with his wife, which according to him must mean that their marriage was still imperfect in spite of all they had both gone through. I insisted that such a happy coincidence was always rare, but he became more and more depressed about what *he* insisted was the only evidence of a perfect union.

"I believe that the nearest I've ever come to perfect love was with a young coal-miner when I was about sixteen," he declared.

On and on Lawrence went that morning about the need for people to think with their genital organs instead of their minds, on and on about the Etruscans, who he was convinced thought with their genital organs, on and on until at last I had to stop what was turning into too long a sermon. I told him that if he was determined to convert the world to proper reverence for the sexual act by writing about it in a novel he would always have to remember one handicap for such an undertaking.

"What's that?"

"Something that Heraclitus and Parmenides must have recognized, something that certainly every Greek poet recognized . . ."

"What is it?" he asked impatiently.

"That except to the two people who are indulging in it the sexual act is a comic operation."

I see now Lawrence's pale face grow paler as he turned round and hurried off with his string bag to eat his lunch in solitude.

Next day he came into my room and said abruptly:

"Perhaps you're right. And if you're right . . ." He made a gesture of despair for the future of the human race.

The strain upon Lawrence of the Great War for Civilization had indeed been unbearable. For him, married to a German wife, pressed for money and in poor health, it plunged him into a miasma of morbid dreams. Then that journalistic scavenger James Douglas attacked *The Rainbow* when it was published by Methuen in 1915 and the book was seized by the police on the instructions of some constipated booby of officialdom who should have been publicly purged. Finally some elderly ass of a magistrate ordered *The Rainbow* to be blotted out.

In the winter of 1920 Martin Secker was already playing with the idea of publishing Lawrence's next novel, *Women in Love*, and even with re-publishing *The Rainbow*. I warmly encouraged this idea, and as early as January Secker was writing to me:

Yes, the economic problem of the novelist without popular sales is very difficult. I could make him an offer to purchase the rights of Women in Love *for £300 and* Rainbow *for £200. On this he could live comfortably in Italy for a year during which time he would finish another book and we might come to an arrangement.*

I put forward a scheme which I thought would be more advantageous for Lawrence and at the end of the month Secker wrote:

I have thought over your suggested arrangement, but the affair is becoming too complicated. To be quite candid I am not at all convinced that he is a commercial proposition anyway and I am lukewarm about reprinting The Rainbow. *I would only do so after I had got clear away with* Women in Love. *I do not want the advertisement of a cause celèbre which can be purchased at too great a cost, and I am advised that as matters stand its publication would automatically constitute a contempt of court. I do not think the authorities would move of their own volition, but some purist busybody would compel them to take notice. I can only repeat my original offer, £300 for all rights of* Women in Love *with the option of following up with* Rainbow *at £200. This I should probably exercise if "W. in Love" did not involve me in any kind of lawsuit and did something to rehabilitate the author. It must not be forgotten that at the moment no bookseller would buy a single copy of the Rainbow even with my imprint unless he dealt in "curiosa".*

If he does not like this proposition I can revert to the original plan of trying "W. in Love" on an ordinary contract, royalties starting at 10%. But I am a little tired of the whole thing and, now Duckworth is in competition, am quite ready to retire in his favour. Lawrence's books are not worth competing for from a money making point of view.

Lawrence had made a trip to Sicily with the Brett Youngs to see the temples at Agrigentum, and sometime early in March he decided to leave Capri and find a *villino* in Taormina for Frieda and himself; Mary Cannan went with them. I have a letter with only "Monday" for a date:

Fontana Vecchia

We're at home in our house this evening—I write by lamplight. Already rather cosy. Returned to Giardini Sat. evening, and waited there till 9.30 when F. and Mary arrived by the accelerato—ach!—and their trunks not with them. We all stayed at Bristol—to-day I skipped to Catania for the trunks—got them all right. Mary has turned in to Timeo—seems a nasty impudent place like Etrangers, only more of it. The woman upstairs here leaves on Thursday morning—meanwhile frigid gulf between two regions. To hell with her—I looked again at the Hindoo muslin stuff—but as the woman was cheeky, with her English, and as the ragged rubbish has a dirtyish look to hell with it. Mary of course darted into the rag-shops like a sparrow into a scullery and emerged with a waistcoat. I shall send you 50 francs when there is ink for a cheque. It is scirrocco [sic] to-day—grey like unshed tears, ages old and still unshed. That wall of mist met me as I left Messina, rolling up the Straits in a wall. There are many devils, little people, . . . dark influences in Sicily! This is the Celtic land of Italy with the old fear in it—I suppose to-night you are back at Piccola—seems across a space—Frieda loves the house, so does Mary—Do you imagine the balcony at night?—the Plough pitching headlong, but the sea on the left, terribly falling, and Taormina in a rift on the right fuming tremulously between the jaws of the darkness—I wonder if I shall write—Heaven save us all! Did you hear that one of F's diamond rings was stolen from the room in Capri? One shouldn't have diamonds voilà tout!—Most bookless here. If you ever have anything I might read and you don't want, remember me. Send me name and address of Land and Water *man, please, for Magnus. Tell me the news; hope all is well.*

D.H.L.

A second letter also dated "Monday" must have reached me a week later:

Fontana Vecchia
Taormina

We've turned in to our house to-night—strange lost soul I feel, with a bit of heimweh for Capri. But I am very grand here in the house of the Cook. Mary has gone in to Timeo tonight also—hateful place, Timeo, our Bristol much nicer, smaller: she stayed with us till to-day, down there—Well, I feel I've reached my limit for the moment—like a spent bird straggling down the Straits. We saw a great V of wild-fowl wavering north up the Straits. Heimweh or nostalgia there, for the North. Yet I am wavering South. But I am at my limit for a year. Consider my exchequer with repulsion based on fear. But best not consider—I hope you won't scorn us too much for moving to Taormina. It was chiefly, I think, the arid sort of dryness of the Capri rock: a dry, dry bone. But I don't know, I feel a bit of a stranger here—feel the darkness *again. There is no darkness in Capri—Frieda said you had pains—do hope they're better. I get a sort of Wehmut. Quoi faire!— Later I'll come to the South Seas—drift and drift. Don't let us lose sight of one another. We are opposite in most things, But opposite poles are not inevitably mutually related. Don't let the world matter—it doesn't matter. I think we met well in Capri—I'll see you again before very long. Let us weave fate somehow together. Hope your book goes—perhaps I shall write here—if only I could care again—or if only the ravens would walk up with the capretto and macaroni. Send me a line—No ink here yet. I hope you got your typewriter safely—and many thanks.*

D.H.L.

A torn scrap of paper with "Wednesday" must have been written when Lawrence was negotiating with Gerald Duckworth.

I enclose Secker's letter—As you please, dear Martin—I'll send The Rainbow *to Duckworth, and get on with him. If he would really like a little foreword by you, would you still do it? I'm staying indoors with a cold for the moment.*

D. H. Lawrence

The next letter tells of Lawrence's break with Duckworth,

Fontana Vecchia
Taormina
22 March

So sorry you are seedy—hope it's better. Brooks wrote and says you are working again. Do hope it goes. I have dreamed twice I was going to the South Seas. I scrapped all the novel I did in Capri—have begun again, got about 30,000 words, I believe, done since I'm here. Rather amusing. But as for me, I may come to a full stop any moment—you never know.

I had a letter from Duckworth, and he wants me to cut pieces from The Rainbow. *It annoys me, so I break off with Duckworth. I wrote to Secker to say I'll take him at his old terms if he is still willing. That too annoys me, to lose all my rights over the books. But I'll be glad to get them off my hands and be rid of the bother of them. . . . Enough of Europe and its ways. If Secker doesn't want any more, then to hell with the lot, and there's an end of it.*

This place is really awfully nice, for greenness and sappy growth and a little stream falling and tinkling, and water cress, and the sunrise golden and the shimmering pallid wide sea over which one walks, ach, treads far off, with one's back on Europe forever.

For people—I know a few already—the permanent evergreens are awful, while the deciduous are even awfuller. But the permanents, the evergreens like Miss Mabel Hill, are too sanctified to snuff at me and the deciduous like the Duca[1] are getting ready to shed themselves from Taormina. So as for people peu ou rien. Save for a slit-eyed Dutch woman and two young men from South Africa, rather nice— I don't like people—truly I don't. And Taormina is a place where I can amuse myself by myself in the garden and up the hills among the goats. I wish Taormina village weren't there, that's all—with Timeo, Domenico, and Villaolatri.

Is Secker coming out? If so, tell him what I say—I should really like to be rid forever of the bother of those two novels. Damn the world. Why is one such a fool as to offer it anything serious di cuore. *I've finished forever—wish I'd never begun. Henceforth, my fingers to my nose—and my heart far off.*

When you are well you might come to Taormina for a little bit although you scorn it.

I wish you had a ship. Such a lovely steam yacht has been cruising off here—now she has gone eastwards, over the pale level flow of the sea. If only I had her! I invoke the ultimate heavens. Ah God, if one had the feet of the sea, and far spaces, and sails that kiss the wind. To sail outwards—outwards, that's the best of our Fontana Vecchia, she's a watch tower of the sea. The young men say Africa.

How is Eric?[2] Remembrances to him. I believe Douglas is in Naples just now, en route *for Greece. Wonder if he'll appear.*

Ethel Smythe is here—haven't met her—but see her in the street. Niente bella. *Frieda is going to write to you—so is Mary. You are the enfant gâté of Capri— save for the gods who screw you with too much pain. I hate pain. To me the elements are lovely, the wind and shadows and the up and down of hills. One should not have any more pain. Assez de cela—it is of this sick world. So rise up.*

D.H.L.

Oh, how is the Solaro house?

[1] The Duke of Bronte (Hon. A. Nelson Hood).
[2] Eric Brett Young.

By April Lawrence was back in England for a time and Secker was writing:

The Lawrence position is this: in his letter he expressed his dislike of parting with his copyrights, so I therefore made him an offer to publish both books, with an option on his next five, at 1/- per copy for the first 2,000, then 1/6 to 5,000 and 2/- after that. This offer he accepted, but I feel most strongly that I must reserve my decision to publish The Rainbow *until after* Women in Love *has appeared and done something to rehabilitate the author—in fact to be guided to a great extent by its reception. Also I must have legal advice to make sure that I was not automatically committing a contempt of court by re-issuing the book. Then, assuming that this is not the case, but that police proceedings are started* de novo, *I am not prepared to invest £1,500 in a cause célèbre to entertain the world of letters. Even if I could afford it, I do not want to be harassed by it. This must be quite clear.*

I have looked up the Times *report of the case* (Nov. 18, 1915). *Mr Muskett for Commissioner of Police, no doubt in a strong Irish brogue, said the book "was a mass of obscenity of thought, idea and action throughout, wrapped up in language which he supposed would be regarded in some quarters as an artistic and intellectual effort". Finally, the Magistrate at Bow Street, Sir John Dickenson, now deceased I believe, ordered all copies to be destroyed and defendants to pay the costs of the proceedings. This is not encouraging.*

Why I want D.H.L. to change the provocative title of Women in Love *to the quiet, even dull one of* The Sisters *is just for the very reason that it is important from D.H.L.'s point of view to be as unprovocative as possible in order to get the book taken anywhere. To give it that title is to tie a red rag on to it. By the way, the copy he wishes me to set up from is the typescript now in America, considerably altered he tells me, which may differ from mine by having all the best bits taken out and a lot of lesbianism written in. So obviously I must see this American typescript first, although I do not imagine of course that what I have suggested above is really the case.*

I feel instinctively that anything to do with D.H.L. is rather dangerous, but I am prepared to take risks justified by what I know to be your wishes that I should give him another chance. I agree that he may go mad if he does not have something in print soon.

I was grateful to Martin Secker for the courage he was displaying; in the mass of verbiage written about Lawrence both here and in America during the last decade I have not seen any recognition of that courage. When *The Rainbow* was finally published without a word deleted or changed the authorities were as mild as their own milky minds. As I had prophesied, they did nothing. However, when Martin Secker was about to publish *Women in Love* Philip Morrell got hold of an advance copy and offered to finance Peter Warlock, the composer, in a libel action. He was furious with an alleged portrait of his wife, Lady Otto-line, in the book, but did not want her to sue. The early copies were called in and Peter Warlock's nickname of "Pussycat" or something like that was changed.

Lawrence's caricatures of various people in his novels and short stories set against their own photographic background sometimes deserved to be jumped on. He lacked the patience to evoke an unrecognizable background for his caricatures. By this time Lawrence believed that the threat of a libel action could only be cruel and deliberate persecution. On top of that the volume of his poems published in Italy was forbidden ingress to Great Britain, and when finally the police closed an exhibition of his pictures at a Mayfair gallery his feeling of martyrdom became acute. By the time *Lady Chatterley's Lover* was published any sense of proportion left to him had vanished.

I was glad to get those letters from Sicily because Lawrence had not seemed impressed by it when he came back from that visit to Agrigentum with the Brett Youngs. Francis declared it was because his hat blew away when they were looking at the temples. I remember Jessica Brett Young's saying to me when they returned from that Sicilian expedition:

"I couldn't help thinking on our way from Naples to Messina how thrilled the other passengers on the boat would have been if they had known who Francis and Lawrence were."

I told her I doubted if a lot of commercial travellers in the orange trade would ever have heard either of Francis or Lawrence. Jessica's romantic illusion was pardonable; less pardonable was that of Jack Squire.[1]

At this date the *London Mercury* was in its apogee. The Squirearchy was out to rule the literary world of London. One of its objects was to bring back the public to a proper reverence for poetry; this involved a campaign against the prosaic influence of novels. The war had given poetry a boost and the neo-Georgian poets were in their glory. In that very March there was a long obituary of my work in the *Mercury* by a forgotten poet called John Freeman, now dead, and dear lovable Jack Squire could not understand why it left me unmoved.

"You were terribly sweet about it," he said when we met two or three months later.

"My failure to protest, Jack, owed nothing to the sweetness of my nature. I was merely amused by Freeman's romantic illusions just as I was amused by yours in that article in the *New Witness* last week."

[1] The late Sir John Squire.

Jack Squire had written about arriving in Ryde with Hilaire Belloc in his boat. While Belloc was making all secure and shipshape aboard, Squire had wandered up into the town to look for a good place for dinner. As he had walked by the houses on that fine summer's evening and seen through the still undrawn curtains the trim parlour-maids putting the last touches to the preparations for the family dinner he had reflected how delighted any of them would have been if he had rung the bell and told them that Belloc and he were in Ryde, and how warmly they would have been invited in to dinner by the owner of the house.

"Do you really believe, Jack, that if you had rung the bell and announced your arrival with Hilaire Belloc that any parlour-maid in Ryde would have done anything but quickly close the door before you could put your foot in it like an importunate tramp? And even if the parlour-maid had gone to the master of the house and told him that a Mr J. C. Squire was in the hall waiting to be asked to dinner, do you suppose that his face would have lighted up with a glow of gratification?"

Jack Squire blinked.

"I think quite a few people in the Isle of Wight would have been glad to welcome Hilary Belloc and me."

"Well, dear Jack, I hope for your sake that your expectation of being able to make the British public read poetry instead of novels will not prove an equally romantic illusion."

Francis Brett Young asked me if I would try the experiment of his brother as a secretary so that if it was a success I might take him with me when I departed for the South Seas.

"Eric is bone idle, but he has a good brain. He's lame but very active with it."

I had to start my next novel, *Rich Relatives*, soon and this sounded quite a good idea. So at the end of January Eric arrived. At the same time Francis and Jessica Brett Young moved up from the Piccola Marina to Il Rosaio. Later on in the spring Francis acquired Fraita, a pleasant small villa looking westwards across a sea of olives where he became an Anacaprese and lived for many years, when not travelling in South Africa or lecturing in the United States.

Francis and Eric had collaborated in a first novel, but totally dissimilar as they were in temperament and outlook the collaboration had not extended beyond that. I found Eric agreeable company; he was not overworked, because the usual tiresome interruptions of neuritis made *Rich Relatives* slow going.

A relic of that March remains in a note from Diana Heiskell after I sent her a birthday present.

My dearest Monty,

I'd rather have "Tom Sawyer" than any other book. I really love it and you too. Thank you with all my heart. Remember we expect you for tea at four.

Your loving Diana

One visit remains vividly from that spring. This was when Kathleen Scott[1] arrived with Peter, who was then ten years old. Carolina was much distressed because he was wearing so few clothes, which she attributed to extreme poverty. I assured her that Peter was wearing so little because his mother thought it was healthy, not because she was poor.

Peter was very much on the spot and arrived one day with three of the blue lizards that are found nowhere in the world except on the Faraglioni rocks. He had climbed up and captured them himself. One of them escaped at Casa Solitaria and got itself jammed in the waste pipe of our wash-basin, and it took a plumber a long time before he managed to extract the dead lizard and allow the waste pipe to function again. I had not seen Kathleen Scott since she passed through New York on her way to New Zealand in 1912, hoping to greet Captain Scott's return from the Antarctic; she looked as young as ever and her personality was as outstanding as it always had been.

Another outstanding personality in a completely different style came to Capri early that summer. That was the Marchesa Casati, whose flamboyant personality has been preserved on canvas by Augustus John. One day I met Munthe on his way down the Phoenician steps from Anacapri to the Grande Marina.

"I am in a great rage," he told me. "The Marchesa Casati wrote to ask me to lend her San Michele for a month and I told her I could not have her at San Michele. Now I have a message to say she is waiting for me at the Grande Marina."

"Can't you send her to an hotel?" I suggested.

"You do not know what the woman is like. She will insist that I lend her San Michele. I am in a rage."

An hour later the Marchesa arrived on the Piazza from the funicular, escorted by an effeminate *cicisbeo*, on whose arm one of her own rested. In her other arm was a gilded gazelle and the *cicisbeo's* other arm encircled its gilded companion. Munthe presented me, and after studying me for a moment or two through a lorgnette she invited me to tea two or three days later. Presently an enormous buck Negro appeared, carrying a blue parrot in a cage.

"I know you don't like driving in a *carozza*, Dr Munthe," said the Marchesa. "Will you take—" she mentioned her Negro servant's name

[1] The late Lady Kennett.

—"up to San Michele? I and—" now the name of the *cicisbeo*—"will drive up later."

Munthe would tell me presently that her Negro servant was being an even greater problem for him than the Marchesa herself.

"I have to find two fowls a day for him. He eats two fowls every day."

"He'll probably eat the Marchesa's parrot if you don't keep him in fowls," I said.

"That woman is impossible," Munthe declared. "And now she is profaning San Michele by putting one of those animals of hers on each side of the front door."

I left Materita and went on to take tea with the Marchesa. Sure enough a gilded gazelle was standing on either side of the heavy front door, which was opened by the Negro servant, dressed now in a blue plush tailcoat and breeches. The inside of San Michele always gave the impression of being more Gothic than Roman, in spite of the relics of ancient Rome with which it was filled. The *cicisbeo* was fluttering about in the entrance-hall to say the Marchesa was waiting to receive me; presently we should be taking tea in the pergola. I passed on to the *salone* and went in. Surprise scarcely expresses what I felt when I saw my hostess lying on the big black bearskin in front of the huge fireplace. The reader may feel equally that surprise is hardly strong enough to describe his feelings when I tell him that the Marchesa was lying there with absolutely nothing on.

"Ah, Mackenzie, I am glad to see you," she said, extending her arm for me to kiss her hand. "I must put on a wrap because we shall have tea outside in the pergola. Go you along now."

I am glad that Augustus John immortalized the Marchesa Casati, but I sometimes wish that he could have seen her as I saw her that afternoon of early summer in Capri upon the black bearskin rug, so appropriately bearskin.

At the beginning of April I had sent the Lawrences some books, including the two volumes of *Sylvia Scarlett* to Frieda. She wrote:

Dear Mackenzie,

You have not only given me two books, but a whole world, just a world that I am walking into, I am just in Spain with the nice fat old woman and Sylvia. That's picaresque, isn't it? You have created a real new free world there, how you have got rid off [sic] all that dull stuffy Englishness! No wonder they dislike you no wonder they attack you—I love this book—Lawrence's new book has something of the quality of yours; I think that same having left all Englishness!—with I suppose the best of England in it— Here I was interrupted. Gilbert [Cannan] turned up— I believe to hit Lawrence in the eye because of the nasty letter he had written. He is Dostoiewski's idiot—But so we told him flat—it looked like he taking money from

M—but he produced a cheque for £75—I doubt whether it would have appeared without that letter. He was highfalluting [sic] of course the old Gilbert—"mais ça ne me lave pas!" To-day he is gone—but I was sorry there is nothing left—I do like the freelanceness of the people in your book—It's a pity you are rich, you ought to be like the people in your Sylvia. I do hope some day in this world, we shall be somewhere together some of us and this rotten show of rotten people will be left behind like old clothes—I wish you would have a rendezvous in London . . . your letter has just come—Mon Dieu donc, what a time you have had—Why don't you and Brooks come? Lawr. says spitefully there will be a rival show at Anacapri . . . with love also to Pauline[1] (I have not forgotten my promise to her). Thank you again.

Frieda L.

You are not nearly proud enough of your work!

Lawrence wrote on April 9th, 1920, from Fontana Vecchia:

I got Secker's letter to-day. It says he will publish "Women in Love" and "the Rainbow" . . . I wrote and accepted. If he publishes at a normal price, it is quite fair and I am satisfied. So far so good.

We received the Scarletts two days ago, and Frieda is reading fast. She likes "Sylvia Scarlett" enormously—says it is a break away into a new world. I am going to read it as soon as she has done. "Mortality, Behold and fear!"

Your letter to F. to-day—also a note from F.B.Y. I am really wretched to think of you so much sick. You will have to leave Capri for a bit—yes, truly. Leave it for awhile—come to Sicily, go to England, but leave Capri for a bit. Nip over here for a short while! Fun!

Yesterday I heard a fumbling on the terrace and there Gilbert at the foot of the stairs in a brown hat rather like yours; gave me quite a turn! thought it was somehow you—not you. He came express from Rome in one of his tantrums because of the nasty letter I'd written him—fume! But—nay, I'll say nothing. The main upshot is that in his indignation he disgorged a cheque for £75 SEVENTY FIVE POUNDS STERLING—as the equivalent of $300 which he had collected from Americans for me. Benone! Fortune so had it that for once Mary wasn't here to tea; and that he had taken a room at Domenico as being a little grander than Timeo. He is tout américain—L'Americanisato! pocket book thick, fat, bulging with 1,000 Lire notes—"these beastly hotels"—"Oh yes, picked up quite a lot of money over there"—"Oh yes, they seemed to take to me quite a lot". "Yes, have promised a quantity of people I'll go back this Fall."

Of what a Fall was there!!

However, we parted as friends who will never speak to each other again.

> *And Life is thorny, and Youth is vain*
> *And to be wroth with one we love*
> *Doth work like madness in the brain.*

[1] Our cat, but I do not remember what the promise was.

M

Poor Gilbert—a soup frill. However, I've sent my check like lightning to the bank, to see if it'll be cashed safe and sound. Aspettiamo. And to-day the filbert returns to Rome, to his dear —— s. "—— is a wonderful and beautiful character" this to my nose. Do you wonder I made a nose at it? "—— isn't a forgiving nature," says he. "Neither is mine," reply I. Assez de ça. . . . "It has made no difference to me." This from the filbert, regarding the marriage of ——. Ça paraît, mon cher.

I had a letter from F.B.Y. But not a word of his landed proprietorship. It's no good, my dear fellow, you may wrestle with him for the tight little island, but he's got his teeth in, so you may as well let go. Now, early, with a good grace and a bonne mine, *carissimo. Tulips, daffodils, all the lot relinquish, let go. À la bonne heure, mon cher, if you* will *invite young writers to Capri. My novel is page 245 and I like it so much, it does so amuse me. I want to wind it up about page 400 MS. rivederci.*

D.H.L.

On "Monday May 10 or 11" Lawrence was writing from Fontana Vecchia:

Had your letter to-day. I've finished my novel—"The Lost Girl"—sent first part to Rome to be typed. Devil it will cost me 1,000 francs. I think it's good, amusing. Secker sent me finicky agreements—however—I signed, except I reserve for myself All American rights and properties. He sounds funky. You'll be able to hold his hand when you go to London—I've read Sylvia Scarlett *and S. and Michael—amusing and witty and alas, only too like life.*

This rolling stone business gets a little heartrending in the end. One is rather busy at it oneself. Poor Sylvia—qu'est-il donc qu'elle cherche? It isn't merely *adventure. She's all the while looking for something* permanent. *Don't like the Christ hankering—sign of defeat: alas, S. and Michael are a wistful pair. I'm terrified of my Alvina who marries a Cicio. I believe neither of us has found a way out of the labyrinth. How we hang on to the marriage clue! Doubt if it's really a way out. But my Alvina, in whom the questing soul is lodged, moves towards reunion with the dark half of humanity. Whither poor Sylvia? The ideal? I loathe the ideal with an increasing volume of detestation—all ideal.*

Yes, I should like to see you before you go to England. Yet I feel I ought to sit tight on the Liras. I am determined myself to hop off the known map by next Spring: shall hoard Martin's dear advances, and shan't buy a Fraita, not even a Pauline. But I should like to talk once more South Seas. *That interests me finally. I have to poke myself to be interested in novels and plays.* Are you really going? *I had by the same post a letter from an American friend in Paris at the moment— also South Seas. He also plans to go. He has a friend in the U.S. navy who knows the South Seas well, knows the natives of the Islands, who love him. He's looking for a ship to get out. He also will look for a place for us. And I am going to have enough money* by next year *to start off. Voilà. Free bird too. Meanwhile I shall cogitate a day or two, and may suddenly appear in Capri one morning.*

At this moment Mary is madly keen to go to Malta, because at the hotel they give you soles and ham and eggs for breakfast, raspberry jam and cream puffs for tea. And she's scared of going away any more alone—begs us to go with her, she buys tickets. I don't know. . . . But if I come to Capri it will be because I want to talk South Seas for the last time before you start. I can't *be* VERY *interested in plays, even my own. I somehow have no belief in the public; only in that other world which is dusky. I love a desert. Don't imagine—since I mention tickets—that it is money which prevents my coming to Capri. I am quite well off as a matter of fact. The Malta affair is a mere excursion, a* niente *on which I would* not *spend.*

But after my novel I am holidaying for one month. Then I should like to start again, with another I have in mind. I feel as if I were victualling my ship, with these damned books. But also somewhere they are the crumpled wings of my soul. They get me free before I get myself free. I mean in my novel I get some sort of wings loose, before I get my feet out of Europe . . . will you believe my luggage hasn't come yet. And do you imagine my weary despair. Frieda sends you herzlich. Auf Wiedersehn—even if it's in Honolulu.

D. H. Lawrence

On Sunday, May 16th, Lawrence wrote:

We're going to Malta to-morrow. Don't know why it sounds so thrilling.— seems so thrilling. Perhaps it'll be a fiasco. Secker says he may be able to serialise the new novel in The Century. *Good if he could! Will you really take the MS to London for me, as you pass? Otherwise I don't believe it will ever arrive. You'll have E.B.Y., won't you? The woman is Miss Wallace, Pension White, 11 Via Vittorio Colonna, Roma 26. I should think she'll have it done by first week in June.*

Secker prefers the title The Bitter Cherry *not* The Lost Girl. My Lost Girl *amused me so—made a film title. But we shall have to let Secker have this as he yields me* Women in Love. *. . . . Don't you think I might possibly have the novel serialised in England? I'm dying to make enough money to trip off.*

The publication of *The Vanity Girl* in May was the signal for a display of enlarged spleen by the reviewers; one might have supposed it to be an infectious disease from their unanimity.

A quotation from a long review in the *Westminster Gazette* will serve as typical of at least three dozen others:

"It is with genuine melancholy [of crocodiles' tears!] *that those who have hoped against hope that Mr Compton Mackenzie's undoubted and remarkable gifts as an observer would, some time, prevail against his fatal facility and the inherent banality of his point of view must peruse his last novel. 'The Vanity Girl' (Cassell 8s. 6d.) bears upon it every mark of library success; it has every passport to a big circulation; but artistically, as the work of a writer in regard to whom Henry James once expressed the liveliest anticipation, it does not exist at all; it*

represents the abandonment of serious intention altogether. . . . Of course, since Mr Mackenzie has the perfect art of the cinematographist, the scene as it unfolds before us is admirably and alertly diversified; it jumps and flickers just like the movies. There is very little he does not know about the Vanity Chorus; but after all, thanks to his assiduous industry, there is very little we do not know either. . . . Although externally modernized, the story is in all essentials true to the type of the Family Herald Supplement, *of the kind of vogue enjoyed in its time by that soothing syrup for the starved romanticism of housemaids, nurses, and typists, 'The Vanity Girl' is assured; but of nothing more."*

This was written by Naomi Royde Smith, an angular arbitress of literary fashion at the sherry parties publishers were beginning to give to baptize a new book. I had met her about eight years earlier when she was hopefully playing Egeria to Charles Marriott after the death of his first wife.

I recall asking Frank Swinnerton soon after the publication of *The Vanity Girl* what I had done to make all the critics turn on me with such evident relish in the attack.

"I think," he replied, "it's because people feel you consider your position so secure that you can afford to live out of England."

Lady Algernon Gordon-Lennox, who had been reading *The Vanity Girl* on her way out to Capri, congratulated me on the truth of the book to life. She was a sister of Lady Warwick and one of the beauties of the Edwardian Court. I felt she might know a little more about life in the peerage than most of the critics. Lady "Algy's" company was one of the pleasures of Capri. She had bought San Michele, one of the four hills of Capri which had formerly belonged to old Prince Caracciolo, and not to be confused with Munthe's San Michele. Here, thanks to the illimitable water supplied by the old Roman cisterns of what had obviously been the site of one of the twelve villas Tiberius built for himself on Capri, she had made one of the loveliest gardens in the Mediterranean and she was still adding to it year by year when she retired annually from the London season. For her Capri was a rest and she was hardly ever seen in the gay crowded life of the island. Those walks with Lady Algy round that great garden, talking about flowers and flowering shrubs, are one of the memorable pleasures of my life and I should presently dedicate to her *The Seven Ages of Woman*. In London after Lord Algernon died on one of his brief visits to Capri, to be buried there in the little Protestant cemetery, she lived in Portland Place, where on my brief visits to London during the twittering 'twenties I could always feel the Great War for Civilization had never happened to interrupt it.

The Vanity Girl would be republished by Macdonald's in 1954 at two shillings more than its original price. This book was dedicated to my sister Fay, who in 1920 had just had her triumphant success in Barrie's play at the Haymarket, *Mary Rose*. I wrote a fresh inscription when it was republished:

"*Dearest Fay,*
I dedicated this Edwardian romance to you when it was first published in 1920. I rededicate to you this new edition thirty-four years later when the Edwardian decade seems as remote as the Regency."

Stephen Gazelee was driven to write to the moribund *Athenaeum*, now being edited by Middleton Murry, which had published an acidulous review under the heading "Mr Mackenzie's Treat":

"I venture to doubt whether your reviewer's condemnation of 'The Vanity Girl' as a 'pot-boiler' and a betrayal of his art (May 14) is justified, and I suggest that it may be the most subtle work that he has yet produced—the picture of a girl of any ordinary middle-class family who . . . comes to subordinate all else to making herself the instrument by which a great family is to be perpetuated and its possessions handed on unimpaired. If I am right in my opinion, great art is displayed in showing the extremes of callousness to relations and friends, amounting sometimes to cruelty, and the perverted self-sacrifice to which this slowly realized ideal, if such it can be called, makes Dorothy Lonsdale capable."

The reviewer replied:

"That Mr Mackenzie is holding up one division of his public for the other to laugh at; that he is taking his sophisticated public to see the funny little animals feed is highly possible. But it is a dangerous proceeding, and we do not withdraw the word 'betrayal'. K.M."

So by some feat of literary legerdemain I was inviting the upper classes to laugh at the middle classes but at the same time writing a *Family Herald* novelette to nourish the "starved romanticism of housemaids, nurses and typists".

My own peace of mind was not disturbed by the critics' reception of *The Vanity Girl*. Knowing that I had enough subjects for as many novels as I should live to write, I was not dismayed by these eager obituaries. What that copy-cat attack on *The Vanity Girl* did effect was to convince me that I must get away from the heart of things for the next two years. I realized that I had had six times as much experience of life as most of my own contemporaries and therefore that I could afford to withdraw from the world for the present. I was not prepared to compete with my juniors by pretending to be younger than I was. Still, it was cheering to read in the *Chicago News* in the course of a review of *Poor Relations*:

"Before the critics could get round to roasting him for 'Sylvia and Michael' Mackenzie comes out with 'Poor Relations'. Authors who write as rapidly as Mackenzie does have a splendid defense against critics; they move ahead so fast that the torpedoes pass under their sterns. . . . Mackenzie has a special place in our literature as the only legitimate heir of Smollett and Dickens. He has their eye for the grotesque in common life and their faculty for swiftly differentiating minor characters. . . . Altogether we find Compton Mackenzie a most significant figure."

I reached London at the beginning of June. Faith had taken Markham House at the corner of Markham Square in Chelsea, one side of which looked out on the noise of King's Road. Presently I went down to Iver to stay with Martin Secker and spend a fortnight in finishing off *Rich Relatives*. I realized Secker was beginning to be rather apprehensive about the arrangement we had come to by which he was to acquire all my books and give me a third interest in his business. I expect I began to display large ideas about its future, whereas he was determined to maintain at all costs his policy of selective publishing. I suppose my mind was so set upon a South Seas adventure that I have forgotten the details. However, in the end, I refused an offer from Pinker to guarantee me £6,000 for two books annually for three years with a 15 per cent. commission on whatever contracts he obtained. Secker had made a three-book contract with Frederick Stokes of America, but Pinker arranged a much more handsome contract afterwards with George Doran.

My mother had started her Theatre Girls' Club in 1915: in 1918 after my father's death she had this formally incorporated as a recognized charity, and the new premises acquired at 59 Greek Street, Soho, were solemnly blessed by the Bishop of London. Now she was determined to give my sisters Viola and Katie an opportunity to shine, and was proposing to turn the Grand Theatre, Nottingham, into a repertory theatre. She had found partnership with Milton Bode irksome and was getting herself bought out of her half share in five theatres. I promised to write another version of *Carnival*, which had to be called *Columbine* because Matheson Lang had acquired an Italian play called *Scirocco* and renamed it *Carnival*. (Twenty years later a third-rate thriller called itself *Sinister Street*.) There is no copyright in the title of a play or of a book provided it can be shown that neither is a colourable imitation of the work thus previously named. Matheson Lang was a cousin of Cosmo Lang, the future Archbishop of Canterbury, and was equally determined to believe that he was infallible.

I succumbed to the prevailing epidemic of squandermania, as it was called, which had followed the restrictions of war-time, and bought a very expensive pigskin dressing-case at Finnigan's in Bond Street and an almost equally expensive dressing-case for Faith.

I had suggested to my mother that her Repertory Theatre in Nottingham should produce Lawrence's two plays. An undated latter of his, probably of that May, expresses his reaction:

Got your letter last night. We were away at Randazzo for 3 days. About the theatre thrilling but terrifying! You know my horror of the public! Well, it's a phobia of phobias in Nottingham. Nottingham! Cursed, cursed Nottingham, gutless, spineless, brainless Nottingham how I hate thee! But if my two plays could be thrown so hard into thy teeth as to knock thy teeth out, why then, good enough.

There are only two plays. "The Widowing of Mrs Holroyd" which Duckworth published years ago and "Touch and Go" which Daniel is publishing this minute. . . . I confess that the very thought of the plays in Nottingham gives me such a fright I almost feel like deserting my own identity. But where the public is concerned I am a veritable coward. . . . My idea of a play is that any actor should have the liberty to alter as much as he likes—the author only gives the leading suggestion. Verbatim reproduction seems to me nonsense. I should like to see the things done and done properly. Oh, if there were actors! I'd like to be there to beat the actors into acting. What terrifying thrills ahead! But I must see you soon. Hang it all, you must be better, not so seedy. I hope to finish the novel in 1 week. If we have to talk plays I shall have to hop over to Capri. But read the plays first.

We went to Maniace to the Duca's. God, what a Duca! Shall write a farcical comedy.

> *Trust your're better.*
> *D.H.L.*

Lawrence's interest in the possible production of his plays in Nottingham was evanescent, as a letter of June 11th from Fontana Vecchia shows:

I didn't write you because I didn't know if you'd gone. I hear this minute from Miss Wallace you are in Rome: so you are en route. How thrilling. With my mind's eye I see Nukahiva. Ah God! Such a lovely sea here to-day, and a great white ship on the wind, making towards the South-East. I'd give my fingers to be off. I read some of Stevenson. Idiot to go to Samoa just to dream and get thrilled about Scotch bogs and moors. No wonder he died. If I go to Samoa, it will be to forget, not to remember.

I read ½ of "The Lost Girl" in type—wonder how she'll seem to other people. It's different from all my other work; not immediate, not intimate—except the last bit: all set across a distance. It just came like that. May seem dull to some people— I can't judge.

Vanity Girl came yesterday—have only just glanced at it. Mary is Hotel Bristol, Taormina.
Send thrilling news—all news.

D.H.L.

Read Herman Melville's "Moby Dick".

It was at the very end of June that I sent Lawrence news of having found what I believed was the perfect craft for the South Seas. This was the ketch *Lavengro*, 134 tons. Her length on the load line was 84 ft.; her beam was 19 ft. She was coppered. She had four boats including a motor-launch. She had a large saloon, four cabins and a smoking-lounge. She had 54 tons of lead as ballast. Her sail area was 6,136 sq. ft. Her price was 7,500 guineas.

I talked about *Lavengro* to Jack Squire, who believed himself to be very knowledgeable on the subject of sailing craft, and he volunteered to drive down with me to Burnham-on-Crouch where she was lying. I remember saying "Billéricay" as we drove through with as much care-free disregard of the right pronunciation of a place-name as a B.B.C. announcer of the future. "Billerícay," said Jack Squire severely. "Not Billéricay."

I wrote enthusiastically about the ketch to Lawrence, who wrote back from Fontana Vecchia on June 30th:

The Lavengro of course thrills me to my marrow. Yes, I'd sail the Spanish Main in her. How big was Drake's ship? Is she steam as well as sails? How many men do you consider you'd want to run her? I pace out her length on the terrace below. Is she a pure pleasure yacht? She sounds narrow in the beam—though I know nothing at all about it. I suppose she's pretty. Why, one would soon learn to be an A.B. oneself: ar at least $\dfrac{AB.}{2}$ *And one could be one's own steward and a good bit of one's own cook. If ever I have any money I'll go whacks in her—running her.*

For It's westward ho to Trinidad. Don't believe Duckworth[1]: he's an old woman. One only needs guts: and his are nothing but lard. We've only one life: best live it.

London sounds sickening as ever. Curse these strikes. I hate Labour and Capitalism and all that frowsty duality in nothingness. What a pity I haven't got a bit of money. I shall have some, you'll see, before long.

> *You can sell Capri. Anybody can have Capri.*
> *I'm glad she's not called the Bible in Spain.*
> *Round the world if need be.*
> *And round the world again—*

[1] The late Gerald Duckworth, a favourite Savilian of mine.

If you do buy her, then I beg you, send me a book where I can learn all about sloops, yachts, clippers and frigates, clewlines and bowlines and topsle gallants, ensigns and mizzens, forepeaks and so on, for I feel it's a question of becoming sea-born.

I shan't pray because I believe Jesus is no good at sea. But I'll invoke Aphrodite and Poseidon and Dionysos, and keep my eye on the Mediterranean.

                                                             D.H.L.

On July 8th Lawrence sent me a postcard:

Am dying to hear about the Lavengro. Hope it's a go. I've got a VERY GOOD *book from America about the Marquesas Islands—"White Shadows on the South Seas" by Frederick O'Brien. It gives a real impression of the Marquesas as they are now. I'll send it if you like. Also Gauguin's "Noa Noa", which is Marquesas too. O'Brien's book published last year, but written presumably 1913-14. Best thing I've read of late year travels. Say if you like it.*

It is hot here, but I don't mind. I wish we could sail away away from Europe. F. talks of going to Germany in August, but I shan't. Expect a letter every day from you.

                                                             D.H.L.

One of the projects Lawrence and I had discussed over and over again that winter was to take a selected group of people to re-colonize the Kermadec Islands, the description of which in the *Pacific Pilot* fired our fancy. True, there was occasionally an eruption on Sunday or Raoul Island, the largest of the group, and it had been evacuated in consequence. I had written to Pember Reeves, who was then the New Zealand High Commissioner and a member of the Savile, asking him to ascertain the views of his Government about such a project. In the very week I saw *Lavengro* he had heard that the Kermadec Islands, over 400 miles north of Auckland, had been leased to a New Zealander.

Nevertheless, for the next few weeks I made great efforts to raise the money for that ketch. Then in August Martin Secker, who had all the while been struggling against the South Seas plan, showed me an advertisement in *The Times* inviting applications for a sixty-years lease of the island of Herm at £900 a year and of the island of Jethou at £100 a year.

"I'm sure this would be much better than going to the South Seas," he urged.

I agreed with Secker that if I could obtain the leases of both islands the Channel Isles might supplant the South Seas in my dreams. Completely convinced as I was that I must withdraw from that post-war world of London, Herm and Jethou seemed to offer the opportunity. I sent in my application, saying that I would not take Herm without Jethou.

As I look back on that July it becomes a whirl in my memory in which sequence vanishes. I go to see Fay as Mary Rose at the Haymarket and find the play impossible in spite of her enchanting performance. Jean Cadell and Ernest Thesiger are good, but Robert Loraine is a bad joke as the young man.

I have one of my goes of pain but insist on getting up next day to lunch with Fay at the Berkeley. Barrie and Ernest Thesiger are in the party. After lunch we go to Berry Brothers at 3 St James's Street where Barrie, Thesiger, Faith and Fay are weighed. I had been weighed a fortnight earlier with Martin Secker—10 st. 12½ lb. and 9 st. 9 lb. I am surprised to find that Barrie weighs only a pound and a half less than I do. I am not less surprised to find that my wife and my sister are both over 10 stone. People had been weighed in that machine since the eighteenth century and our weights are recorded with Charles James Fox and other famous figures of the past.

To-day it is high time that Lord Boothby got himself weighed in this historic establishment. Charles James Fox reached 13 st. 12 lb. in "Boots and Frock". Would Bob Boothby beat that in "Shoes and Dittos"?

I meet Noel Coward, who is an ebullient twenty-one, full of the exitement of his first play, *I Leave it to You*: I see him bobbing along beside me past Devonshire House and hear him telling me about war's having been declared on him by the Sitwells. My most vivid memory of the play is losing a pearl-stud from my shirt-front.

At the beginning of the month I met Rebecca West at one of Violet Hunt's parties on Campden Hill. That huge futuristic head of Ford Madox Hueffer was still in the little front-garden of Holly Lodge; Ford himself was in Paris with the *avant garde* of literature.

Rebecca was half through her novel *The Judge*, which according to H. G. Wells was an addled egg on which she should give up sitting. I thought it was very good and suggested she should go out to Capri when Faith went back in the autumn and somehow finish *The Judge*. She had written some viciously clever hostile reviews of my books and I asked her why the critics had all turned against me. I can see now her expression under the floppy summer hat she was wearing and recapture the very tone of her voice as she turns and asks:

"Are you surprised? Don't you realize that you've been given much too much for people to bear it?"

Rebecca told me that H. G. would like to meet me again and I went along to Queen's Gate, where he and I talked about that dramatic version of *Kipps* I had made fourteen years earlier and wondered whether Ideal Films would produce it as a film. They had just acquired the rights of *Sinister Street* to be included in a series of novels old and new with which they were proposing to infuse life into the British cinema.

I had tried to persuade one of the cinema companies in England to give me a craft that could be made to look like an eighteenth-century schooner with half a dozen actors and actresses and let me go out to the South Seas and make films of *Treasure Island*, the *Mutiny of the Bounty*, the story of Bully Hayes, the story of that preposterous Wesleyan minister Shirley Baker who had terrorized Tonga in the 'nineties, and two or three other tales. I suggested such an undertaking would require three years and offered to play in all the films myself. The notion much appealed to Lloyd Osbourne, who considered coming out himself to play Long John Silver with myself doubling the Squire with Ben Gunn.

Such a plan was rejected as ridiculous by a British cinema company.

"To begin with, costume films don't appeal to the cinema public," I was told. "And anyway if we wanted to make a film about the South Seas we can get all that's necessary for the South Seas with a couple of palms stuck in the sand at Southport."

It is not surprising that British films were so slow in making any impression on the rest of the world while minds like that were running them.

Pinker was on the verge of selling *The Vanity Girl* to Paramount for £3,000, but at the last moment they decided the American public would be unable to accept the marriage of the heroine to the financier and that if the film ended with the death of her husband in action it would be unsatisfactorily sad. So the deal did not go through.

At the end of July I went up to Oxford for the Magdalen Gaudy. The only other two of my contemporaries at the dinner were Harry Pirie-Gordon and Hugh Francis. I found it all a little melancholy; the modernization of Gunner's room by Gynes deepened that melancholy.

On August 20th I was notified that the Treasury had accepted me as the tenant of Herm and Jethou. Martin Secker was jubilant and we arranged to go over to the Channel Isles at the weekend to visit my exciting acquisition.

We crossed by the day-boat from Southampton, putting up at Gardiner's Royal Hotel in Guernsey. Next morning we went to see Victor Carey,[1] the Receiver General, to conclude all the signing which accompanies such occasions. Carey told me I had been lucky in being able to persuade the Treasury to let me have both islands. It seemed that in 1881 Colonel Fielding, the tenant, had indulged in smuggling brandy from Jethou to England; he had been depried of both islands and a rule had been made that they should never both be held by the same tenant again.

Herm had been for many years in possession of Prince Blücher von Wahlstatt and when war was declared on Germany in 1914 Prince

---

[1] The late Sir Victor Carey.

Blücher had been deported. His son, Count Lothair, was a British subject and had been allowed to serve as a subaltern in a British labour battalion. Prince Blücher had married a beautiful young Radzywill and almost immediately afterwards Lothair had married her elder sister; he and she were living in Guernsey. Prince Blücher had naturalized wallabies on Herm, and when the island was occupied by a detachment of South Staffords under the command of Herbert Hughes[1] none of the men would go out patrolling at night alone, because one of them had been attacked by a ghost.

"It must have been a wallaby that went jumping by him in the dark," Hughes laughed.

"You should have incorporated that wallaby in a folk-song," I told him.

One of the provisions of the lease set out that visitors were to be allowed to land on Herm twice a week to visit the unique shell beach on payment of a toll of sixpence, of which the tenant had to pay twopence to the Treasury, representing King George V's inheritance from the Dukedom of Normandy. Visitors could be excluded entirely from Jethou, the last tenant of which had been Sir Henry Austin Lee.[2]

I can feel the magic of Herm still when I remember the time I stepped out of the *Watch Me*, the island boat with her bearded skipper, and walked up the steps to set foot for the first time upon the little granite pier. I extract from an article about Herm which I wrote for *The Times* about a year later a few paragraphs to give a rough idea of it.

"Herm is three miles from Guernsey and 30 miles from France; the Little Russell which separates it from Guernsey is a dangerous water beset by rocks, tides, currents and winds. The diminutive harbour of Herm was constructed in the days when granite was quarried from the island, the quality of which may be observed by walking down the steps from Carlton House Terrace to the Mall; their edges are as sharp as on the day when they were cut. The Herm quarries have long been abandoned and they are fair spots now, the sides covered with ivy and honeysuckle, the depths green with ferns, the shelves bright with gorse and blackthorn, the crevices and fissures stuffed with moneywort and seapink, with sheep-bit and campion in their seasons. From the harbour near which are an old inn and a dozen cottages, a road winds up a steep 250 feet to the Manor House.

"Trappist monks who held the island for some time about forty years ago planted the Monterey pines (*insignis*) and the Monterey cypresses (*macrocarpa*). There are elms and silver poplars and, I regret to add, blue gum trees, the rattle of whose leaves in the wind is like a bunch of

---

[1] The late Herbert Hughes of folk-song.
[2] Sir Henry Austin Lee, K.C.M.G., d. 1918.

rusty keys in the hand of a caretaker. The banks are thick with prim-
roses, bluebells and foxgloves in order of blooming, and halfway up the
road a meadow ascends between coppices of blackthorn to the top of the
world and beyond that to a grove of pines planted by my predecessor.
That grove on the highest point of the island is a magic place. Prince
Blücher was less happy as a builder than as a planter, and he made the
Manor House what is externally as ugly a building as may be seen in
Europe. Nevertheless, there is a chapel of the early fourteenth century
attached to it, and embedded among its castellation is a little house of
the eighteenth century. The garden of the Manor House surrounded by
pines and a wall of Cyclopean dimensions, is intersected by broad ilex-
bordered walks that are worthy of the Borghese Gardens.

"Outside the garden the road runs north and south along the spine of
the island. Southward it disappears in gorse and heather on the top of
high cliff. Northward it runs past the farm buildings between meadows
and fields until it ends in what is called the Common, though why a
proprietary island should possess a Common I do not know. This tract
of land is dominated by two isolated hills called the Grand Monceau
and the Petit Monceau, solemn aspectful hills from the summit of
which runs a long chain of cromlechs. All about here are megaliths,
mostly stone circles and kysts. Nine mighty menhirs are shown in a map
of Henry VIII's time; these must long ago have been carried off by
pirate builders, and nothing remains except an obelisk which was
evidently maintained as a day-mark for mariners.

"The Common is rectangular and the beaches, glorious beaches
composed of shells, lie due east, due north, and due west, each about
half a mile long. Short sweet turf predominates, interspersed with sandy
drifts and beds of glaucous reeds. Bushes of eglantine grow among the
reeds; in June the whole surface of the Common is starred with the little
burnet rose (*spinosissima*) and the air above is sweet with the fragrance
of it. The east side of the island is sheer to the jade-green sea, although
at low tide once can walk among the granite boulders at the foot of the
cliffs and explore a dozen caves, one of which is the colour of lilac
and full of sea-anemones like strawberries, and another of which drips
with what apparently is blood. The island is about five miles round
and a mile and a half long. The farm has a hundred acres of arable
land."

As we walked round Herm upon that sunny September afternoon I
felt what Dorothy Osborne felt when three centuries earlier she wrote
in a letter:

Do you remember Arme (Herm) and the little house there? Shall we go thither?
That is next too being out of the worlde, there we may live like Baucis and

Philemon, grow old together in your little cottage and for charity to some ship-wrecke stranger obtaine the blessing of dying both at the same time.

How idly I talk!

Eric Brett Young did not fancy living on Herm, and for that I was glad because by now I had decided he was not what I wanted as a secretary, and I was saved from having to tell him this myself.

On September 12th Lawrence wrote from c/o Thomas Cook, Florence:

Dear M.

What is this I hear about Channel Isles?

The Lord of the Isles.

I shall write a skit on you one day. There will be a lady of the Lake in it, and a rare to do between the pair.

I am sitting in a rambling old explosion-shattered villa out under Fiesole: like it. Douglas away with his amico, Reggie back from Capri, rather shaky. . . .

My novel jerks one chapter forward now and then. It is half done. But where the other ½ is coming from, asks the Divine Providence.

Frieda gone to Munich—enjoying Germany; peasant drama and marionettes and return to innocent bare-footed dance under heaven. One of the reactions with sentimental naiveté, I presume. At same time she says there is a very bad feeling between French and German now brewing. She proposes to come back early October. Suppose we shall dribble our way to Taormina.

I bought a very nice old travel book. "An Account of the Pelew Islands" by Captain Williams wrecked in the "Antelope" on those shores 1783. It is a quiet, very pleasing narrative and a book something like your Mariner's Tonga. . . .

If only it were about the Channel Isles, I'd send it to you.

Tell Secker I sent what proofs came—from Venice, about a fortnight since. Nothing has come to me later.

Very hot still here and no rain to speak of. Am alone in this villa at San Gennaio—save for gardener's family at the back.

Tanti saluti,

D.H.L.

I think it must have been that very heavy pigskin dressing-case into the acquisition of which I had been lured by squandermania that made me decide I must have a valet to deal with it. Anyway, I engaged at a wage of £3 a week Thompson, who had been the valet of Lord Lansdowne. Perhaps he lacked some of the richness of Jeeves, but as a guide to high life below stairs he was superlative. He had endless tales of his late master.

"I always had to know when to change his blotting-paper. If I changed it too soon he would ask me how I thought he could afford the extravagant way I treated his blotting-paper. If I left it too long he would ask me if I was trying to spoil his handwriting by giving him blotting-paper that wouldn't blot. Once he wasn't satisfied with the way I had polished his boots. 'Thompson,' he said to me, 'am I or am I not a Marquess?' 'Yes, my lord,' I said. 'I ask if you consider those the boots of a Marquess?'

"But he had to admit sometimes I was right. I remember once him telling me it wasn't ribbons and stars and when he came back he said: 'Thompson,' he said, 'you was right.' Oh, I must give him that. He was never afraid to admit when he was in the wrong. One of my bothers was that his lordship liked to sleep in cashmere sheets and her ladyship always wanted linen sheets. My goodness, when I think of the arguments I've had over their bed when we've been staying at Chatsworth or Belvoir or wherever it might be away from Bowood. Her ladyship's maid would insist that his lordship's cashmere was too much on her side and then I'd have to argue his lordship couldn't sleep on two feet of cashmere. Oh, it was chronic, specially at Windsor where the housemaids always used to create about those sheets."

And then Thompson's talks of etiquette below stairs:

"When we were at Windsor it didn't matter whether we'd been loading all the morning, we had to be in black coats for lunch. We were always given the precedence of our masters. So I was always right up near the top of the table. Among ourselves we always called ourselves by our Masters' name. I'd always be 'Lansdowne' for example, if any of them spoke to me. When the time came for the sweet the butler and the housekeeper used to get up and go into the housekeeper's room where us valets and lady's maids were to follow them."

On October 7th Lawrence was writing from Venezia:

Dear M.

I have been hearing about the islands, Herm and the one ending in "hou". They sound rather fascinating. Are you going to farm Herm?—and who is going to be your farmer? I've half a mind to come and help in the stormy Channel. Tell me about Herm, anyway. Are you going to make a Cinema studio on Herm really, or is that just gossip? They sound expensive, but probably you can make them pay.

I expect Frieda here to-day—then we shall go almost at once to Taormina . . . want to get back and work; have done nothing but a little book of vers libre, which please me. I can't do anything in Venice. Italy feels awfully shakey and nasty, and for the first time my unconscious is uneasy of the Italians. I wonder how you find Nottingham. I dread it for you because I loathe the town. But I hope all goes merrily. Tell me about it.

I'll write to my sister. You might have tea with her in some café. She lives out of town.

Yrs,

D.H.L.

My sister is Mrs Clarke, Grosvenor Rd, Ripley nr Derby. She comes to Nottingham every Wednesday.

My memory of directing the rehearsals of *Columbine* at Nottingham that autumn is cloudy. However, I do remember sharply an extremely sympathetic and extremely able young editor of the *Nottingham Journal* whose name was Cecil Roberts. He wrote a "Silhouette" of me in his paper from which I hope the Cecil Roberts of to-day will not mind my quoting a line or two:

"I have reviewed all his novels with the exception of his first from which task age alone incapacitated me, and I have yet to experience a better thrill of anticipation than that aroused by the publisher's advance copy."

From ten years earlier at the Alhambra two of the quartette *Chintz and China* in Pélissier's revue *All Change Here* appeared in the dressing-room scene—Nellie Digby and Christine Maude. Christine Maude, of whom I wrote in my Fourth Octave, was the original of Jenny Pearl; for her that scene every night in the Grand Theatre, Nottingham, was an amusing interlude before she was once again Mrs John Mavrogordato and the mother of a small son. She did not continue to act in the play when it went on from Nottingham for a fortnight to Kennington and then for a month to the Prince's Theatre in London.

On October 25th Lawrence wrote from Fontana Vecchia:

Dear M.

Your letter to-day. We got back here last week—peace and stillness and cleanness, flowers, rain, streams, birds singing, sea dim and hoarse: valley full of cyclamens; poem to them among other vers libre.

Today Lost Girl, brown and demure and anything but lost looking. Glad you were amused. She looks testamental.

Heard from my sister who saw Columbine and loved it. Heard from my elder sister, that Nottingham thought it a great success.

Heard all about Herm from a man called Hansard: sounds very lovely. I must come and see it next year. Meanwhile write me more about it. Who is going to farm it? How many houses? Are you letting or having a farm bailiff? News!

We are quite alone at Taormina. I haven't been out to see who, English, is here. Feel I don't want. Prefer to be quite alone this winter, rather than that sort of well-to-do riff-raff, Ducas, etc. Don't feel at all drawn to Capri—do you? N. Douglas has gone to Mentone with his René.

Frieda back very chirpy from Germany: me pledged to go there in spring. Who knows what spring will bring.
You seem all business now.

D. H. *Lawrence*

The Repertory Theatre lasted for over two years at Nottingham, by the end of which my mother had lost too much money to carry on. Nevertheless, later on she started a repertory theatre at Cheltenham and managed to lose a good deal more.

Faith with Rebecca West went to Capri in October before the play came to London.

Meanwhile, Ideal Films had been going ahead with turning *Sinister Street* into a film. I was taken to see some of the "rushes". To my consternation I was shown Lord Saxby in full regimentals of the Welsh Guards, bearskin and all, riding along a country lane to have tea with Mrs Fane.

"But look," I protested to the two little Jewish brothers who were managing Ideal Films, "a Colonel in the Guards would not go to tea in the country dressed up like that. He must be in mufti."

The two Rowsons smiled.

"What you must try and understand, Mr Mackenzie, is that the cinema audience wants rómance. We must give them rómance. There's no rómance in a suit of dittoes."

That was the last I saw of *Sinister Street* as a film. The caricature of *Sylvia Scarlett* made later in Hollywood for Katherine Hepburn to star in I avoided altogether. I also managed to avoid seeing more than two or three rushes of the second film of *Carnival*, made in the 'thirties. Of the third film of *Carnival*, made by Filippo del Giudice in the 'forties, I thought I had managed to avoid seeing even one of the rushes. Then one evening in April 1947 I was sitting next Sir Mark Young, the Governor of Hong Kong, at a performance of a dreadful film about Paganini in which Stewart Granger was starring. Suddenly in the interval a trailer of the third *Carnival* film appeared. I just caught a glimpse of Michael Wilding in a cloak before I buried my head in my hands.

The Governor protested,

"You mustn't do that. The owners of the theatre will lose face and I shall be held responsible."

So I had to look at two or three more rushes, thankful to Providence that Paganini had been the chief figure on the screen that evening, not Jenny Pearl. It was not until 1949 that *Whisky Galore* was able to make me sit through a film based on one of my own books, and for the first time recognize some of my own characters.

London was becoming more and more oppressive. Not even the

N

pleasure of reading Mrs Asquith's lively memoirs lightened the gloom of that late autumn. The damnable way in which the Coalition Government was handling Ireland was heavy on my spirit, and the stupid way in which they were handling the Greek situation after the return of King Constantine by the universal demand of the Greek people did nothing to lighten it.

Not even an invitation from Edmund Gosse to attend an annual dinner he gave for Mr Asquith could keep me in London. I much regret now my failure to meet one of the very few politicians I could wholeheartedly admire and respect. I have a souvenir of that invitation in a note from Gosse:

> 17 Hanover Terrace,
> Regent's Park,
> N.W.1.
> *December 8, 1920*
>
> *My dear Compton,*
> *It was a sad disappointment, for you would have been the life and soul of the party. But I look forward to a happier occasion. It was very kind of you to give me good warning. George Moore takes your empty chair.*
> *Glory to Herm and its new ruler! Peace to Jethou!*
> *Ever Yours*
> *Edmund Gosse*

I stayed at Gardiner's Royal Hotel on the front at Guernsey, getting over to Herm occasionally on fine days during December; I soon began to realize that running an island of 400 acres is not so easy as it had sounded. I was lucky to make friends at the Guernsey Club with a sympathetic architect, R. V. Quilter, with whom I made an arrangement to superintend the alterations necessary at Herm for a regular salary. At the Club, where we played pool with as much passion as they played snooker at the Savile, I made friends with Lothair Blücher. He and the Countess had an agreeable house in which were some of the David pictures looted from Paris by his great-grandfather after Waterloo. Poor Lothair was a sad man; he had felt strongly the refusal of the military authorities to let him have a commission in one of the fighting battalions. He was worried, too, by the way the Czechs were confiscating estates of his in Bohemia.

After dinner one evening Countess Blücher said to me suddenly:

"I am badly worried about you. When the British Government expelled my father-in-law, my sister, who adored Herm, solemnly prayed to the island spirits that they would bring misfortune to the next tenant. She would never have done that if she had ever met you. I am worried."

At the time I lightly dismissed what was in effect a curse, but promised the Countess with half a smile that I would do my utmost to appease the spirits of the island.

The first problem I had to settle was where I was going to live on the island. Lothair and his wife had lived in the old inn which was close to the harbour. This they had made comfortable, and it was now known as the White House. I felt I should not want to live indefinitely so near to the sea's edge on account of the confounded sciatica attacks; at the same time I could not see myself at home in the Manor House. In the end I decided to make my own headquarters a cottage looking into the garden some twenty yards away from the Manor, but that was later. Meanwhile there was plenty for Quilter to do in getting the farm buildings back into good order, not to mention nearly a dozen cottages.

During the war Herm had been farmed by an amusing drunkard called Wheadon who was still living in a small house above Belvoir cove, which had been the private bathing-beach of the Blüchers. Fortunately Harding, who had farmed the island for Prince Blücher and had continued to do his best for it in spite of Wheadon's irresponsibility, was still on Herm and I immediately took him on as my farmer.

Harding was one of the most precious figures my memory holds. He had come to Herm over fifty years ago to Colonel Fielding from the Druids' Lodge Stable in Wiltshire where he had been an apprentice. Not a day passed without his having some tale of the past. I hear him now describing the life of an apprentice jockey in the 1860's.

"We were locked in every night above the stables and there were iron bars on the stable doors, and the littlest thing we did wrong we got it with the whip we called Long Tom."

And would that I could remember the story of three poachers called Savage, Tripe, and Snipe, but alas, only their names remain.

One day when he was telling tales of the cock-fighting on Herm, which some of the young and not so young Guernseymen used to attend surreptitiously, he showed me a cock's spur, "wicked, bean't it?" he commented, but a twinkle in his eye let me know he had not enjoyed the sport less for its cruelty and illegality.

The cover for that cock-fighting at the old inn was a skittle-alley, which was now used as a store-room.

In spite of not having seen his native Wiltshire for fifty years, Harding had not lost a single tone of that rich dialect. He sighed for the agricultural glories of Herm's past in the days of Colonel Fielding, since when its glories had grown dimmer each year until Wheadon had snuffed them out completely.

"Darn it, Wheadon didn't know nought about a farm. Even the old ram was too good for him. 'Damn his blood, do he think he be the boss of this island? I'll show him,' but it were the old ram as showed Wheadon. And did I laugh when I seed him chasing Wheadon three times round the little barn? And he was a great one for a barrel of beer. 'I can do more when I'm drunk than any other man on the island can when he's sober.' "

I enjoyed Wheadon's company and was sorry in a way to see him go, though he would have been a problem if he had remained. When I think of those talks with Harding, who was small and thin as one might have expected in somebody who once was going to be a jockey, I am glad to remember his saying to me after a long gossip that I did make him sweat with laughing.

Harding's only child was married to Captain Attewell and they were both living in the White House until the farmhouse was put in order. Attewell had been a sergeant-major in the Royal Fusiliers whose gallantry had earned him a commission in the war. I liked him at once and offered him the job of agent or factor. His devotion and loyalty to me were so complete that I could never bring myself to hurt him by telling him when he did something really stupid, and only too often he would do very stupid things.

Our transport was the *Watch Me*; a sixty-year-old vessel with an auxiliary engine that was continually breaking down. Captain Mauger, the white-bearded skipper, was an extremely competent mariner, but like most competent mariners considered that his boat was much more important than the people in it, or for that matter the people on the island. He had as his number two a temperamental but excellent seaman, Freddie Zabiela, whose origin nobody ever discovered; opinion as a whole inclined to the theory that he was a gypsy.

My visits to Herm that December were determined by Captain Mauger's opinion of the weather. On one occasion I insisted on crossing and had to spend the night on the island, sleeping on a mattress in the as yet unfurnished White House, after which I never ventured again to over-ride Captain Mauger's decision about the weather. Thompson, who had had to sleep on the floor without a mattress, told me firmly that he thought I should listen next time to what Captain Mauger said.

So December passed into January after a jolly Christmas at the Royal Hotel with lots of dancing and plenty of good food.

On my thirty-eighth birthday *Rich Relatives* was published by Secker and received by the critics with a kind of compassionate generosity after *The Vanity Girl*. Probably the prodigal son was treated by the other guests with the same kind of compassionate generosity when they were tucking in to the fatted calf provided by his lovable old father.

Three days later I left Guernsey for Herm.

ABOUT a week after I had established myself on Herm I wrote to tell Martin Secker I thought I had made a mistake. Herm looked like being a much heavier responsibility than I had realized. Secker, who felt partially responsible for my abandoning the South Seas for the Channel Islands, wrote back reassuringly; the temporary anxiety about the future passed. I was soon absorbed by the multiform problems that possession of an island like Herm entailed, and my sanguine temperament convinced me I could solve them and make Herm pay for itself; that eternal creative urge was asserting itself.

De Putron, who ran the Caledonian Nurseries in Guernsey, entered into my floral plans for the future with enthusiasm, and for the next ten years I should obtain from him invaluable help. He wrote to Sir Frederick Moore, the head of the Glasnevin Botanical Gardens in Dublin, to ask if he could suggest a young gardener for Herm. Sir Frederick recommended as the most promising member of his staff a young man of about twenty-four, already married. Keegan was a gardener of great skill and remained with me for over ten years.

The other necessity was an estate carpenter, and I was lucky enough to engage George Macdonald, slightly lame, but a master of his craft. He was the son of a sergeant in a Highland regiment quartered in Alderney who had settled there when he left the army. Mrs Macdonald was also of military Highland origin. The Macdonalds came with me when I moved from Herm to Jethou and later to Inverness-shire. When I moved to Barra they went back to work for my successor in Jethou; even the Germans left them there during the occupation. Macdonald is now dead, but I still hear every Christmas, Easter and on my birthday from Mrs Macdonald in Alderney.

On February 7th Lawrence wrote from Fontana Vecchia:

Dear M.

We had your three postcards from Herm, with much interest. I didn't answer because you said a letter was following.

I should like awfully to come to Herm for a week or two in the early summer. Would there be anywhere where we could have a lodging? And where my sister could come and stay with us for a fortnight? They insist I should go to England, but I loathe the thought of going to England, and it might by great fun to meet in Herm. I am so wondering what it is all like: if it has that Celtic fascination.

I am fighting my way through various pieces of work: and through life. It works out to a long fight, in which one doesn't emerge as much of a winner so far. Heard from B-Y. Off for Jo-burg.

Hope you're well,

D.H.L.

I saw Lawrence two or three times in London later that year, but to my regret he never managed to come to Herm.

I had a great deal of pain that February. Lying awake all night, I read a novel called *Main Street* which had been sent to me by the American publishers Harcourt Brace. Next day I telegraphed Martin Secker to make every effort to secure British rights; unfortunately Hodder and Stoughton beat him to it. I wrote to Harcourt Brace and received a letter from Sinclair Lewis at *1639 19th Street, N.W. Washington, D.C.*—*but written, this March 19th, on three strips of stationery, picked up at Chicago, where I have been quasi lecturing!*

Dear Mr Mackenzie,

My publisher has sent me a copy of your extraordinarily generous letter about "Main Street". I wish I had an adequate way of thanking you. I hope that perhaps I may some day encounter you in London. My wife and I are planning to go abroad, for a year or two, this coming May and some time I may be so fortunate as to have a drink with you in some consolingly unprohibited inn at Capri.

I wonder if you know that in an earlier novel of mine, "Free Air" (which bears such relation to "Main Street" as your "Poor Relations" does to "Sinister Street") I had a prairie youngster discovering "Sinister Street" and in it finding a revelation of the Great World which, in his horrible little town, had been denied him . . . and in another novel "The Job", the drab heroine attains to "a library of Wells and Compton Mackenzie and Anatole France" and so is at last happy. . . .

From these references you may guess my admiration for your books and my consequent pride in your liking for "Main Street".

It's Mackenzie with a small "k" isn't it? That's my memory of it, but, damn it, in this abysmal house of a Kind Relative, where I am being dutiful for three days before returning to Washington, there is, of course, nothing in which to look it up.

Hodder and Stoughton are to publish "Main Street" in England. Some time in June, if you happen to be in England won't you send me a note c/o Hodder, and let me come round and say how d'ye do to you? I rather fancy my wife and I will find a small house in Hampstead and stay there till, say, October.

Thank you for your letter!

Sincerely yours,

Sinclair Lewis

Main Street appeared and was dismissed by the *Times Literary Supplement* in half a dozen lukewarm lines. I wrote to protest, but my letter was not printed.

On July 12th Sinclair Lewis wrote from the Poldhu Hotel, Mullion, Cornwall:

Dear Mr Mackenzie,

I have just been turning over the pages of "Sinister Street", thinking of the pleasure I shall have in re-reading it. I've read it twice before. Three years ago when my wife and I were getting ourselves to stay as long as we could in a dull little Middle Western town I used to read just a bit of it every day as an antidote to get me through the day . . . this is perhaps one of the few times that your book, which has been to most readers a pure delight, was also at once a Social Document, and an opiate—or, as we say in the States, a shot of dope!

Thank you for your invitation to Herm. I wonder if we might come in late August when we shall be in Kent . . . when we shall be settled and when I shall have done enough of the novel I began on July 5th so that running away will begin to be attractive.

This is a dull amiable place—admirable for writing and amusing to explore . . . the wife of the vicar summering here has just discovered that the vicar over at Mullion is guilty of Catholic practices. God! So, one who was reared a Minnesota Congregationalist cannot quite get up the proper sympathy . . . if I do not hear from you, I'll write to you in August.

Sincerely yours,
Sinclair Lewis

I have written of Schofield, that vicar guilty of Catholic practices, in my Fourth Octave, and of my preaching, morning and evening, at the patronal festival, and in my Third Octave of that thumping headache I once had in the Poldhu Hotel, never to be repeated.

On August 21st Lewis was writing from The Bell House, Bearsted, nr. Maidstone:

Dear Mackenzie,

Indeed, it would suit us very well indeed to come about September 20th instead of mid-August. There is to be a new governess for our four-year old and she will not appear till the first of September. Write me again sometime in September, won't you, please? And how does one go from here to Herm, without being engulfed in the mighty waters to the high detriment of American Realism (if any?)

We have this amiable half-timbered cottage till October 1st, a quiet place in a village green, and daily I struggle against an enormous novel. It seems at present highly improbable that any Human being can ever write all that my scheme calls for—improbable and, in a world where one can watch geese marching across the village green, rather undesirable.

Sincerely yours,
Sinclair Lewis

Was the novel to which Lewis alludes in that letter *Babbitt?* To my great disappointment the visit to Herm failed to come off and all I saw of him was at a very brief meeting we had in London when he was on the point of leaving England. To my mind the major novels of Sinclair Lewis are incomparably better than any that have been produced since in his genre. I was most pleasantly suprised when he was given the Nobel Prize; the Nobel Prize is seldom awarded to a novelist who has achieved the popular recognition which makes him suspect for academic opinion. Theodore Dreiser's *An American Tragedy* was, and for all I know may still be esteemed; I have never been able to tolerate the utterly execrable English in which it is written to read it through.

Some time that February I bought two horses in Guernsey. They arrived on the *Helper*; Edmund Gwenn was on board on his way to Sark. He introduced himself and then proceeded to assist most efficiently in the disembarkation, explaining that this had been one of his jobs during the war. On his way back from Sark next day Gwenn stopped at Herm for a few hours and I recall two of his stories.

One was of Henry Ainley at Shoeburyness, who as a cadet was not attending to the Instructor and on being ordered sharply to pay attention replied, pointing to the view, "Isn't it beautiful?"

Another was of an R.S.M. in the Gunners. One day word came that the Sergeant-Major wanted to see Driver Gwenn. Gwenn, wondering what military crime he had committed, went along to the Sergeant-Major's office. The great man was twisting his waxed moustaches with one hand and turning over papers with the other.

"Driver Gwenn," he said without looking up, "I see by your military history that before you joined the Royal Regiment of Artillery you were an actor. At the sports next Saturday you will dress up as a woman and amuse the women and children between the events. Right about!"

"And did you?" I asked.

"Oh yes. Driver Gwenn was not in a position to disobey the Sergeant-Major."

I had started *The Parson's Progress* but by the beginning of February I had realized that it was going to be a very long book and for two or three days I played with the notion of writing the last book in my agreement with Secker. I sketched out *The Seven Ages of Woman*, but in the end I decided to stick to what was now to be called *The Altar Steps*, ultimately the first of a trilogy of which *The Parson's Progress* would be the second volume.

Hamlet, a three-month-old black Great Dane puppy, was a great amusement. I recall Dora Giles, one of our maids, coming in much excited to say Hamlet had eaten half the Visitors' Book and adding,

"It's a wonder he didn't get hold of that man." That man was a terra-cotta statuette of the Belvedere Apollo.

A young Liverpool journalist called James Eastwood, who was stranded in Guernsey where he had come for his health, wrote to ask if I could make use of his typing and shorthand. I liked him and early in that spring he was housed on Herm. About the same time I felt that Nellie Baker and Hilary, her baby of fifteen months old, should be given asylum on Herm. Eastwood was excellent at dictation, but only Nellie Baker was able to tackle my handwriting and, although there was a certain amount of dubiety on her side of the family, Faith strongly approved of my suggestion. So "Mrs Blake" arrived, bringing with her a young woman who, justifiably or not, called herself Mrs Whybrow. Ethel Whybrow, who had served in the W.A.A.C. during the war, kept me steadily entertained with hilarious stories about female military life. Another permanent feature of Herm during that spring and summer was Donald Rea, a young parson, who had had a breakdown of health, and became well again by cutting more bracken than any individual had ever cut before. He was of great service to me in writing *The Altar Steps*, and is now Canon Rea of Diss in Norfolk.

The glorious weather of 1921 which began in March and lasted until October was disastrous for my first and last attempt at farming. To add to our difficulties old Harding got a bad leg and had to go into hospital in Guernsey. When I went up to see him the night before he left the island he told me a story of long ago when he had been given a packet of cigars which he had put in his pocket beside a powder-flask.

"I were smoking a cigar and without thinking what I were doing I put it quickly in my pocket to take a shot at a rabbit. My goodness, what a bang, and they cigars come out of a new worsted jacket I were wearing like bullets. 'You'm burning,' they all shouted at me. Well, what a darned silly remark, eh? As if I couldn't see I were burning. I were out of that new worsted jacket as quick as they cigars."

Not a drop of rain fell and the water supply on Herm was getting terribly low. A dowser came over, by whom I was not impressed. The crops were all suffering from the drought and the twice-a-week trippers were a great trial. Eastwood was given the job of collecting the sixpenny toll. The unwelcome visitors were allowed to walk about a mile along the road across the Common to the shell-beach, and most of them were content to do this; but of the 150 who reached the little harbour twice a week about a couple of dozen always had to believe that the freedom of the island was conferred upon them and in spite of having about a mile and a half of beach on which to picnic and collect shells and from which to bathe they would find their way to Belvoir cove and bathe there. Others would go wandering all over the island; they were a sad nuisance. On one occasion, Hamlet arrived back from Belvoir with a girl's panties, and presently I received a letter of protest from a young woman to ask why I did not keep my dangerous dog chained up. Decent people were turned into savages by the mere fact of having paid six-pence to land on a small island. I used to get letters complaining of the insolence of the young man who issued the tickets; that was Eastwood.

Faith arrived in Herm from Rome at the beginning of June. She had been enjoying a delightful visit to Ravello, where Stuart-Wortley and his wife Edwina, the famous soprano, had a villa. Faith obviously sighed for life in Italy, although she did her best to adapt herself to the complicated problems of the small island with which she believed I had foolishly saddled myself.

At the beginning of July the King and Queen arrived in Guernsey, the Royal yacht being escorted by the cruiser *Cleopatra*. General Capper,[1] the Lieutenant-Governor, kept issuing contradictory instructions about our dress for the occasion; Faith and I arrived in Guernsey to stay at the Royal Hotel with enough luggage for a month's stay instead of two nights. Thompson was critical of the Governor's failure to issue proper instructions about the clothes to be worn as he unpacked my Marine whites, a grey tail-suit and grey top-hat, and a black tail-suit and silk hat, the last of which had been the final instruction from the Governor on the morning before the royal visitors arrived.

To my pleasure Claude Kirby was on board the *Cleopatra* and we had a jolly lunch with Captain Stopford.

"My liberty men are wonderful," he told us. "You might think they'd find the cheap drink in Guernsey a temptation. Not at all."

Gin was 3s. a bottle and whisky 3s. 6d. Eheu fugaces!

Soon after this it was time to go ashore, and the tide being low we had to walk up a lot of steps at St Peter Port before reaching the top of the harbour. All the way liberty men, obviously very tight, supported one another as they tried to salute their Captain on his way up. I can see now Stopford's expression as he stared in front of him without seeming to notice his liberty men. Claude Kirby and I tactfully pretended that we, too, had not noticed those liberty men.

The Governor had made rather a mess of things for the disembarka-tion of their Majesties. Queen Mary had to walk 400 yards on that blazing day to the Royal car, and she looked really angry. The King was in naval whites and was better able to stand the sun.

In St George's Hall the King was to receive the homage of the Bailiff and the States of Guernsey, and also of the Seigneur of Sark. The Seigneur, who was known irreverently as "Moppy" Collins, was a splendidly eccentric character. He had to kneel and put the palms of

[1] The late Major-General Sir John Capper, K.C.B., K.C.V.O.

his hands against those of the King and offer his homage in Norman French. Somehow he knelt on the other side of a big tub of hydrangeas, and for a minute or two he and his feudal lord were bobbing about after one another round those hydrangeas before the Seigneur was kneeling in an attitude of feudal homage, palm against palm. Then his Majesty had to read his gracious reply to the States of Guernsey and in looking for his glasses he dropped the paper; I see again the magnificent gesture with which Queen Mary, who was holding a duplicate script, swept her arm in front of King George to turn herself as it were into a lectern from which he could read the gracious reply.

In the afternoon we went up to Government House to stand in a respectful line of Guernsey notables along which their Majesties walked while his Excellency named us one after another to bow or curtsey. That night there was a ball at the Old Government House Hotel, from which we went on at 3 a.m. to Gardiner's Royal Hotel, where we danced for another hour.

Next morning I walked round Herm with Maurice Headlam of the Treasury, who was full of compliments for the way I was getting down to the job of improving the Crown property administered by the Treasury. There was an amusing incident when the Royal yacht approached Herm on her way to Sark. A week or two earlier two shire mares I had bought for £100 apiece from George Sandwich had arrived from Hinchingbrooke. When they saw the Royal yacht approaching Blossom and Flower, as they were called, plunged into the sea and swam out a quarter of a mile, obviously feeling that they must pay homage to their Majesties on board; it was quite a business getting them back ashore, and no sooner were Blossom and Flower safe than our cowman came hurrying down the drive to say that Mildred, the new heifer, was down with sunstroke. Lothair Blücher had sold me Mildred, who came from one of the Guernsey prize herds, for only £25 because she had a small black patch on her nose. That ruled her out of ever winning a prize in a show but did not detract from the possible value of her progeny in the herd I was hoping to build up on Herm.

That blazing summer went on. Sheila Kaye-Smith came over from Sark two or three times with Trevor Blakemore. She looked absurdly young for her age but made no pretence of being younger than she was. She had already written several good and successful novels and was extremely modest about her considerable attainment and always kind about others. She had had an unsatisfactory love-affair with W. L. George, who had a vogue for some time as a novelist and made great play of being half-French. He and Munro ("Saki") had competed in cynical witticisms before the war, but Munro had joined up early and been killed, whereas George had managed to avoid any form of active service in what he called the Great European Bore. W. L. George was excellent company but there was something faintly sinister about him.

Sheila Kaye-Smith was already contemplating Catholicism and had some long and earnest talks with me about such a step. I was never a good proselytizer and no doubt I was careful to point out the disadvantage for a novelist of becoming a Holy Roman. I remember her with affection.

Another visitor was Captain Lance Sieveking, with whom I spent a plasant day which he has recorded in his excellent book *The Eye of the Beholder*.

Herm was beginning to seem too heavy a responsibility, and I was beginning to think of the South Seas again. George Lloyd, who was now Governor of Bombay, wrote to ask me to stay with him next winter, and I played with the notion of going on from Bombay to Colombo and thence to Australia with the South Seas as an ultimate goal.

I believe if Lawrence had come to Herm that June I should have decided to join him when he started off for the Southern Hemisphere.

On September 13th George Lloyd was writing from Government House, Gareskhind:

We will have you any time you care to come barring Nov. 17th to 24th when the Prince is here and we are full to the roof. Even if you wanted to come then we would find you a bed somewhere adjacent.

I should not think you were the least good at farming and you had better give it up before you go bankrupt, but I rather envy you your islands. Will you let me come and stay with you there some day when I come home?

On December 9th George Lloyd was writing from Government House, Bombay:

I am so sorry you cannot come out this winter. . . . I shut my eyes and think of the amazing portraits that lie before you to paint, especially some of those under G.H.Q. canvas at Imbros—Colonel Ward and that curious congerie of old Generals whose names I have entirely forgotten and who are now probably talking about it all in Cheltenham and Brighton clubs! . . .

I still regret that I never visited George Lloyd in Bombay. I hope I have been able to preserve something of that remarkable man's personality in *Gallipoli Memories*.

The Altar Steps was becoming a more and more formidable task, and what between recurrent bouts of pain putting me to bed for nearly a week at a time, the ever-growing expense of Herm, the continual interruptions of visitors and the merciless drought, I was oppressed by the reflection haunting sleepless nights of pain that in acquiring a 60-years lease of Herm at £900 a year I had made a grave mistake.

John and Christine Mavrogordato with young Nicolas spent some weeks in one of the cottages; Christopher and Alice Stone with Felicité Chinnery came to stay at the White House. Felicité, who was about eighteen, found in me a sympathetic listener to her stories of the way Mother could not understand why, those familiar stories for generations of Mother's inability to understand eighteen's emotional problems; Felicité and I used to sail away to Jethou, which was already beginning to seem an escape from the complications of Herm.

Earlier that summer Martin Secker had come to spend a week on Herm with Rina Capellero, a charming and extremely able Italian girl who had come to his rescue when his lack of Italian was involving him in difficulties on the way to Capri last year. In due course Martin would marry Rina and produce my godson Adrian; Adrian would one day marry Anthea, the daughter of Felicité Chinnery and Tommy Fairfax-Ross.

My mother came to Herm with Fay's small son Anthony, who distinguished himself by leaving Nicolas Mavrogordato marooned by the incoming tide upon Dog's Island, a large rock by the entrance of Herm harbour which I had presented to the two boys as their private island. We heard about now that Fay, twice a widow, was to marry Leon Quartermaine, who had taken Robert Loraine's part in *Mary Rose*.

I used to drive my mother round the island in a mid-Victorian chaise with an ancient pony, a chaise just like the one in which Queen Victoria would drive around Balmoral with John Brown in attendance. My mother, always sanguine and always creative, thought I should develop Herm as a holiday resort and retire myself to Jethou. She was so captivated by this idea that, feeling her imagination was no longer required to maintain the Theatre Girls' Club and the Nottingham Repertory Theatre, she was determined to invest money in Herm's future as my partner. My mother and I were a disastrous couple when it came to spending money.

In September James Eastwood and "Mrs Blake" announced that they were going to get married, which they duly were by Canon Hickey in one of the two Catholic churches in Guernsey. Canon Hickey and I had not found ourselves in accord; he was one of those Catholic priests who affected that maddening Anglican voice for prayers and had refused to say Mass even once a month on Herm. I had found in Father Bourde de la Rogérie a priest more after my own heart. He was in charge of the little French church built by the *emigrés* of the Revolution in the shape of a sailing-vessel upside down, and he was a man of saintly simplicity whose congregation consisted mostly of humble folk. I was proud to rent two chairs in his church.

In that September I had decided to acquire a reliable motor-boat with auxiliary sail which would be used for our plan to develop Herm next year as a tourist resort. I had already given Thorneycrofts the order to build such a boat but I felt that I must have Adam Robertson, my chauffeur in Athens, as my engineer. Robertson now drove for Sir Mansfield Cumming, who was still the chief of M.I.1 (C), with headquarters near Southampton. C was not at all pleased when Robertson told him he was leaving to come to me and I received a letter of protest in that familiar green ink. However, he forgave me.

Thompson had been becoming a bit of a problem. Life on a small island was encouraging him to drink too much, and when he heard of Robertson's forthcoming arrival he became jealous for his own position and drank much too much. At last I had to say he must leave me. I was glad when I was able to give him a good reference and hear that he had been engaged as groom of the chambers by the new Lord-Lieutenant of Ireland, Lord Fitzalan, just appointed in the hope that a Catholic Viceroy might help to clear up the dreadful mess the Government were making of Ireland.

Faith went back to Capri for the winter at the beginning of October; I hoped that by spring the Manor would be ready for our occupation. At present the only rooms ready were the billiards-room, where Attewell and I used to play with liturgical regularity a solemn game every evening before dinner. Here Macdonald had put up shelves to hold the library of the late Dean Jeremie of Guernsey, which I had bought for the ludicrous sum of £50. I had no time then to go through the 4,000 volumes, but there were many fine calf-bindings and merely as a decorative background for the billiards-table £50 was very cheap.

Hardly a month after they were married James and Nellie Eastwood told me they wanted to leave Herm. Eastwood felt that he must again assume the responsibilities of journalism to meet the responsibilities of married life. I wished them both well, and indeed I could feel relieved that Nellie's future, which had been a problem for Faith and myself, had presumably been solved.

I had devloped a polyp in my nose which Dr Carey said should be removed. I went up to London to see Tilly, who had operated on my father's throat. He said that the polyp was a simple matter but that I ought to have my antrum scraped. That meant going into a clinic for the operation, which was successfully performed. I came to from the anaesthetic to find myself holding the nurse's hand, and saying:

"Nurse, this is in every sense of the word a bloody operation."

I was not more than a few days in the clinic, and when I came out I went to stay at the Savile.

One evening about ten o'clock I went into the billiards-room, hoping to find a couple of members playing the Savile game of volunteer snooker. This seems the moment to set on record that in Savile snooker the green and yellow balls are banished and the brown ball, promoted to score eight, is placed on the spot in baulk, and the blue, pink and black balls on their regular snooker spots with their regular snooker values. After potting a red ball the player may volunteer for any coloured ball and forfeit its value if he fails to pot it. This game was already sacred when I first joined the Club in 1912, and I recall the sense of profanation when members of the Arts Club, to whom we were offering hospitality, occasionally played a game of pool, which was the Arts Club game.

On that November night the billiards-room was empty and, wondering where everybody was, I sat down on the small seat for two that stuck out on the right-hand side of the fireplace, for I had come into the Club out of a night of chill November rain. I was sitting there, no doubt meditating on the problems of Herm, when W. B. Yeats came in.

"Ah," said the poet in his most hieratic voice. "I'm glad to see you. I hear you have been taking an interest in astrology." With this he sat down beside me in the ingle. "As a student of astrology," he continued in those hieratic tones, "you'll be interested to know that I was born at an exact sext between the planet Venus and the planet Mercury." Then lowering his voice in reverence he added: "Indicating thereby the birth of a major poet."

At this moment there loomed in the billiards-room the massive form of Sir Ray Lankester.

"Ah, my dear boy," he grunted, "I'm glad to see you. I was just going to write to you."

With this he sat down heavily on the other side of me and I found myself squashed between the two great men.

"Yes, I was going to write to you about getting some green tree frogs for your island," Sir Ray told me.

Yeats now went on.

"In my sixth house is the planet Herschel, ill aspected by Saturn, indicating from time to time bursts of most unwelcome publicity."

"Yes, I was staying two years ago with some friends on the Riviera," Sir Ray continued. "And over the dining-table on their terrace hung the bough of a carob-tree on which these charming little creatures, bright emerald-green, used to sit and chirp and chirp all through dinner."

Yeats came in again.

"In my seventh house is the Moon, indicating money accruing at times but vanishing with equal rapidity."

Ray Lankester prodded me.

"Who is this fellow?" he muttered.

"Yeats," I whispered.

"Um?"

"W. B. Yeats."

"Um?"

"The Irish poet."

"Never heard of him. What's he talking about?"

"Astrology."

"*Bloody* fool!" Sir Ray ejaculated in a gasp of amazement.

Junior though I was, I felt by now it was imperative to introduce the two great men to one another.

In spite of that beginning they became friendly in the Club. In the following year when Yeats was awarded the Nobel Prize Edmund Gosse said to him, with his claws out:

"I hope you don't think, Yeats, that you've been awarded the Nobel Prize for your services to literature."

I see Yeats now in a black cloak backing away from Gosse like a rook in the wind.

"Ah, no, no, Yeats. You've been awarded the Nobel Prize on account of your hatred of *us*."

And then from behind came the voice of Sir Ray Lankester in protest:

"Why can't you leave the poor wild Irishman alone, Gosse?"

I have only one other memory of Yeats in the Savile, of which he was never such a Savilian as Lankester, and that is of seeing him pick up a popular book about mathematics just published by Stanley Unwin. Was it called *Mathematics for the Million*?

"Ah," Yeats observed dreamily as he put it down again. "More religion for the suburbs."

Ray Lankester used to write a weekly article about zoology in the *Daily Telegraph*, and was at one time director of the Natural History Museum. I was in his good books because I had once contradicted him and had been right. One day I happened to remark in his hearing that the Blue Grotto in Capri got its colour by facing north.

"Nonsense," Sir Ray commented in a voice of utter contempt. "The Blue Grotto faces south."

"No, Sir Ray," I insisted. "It faces due north."

"Go and get an atlas," he ordered in the tone of a master at the school of which we were both Old Boys.

In the atlas I was able to show to Sir Ray Lankester that he was wrong.

After that he had for me what I may call an affectionate avuncular regard. Of many stories I could tell of him I shall allow myself one.

He was talking to me once about his time at the Natural History Museum and of the way he had to put the board of governors in their place.

"They were always trying to assert themselves, you know. On one occasion I changed the arrangement of the birds' eggs without consulting them. So they sent for me and said I must put them back as they were originally arranged. 'You're making a great deal of fuss,' I told them, 'about what after all is only a collection of coloured farts.' That stopped their nonsense."

At Devonshire House in the year of the Great Exhibition Charles Dickens had obtained the gracious patronage of the Queen and Prince Albert for the performance of a play by Lord Lytton by friends of Dickens in aid of some charitable scheme of his. In the cast were Dickens himself, Tenniel, Cruickshank, Wilkie Collins, Douglas Jerrold, Mark Lemon and others of the Dickens circle; my grandmother, Emmeline Montague, who had retired from the stage when she married but acted from time to time with Dickens' amateur strollers, played the heroine. Now, seventy years later, *Not as Bad as We Seem* was to be revived at Devonshire House in aid of the David Copperfield library for children in the house in Somers Town where Dickens had once lived. Ivor Novello, William Orpen, Alfred Noyes, Gilbert Parker, Pett Ridge, A. A. Milne, W. H. Davies, W. B. Maxwell and others more or less well known were in the cast. My sister Fay was asked to play her grandmother's part but could not be released from *Quality Street* at the Haymarket, and Tennyson Jesse played the heroine instead.

It was an execrably bad play and most of the performers were as wooden as the play. Indeed, the only exception was young Ivor Novello, who played excellently the part once taken by Charles Dickens himself.

When the play was mercifully over there was a quadrille in which three of Dickens' grandchildren and myself danced; this was led by Neville Lytton and Adeline Genée. Other dancers were Alfred Noyes, Gerald Duckworth, and, at the very top of her form, Margot Asquith. The men were dressed for the reign of George I with shrunken Ramillies wigs; it is about the most difficult costume to carry off without looking as if one were in the only dress left which could be hired from a costumier for a fancy-dress ball. The women wore the crinolines of 1851 and were much more at home in them than the men in their knee-breeches and ugly wigs. There was an awkward moment when Mrs Asquith tried to show the great prima ballerina how to dance a quadrille, but luckily she spotted that one of the buttons at the side of my silk knee-breeches was undone and seeing me make a grimace as I leant

o

down to button it plunged down quickly and buttoned it herself. I had not yet come to enjoy the privilege of friendship with Margot Asquith, and what I shall recall of that remarkable woman must wait for another Octave.

That crowded evening wound up at midnight with fairy lamps in the garden to welcome Queen Alexandra's 77th birthday as December 1st came in. That is what some of the papers reported; others said the fairy-lamps were lighted to welcome the spirit of Christmas so much loved by Charles Dickens. One may surmise the advertising editor already had his eye on the Christmas shops; even as early as 1921 the hallowed and gracious time was being profaned by commerce.

After the play—in which I had walked on with Justin MacCarthy as a watchman—I found myself in the dressing-room beside W. H. Davies, whose poetry was always a delight to me. Suddenly he asked me if I knew Max Beerbohm.

"He's a cruel man, isn't he?" Davies said.

I assured him that was the last epithet one could apply to Max.

"It's not his pictures I'm talking about. All I know is he sneered at my wooden leg."

"That's impossible," I declared.

I could not extract from the foolish little man what Max had said which he had mistaken for a sneer. I resented such a slur on Max Beerbohm; at the same time I could not be angry with the little man whose vision of life was as simple as a child's in spite of his long experience as a tramp.

"You just misunderstood something he said to you. Max is a very shy man and completely incapable of sneering at anybody's misfortune."

But the poet was determined to hug his grievance.

As I pulled on the silk knee-breeches for the quadrille I winced at a stab of the sciatic nerve.

"Sciatica," I said quickly. I did not want Davies to tell people I had been mocking his limp.

This memory of Devonshire House, which immediately after that last function ever to be held in it was to be pulled down, reminds me of meeting Michael Arlen one morning on that broad pavement in Picca-dilly, along which one could saunter in those days. He asked me to have a drink with him at the Berkeley.

"I've a lunch at 1.30 but there's plenty of time for a cocktail."

The head-waiter paid him the respectful attention that head-waiters kept for somebody who was known as a social figure. Over our dry martinis we had an agreeable chat, but when it came to my turn Arlen said he must get off to his lunch. The head-waiter presented the bill for two dry martinis; it was five shillings. Then Arlen put two fingers in his waistcoat and produced two pennies, which he handed to the head-waiter.

"Thank you, Mr Arlen," said the head-waiter with genuine respect and without a trace of sarcasm.

I realized that he recognized the rock of Ararat in Michael Arlen and found that twopence worthier of his appreciation than the effusive florin he would have been tipped by an American or the nervous shilling pushed towards him by an Englishman. As for me, I registered it in my memory as one of the brave deeds I had witnessed in my life and reflected how unlikely it was that I should ever be brave enough to tip a head-waiter twopence after two dry martinis, even at a station hotel. To this day when I look back to that drink with Michael Arlen at the Berkeley I am filled with something like awe. No wonder the Armenians have been able to survive the massacres and outrages of the brutish Turks.

I was in a state of continuous anger that autumn about the way the Government was handling the Irish situation. I had an admiration for Lloyd George, but I felt he was betraying his race. One could find excuses for an English politician but not for a Welshman. I had to walk out of a house before dinner because Sir Hamar Greenwood, a Canadian who had been made Secretary for Ireland, was a guest and I could not bring myself to shake hands with him.

I recall seeing a Black and Tan swaggering along past the Criterion Restaurant and pushing people into the gutter; he had as foul a face and as brutal an expression as I ever saw. I had the pleasure of pushing him into the gutter and I should have been involved in a fight if a constable of the C division had not dealt with the blackguard.

It was a relief to find in the Savile quite a few members who were as much shocked by the Government's behaviour over Ireland as I was.

When military service had denuded the Club of many of the male staff the Savile house committee had decided after much preliminary trepidation to engage a female porteress to take the place of the departed Christie. Nellie Boyte stayed on that autumn with Lawrence, the new porter. I decided that when she left Nellie Boyte would be just the right person for Herm, to take the place of Nellie Eastwood, provided that she had enough intelligence to deal with my handwriting. So, soon after Christmas, Nellie Boyte came to Herm; now, 42 years later, though no longer on active service, she is still with us.

Ned Stone had been much worried by Nellie Eastwood and her husband leaving Herm. Apparently the job on the *Liverpool Courier* for Eastwood, which was the reason Nellie had given him for leaving, had not materialized, and Ned was being called on for financial help by advancing Nellie the allowance she was given under the terms of my father-in-law's will.

It may have been the problem of that daughter his mother had adopted when she became a Catholic that made Ned write to me how worried he had been by Faith's illness in London, where she had been for a fortnight on her way back to Capri. The doctors called it anaemia, but he felt that giving up her sculpture (which she had done on account of the rheumatic effect of the damp clay) had left her without having anything definite to do and so a feeling of uselessness. *My mother had the same sort of illness for years after she became a R.C. and could not take part in the life of the school at Stone House; she was away from home for a long time and the doctors said there was nothing really the matter with her.*

Axel Munthe had warned me four years ago that Faith must always have something to do by which she could express her own personality and not feel that it was being overshadowed by mine. I had hoped she was going to find her own way of self-expression through sculpture, but when she abandoned that she surrendered to ill-health and after being a problem for doctors in Capri last winter she became a problem for doctors again this winter both in Naples and in Rome. Luckily I should be able to find a remedy for Faith's depression about herself in this year of 1922 which had just begun.

I must record one more brief extract from that letter of Ned Stone's, seeing that one of the dedicatees of this Octave is the subject of it:

Reynolds has had his first half at Eton and seems to be getting on all right; he is very backward but has brains, though I don't suppose he'll ever distinguish himself scholastically.

Reynolds must have wisely decided already that there was enough scholastic distinction among the Stones, and we can be grateful that he discovered for himself what he wanted to do and do it so triumphantly.

Christopher, urged on by his wife, was writing novels, which were not having any success and in which he himself took small interest. The remedy I found for Faith's depression would also relieve Christopher from writing any more mediocre novels.

I made a great effort to finish *The Altar Steps* and managed to do so before January was out, thanks to Sylvia my Siamese cat, now seven months old. She had reached us as a very small kitten at the end of July to keep a grey Persian kitten company. I called them Sylvia and Lily because Sylvia was immediately in command. She ordered about a Sealyham puppy called Stella from the moment the latter arrived, and within a fortnight of her own arrival she had Hamlet, my Great Dane, under control. He used to sleep stretched out in front of the fire in the drawing-room at the White House which I used as a study now that

Faith had gone to Italy; Sylvia considered Hamlet's stomach made an ideal cushion after I deprived her of Lily's services for this purpose, and if he tried to turn over she used to growl and bite the end of his tail. I gave Lily away because I did not think she would ever be able to develop her feline personality under the domination of Sylvia's. The latter, when she was not much more than two months' old, used to sit in the big bay-window at the White House, growling at the sight of the trippers coming up the harbour steps. She was not a cat for the Show of the Siamese Cat Club with her stumpy double-kinked tail, but she was a Margot Asquith-cum-Dame Ethel Smythe of cats.

At dinner she always sat on my left on the table without moving until the filberts came in. Then she would crouch as she watched me peel a filbert before I threw it to roll along the floor, when she would chase it round the room until she jumped up on the table and dropped the nut from her mouth for me to throw it again.

I was writing to Faith:

Sylvia has been in a deliciously naughty mood all the evening, crying for the moon; or in other words to get on top of the Chippendale bookcase. Failing to achieve this, she deliberately tore up a whole copy of the "Exchange and Mart" and then upset six books from the piano, after which she chased an apple round the room. She never leaves me and has at last settled down in my lap. She is loved by everybody and is as fat as butter. Hamlet looks as if a wasp had settled on his nose when she sniffs it. She bit his tail so hard the other evening that he jumped up with a howl.

After dinner when I went into my room to work she would sleep on Hamlet's stomach until the time came for him to go to his kennel at about eleven o'clock, when the household retired and left me to work on by the light of a greenshaded colza oil lamp beside my invalid chair. After clearing off any doggy hairs left from the use of Hamlet as a cushion, Sylvia used to jump up and settle herself beside me while I wrote on and on, sometimes till four or five in the morning, when she would accompany me upstairs to bed and sleep beside me as Pauline used to sleep beside me at Casa Solitaria. The company of that dearly loved cat through those nights of difficult writing undoubtedly gave me the ability to carry on for what was often seven hours at a stretch without getting out of my chair, not wishing to disturb Sylvia.

At the end of December that article from which I have already quoted was published in *The Times* and led to rather a heavy mail from people who had enjoyed it, some of whom were anxious to come and live on Herm, for the privilege of which they offered their services in a variety of shapes, none of them except one in the least likely to fit into place in Herm.

By the end of January the cottage joined to the Manor by a covered way was nearly ready for occupation. The shelves were up; the books from Capri had arrived and were being unpacked.

In that article I wrote:

"For years I have prayed, like Abraham Cowley: 'May I a small house and large garden have and many books.' In Herm I have a cottage full of books actually in the garden, facing south with a view of trees and an ancient round tower. I shall cover the cottage with an amazing Chinese honeysuckle (*Lonicera hildebrandii*) a winter-flowering clematis (*C. Indivisa lobata*), a plumbago, and the rose Fortune's Yellow. The verandah will be hung with that Japanese wistaria (*multijuga*). The small square of garden in front will be planted with *Magnolia campbelli* (a Clara Butt tulip become a tree); *Crinodendron hookeri* (great six-sided rubies pendant from dark lance-shaped leaves, that would have made Sinbad's mouth water); *Eucryphia pinnatifolia* (a white St John's wort become a tree, perfumed with hawthorn and blossoming in August); and *Embothrium Coccineum* (beside which the burning bush of Moses would seem a waiting-room fire). Will any gardener call me unblest?"

A young man of 23 working in an office of the *Sheffield Daily Telegraph* read those words and made up his mind he must come and garden on Herm. He had promised his father, after two years at Oxford when he was demobilized from the Coldstream Guards, that he would work for six months in the office of the family business, of that newspaper which in a year or two the Kemsley Empire would acquire for over a million pounds. That six months was nearly up and Mr Leng Senior made no attempt to persuade his eldest son Basil to continue to work in a job he did not like and therefore from which he was unlikely to derive much benefit.

Basil Leng sent me a very long letter, from the odd spelling of which I recall "extreem", to ask if I would take him as an unpaid gardener on Herm. What decided me to suggest an interview were not the "whys" and "wherefores" of his reasons for wanting to come to Herm but his allusion to an attempt he had once made to grow *Buddleia madagascarensis*, which I had once tried to grow long ago in Cornwall without success. The mention of that white buddleia took me back to those days when my first novel was jogging round the publishers and I made up my mind not to write any more novels until *The Passionate Elopement* stood as a volume before me; I would turn all my creative energy into horticulture. Why should any young man who did not desire to devote his future to cultivating the *Sheffield Daily Telegraph* not devote it instead to the cultivation of flowers? I wrote to Basil Leng, accepting his offer to visit me on Herm and face an interview. In that offer he asked if I had *Mitraria coccinea* and suggested bringing a couple of them with him; it had done well in North Wales. As it happened I had not yet planted that small shrub with little orange-red flowers, I was surer than ever that Basil Leng was the kind of young man I wanted on Herm, and when we met I realized at once that he was the very person for the island; it was settled that as soon as his time in Sheffield was up he should come to Herm. His father wrote from their house in Harlech, asking me to urge Basil to complete his forestry studies, but I was able with complete sincerity to write to Mr Leng and tell him that his son was much more likely to make a name for himself out of horticulture. So at the end of January Basil Leng arrived on Herm and, disdaining luxury, lived at first in a cottage with nothing more than a bed, a chest of drawers, a table and two chairs.

I wound up that article on Herm:

"Most people ask me what I do with myself on Herm. Island-lovers ask me how I find time to do my own work; I need hardly say that the island-lovers understand the real difficulties of life there. I write at night, and even then on moonlit nights I grudge the time. I could easily amuse myself for ever watching birds. The birds of an island like Herm are even more delightful than the birds of a mainland, because one gets to know them individually. My favourites are those who, like the linnets, the blackbirds, the ravens, the oyster-catchers, the gulls and the curlews, pass their whole life on Herm. But there are many other birds that all through the winter spend a day or so with us at a time, and in spring we are a popular honeymoon resort for wheatears, cuckoos, and puffins. There are two winter visitors, a yellow wagtail and a chaffinch, whose wives evidently dislike small islands. They arrive in October and join their ladies again at the end of March, probably at Deauville or some fashionable French resort. They must be real island-lovers to stay so long, for they are much jostled by the Herm sparrows, who resent their presence in the farmyard. On halcyon days in winter I have seen the kingfisher flying out over a calm blue sea, and they nest in Jethou.

"Jethou is a really small island about a mile round; but it has an exquisite wood of sweet chestnuts and pear-trees, an umbrageous mulberry tree, an old cannon, a haunted house, white pimpernels, yellow forget-me-nots, and a wonderful view of Herm.

"But whatever one may write or say about an island like Herm, of its romantic history, of the pirates hanged there in chains, of the treasure found and the skeletons dug up, of the neolithic monuments, of the monks and wreckers and quarrymen and smugglers who have lived there, of the trippers who twice a week in summer cross from Trinidad to Tobago for their cannibal feasts on the shell-beach, leaving more than one footprint to horrify us Crusoes when they have departed—whatever one may say, the island will keep its secret.

"The other day my engineer (Adam Robertson) was appealed to in a London shop by two young men behind the counter who wished to settle an argument. One had maintained that Herm was in the Falkland Islands and had been taken from the Germans during the war.

" 'You're wrong,' said Adam Robertson.

" 'There you are,' exclaimed the adversary, 'I told you it was somewhere near Jutland.'

"Robertson related this when he came back. We were walking on the road from the harbour toward the Common. The clouds were black and silver between rain; a perfect rainbow spanned two of our small hills. All the blackthorn boughs were stained to a rich maroon on which patterns of glaucous lichen stood out with mysterious intensity.

" 'After all, I thought, do I myself really know where Herm is?'

"Our cottage casements open on the foam of perilous seas in faerielands forlorn. Only guide-books give us a geographical existence, commend our shell-beach and our bathing, and call us the smallest and least interesting of the Channel Islands. But guide-books are useful only for mountains; they know nothing about islands."

J. M. Barrie was as vague about the antecedents of Herm as those young men in the London shop. On January 9th, 1922, he was writing from Adelphi Terrace after I had written to congratulate him on his O.M.:

Thank you heartily for your letter and the kind thought that prompted it. May we meet again when you come out of that island, which I know not where it is, being hopeless as a geographer and not unnaturally puzzled by "C.I.", but Herm seems to me to suggest whaling regions, tho' now I think of it I believe the word is Sperm. All happiness to you at any rate in the New Year.

WHEN that New Year came I was hard at work writing *The Seven Ages of Woman* which Secker would be publishing in the autumn. In February I decided I must look for a husband for my beloved Sylvia and one morning Nellie Boyte came in with a male Siamese kitten which had arrived from a reputable cattery. Sylvia, whose head was on the pillow beside me, growled at the new arrival and retreated to the bottom of the bed, where she bit my toe to make obvious her disapproval of the new arrival. That reputable cattery had behaved most disreputably by sending me a kitten from a cattery infected with that cursed enteritis; the poor little newcomer was dead next day. Three days later Sylvia was struck down. I had succumbed to one of my bad goes, and it was Nellie Boyte and Dora who sat up with her for two nights; they were unable to save her.

The thought of sitting in that chair without that beloved cat beside me was more than I could bear; the thought of sitting at the dinner-table without her at my elbow was intolerable. I could stand the White House no longer and two days later I moved up to the four-roomed cottage beside the Manor. Two rooms had been knocked into one for my book-lined study; on the other side of the passage was my bedroom; the two bedrooms above were occupied by Nellie Boyte and Dora.

As I write of Sylvia's death I have just lost my beloved white cat Blanco. I have told some of his story in a book which will be in print by the time this Octave appears. The book is called *Little Cat Lost*, a title all too sadly appropriate now. It was not Blanco's habit to sit beside me, but on his last afternoon with me he came up and sat for a while beside me before going out on his regular nocturnal adventures. That night there was a terrific thunderstorm and next morning he did not arrive as usual to lie beside me in bed. Whether he was struck by lightning or killed by a passing car we shall never know. He was stone deaf and would not have heard the thunder or the approach of a car. I have had other much-loved cats, but the two lives whose loss I have felt most deeply were those all too brief lives of my first Sylvia and Blanco. I do not apologize for this expression of grief. Those fortunate people who know and love and understand cats will give me their sympathy; those unfortunate people to whom cats are strangers will shake their heads over what they will think is mere sentimentality.

It was a habit of mine when worried by monetary or other problems to restore my spirits by ordering a new suit. In the late autumn of 1920

I had been walking along Bond Street at dusk of a depressing day and asking myself if my acquisition of Herm and Jethou was a rash undertaking; as a sedative I went into my tailor's in Grafton Street and ordered a green tweed suit. In the artificial light at Forster's I misjudged that green. When the suit arrived it looked as if it had been made from the cloth of a billiards-table; I had to send it back to be dyed a rich brown. A year later I was walking up Bond Street on a foul November evening. Convinced by now that the acquisition of Herm had been a rash undertaking, I was tempted to turn into Grafton Street, but remembering the mistake I had made in choosing that green tweed, I decided to buy something else. I had had a letter from George Sandwich that morning in which he had enquired after his two shire mares and my mind went back to Burford and playing George Montagu's Aeolian organ. "Of course," I said to myself. "That is what I need in Herm." It was close on six o'clock when I went into the Aeolian shop in Bond Street and enquired about an instrument. I think it must have been the first enquiry they had had for a long time, because in spite of its being so near to closing everybody in the shop seemed excited. There was only one instrument left and I bought it after signing a hire-purchase agreement and arranging for its dispatch to Herm.

"And let me have a catalogue of your rolls," I added.

There was a hurried search for a catalogue, but none could be found. However, the manager promised that a catalogue should be sent to me as soon as possible.

A fortnight passed before that catalogue arrived. I opened it eagerly to look for Beethoven and Mozart symphonies, for the Fifth and Sixth Symphonies of Tchaikovsky and for that *Marche Slav*, a performance of which on winter nights at Burford had almost persuaded me that I was a conductor *manqué*. Not one of them was listed any longer among the rolls of the Aeolian.

There was nothing except selections from musical comedies and a quantity of what is called light music on which I felt my manipulation of the various organ stops would be wasted.

I wrote to the Aeolian people to say that the deal was off unless they could supply me with the rolls of classical music which had been obtainable sixteen years ago. They wrote back to say how much they regretted being unable to supply the rolls I wanted but found themselves unable to cancel my order on account of the difficult position it would put them in with the hire-purchase company. After a further exchange of letters the Aeolian people asked if I would agree to exchange the organ for a gramophone. I wrote indignantly to say that nothing would induce me to have a gramophone. I had had a gramophone twelve years ago in Cornwall and except for records of Caruso and Harry Lauder the gramophone was useless. More correspondence ensued and finally, as I could not get out of the hire-purchase agreement, I agreed most unwillingly to accept the Hepplewhite model of a Vocalion Gramophone. I was agreeably surprised to find in the catalogue a few records of chamber music in their pink labels and some band records of good music in their less expensive blue-labels.

I was in bed up at the cottage, recovering from one of my attacks, when the Vocalion arrived with its records. I picked out a shortened version of Schumann's Piano Quintet on two double-sided pink discs and Robertson put on the first movement. I had expected to hear nothing more than the scratchy buzz of a violin record in 1910 and a piano sounding like somebody tapping a tune on his front teeth. Instead, I heard music.

"There are other gramophone companies besides the Vocalion, aren't there?" I asked Robertson.

"There's H.M.V. That's the biggest."

"What's H.M.V. stand for?"

Robertson tried not to look surprised by my ignorance.

"His Master's Voice."

"I must find out their address and get hold of their catalogue. H.M.V. you say? Yes, I seem to remember now hearing records from them in Cornwall. Yes, of course! There's a picture of a dog listening to a horn."

So the H.M.V. catalogue was ordered and duly arrived; then Robertson discovered there was a company called Columbia, and their catalogue arrived.

The only complete recording of a classical symphony was in the H.M.V. catalogue; it was Beethoven's Fifth conducted by Nikisch, and ludicrous though the reproduction would sound to-day it remains for me the finest interpretation I have heard on a recording. There was no chamber music in the H.M.V. list except shortened versions of an occasional movement from a quartet on one side of a black-label and on the celebrity single-sided red labels there were two or three excerpts of chamber music played by the Flonzaley Quartet.

Presently I should be discovering two or three ten-inch red labels of an Italian conductor called Toscanini conducting the orchestra of La Scala in brief extracts from Beethoven symphonies. These were not stocked by British dealers but had to be ordered from Italy.

Columbia had been more enterprising than H.M.V. with several semi-complete works of chamber music, including the great Mozart string quintet which had been recorded during an air raid. Soon I should be enchanted by Galli-Curci and Alma Glück, spellbound by early recordings of Caruso before he set out to rival Tamagno as a *tenore robusto*, captivated by Pol Plançon's *basso cantante* and by every one of John McCormack's records, which I bought after hearing his record of *Oh, don't you remember sweet Alice, Ben Bolt?*: I had acquired this not because it was sung by a great tenor whose voice I had never heard on the concert platform, but because of its association with Trilby. I suppose the unwashed unpruned beatniks of to-day never read about George du Maurier's Bohemia; a pity.

No more about those first records; enough to say that I was once again absorbed by a *grande passion*. I was writing to Faith early in that spring:

I have gramophilia badly, and now have 221 records, but hope to have 200 more soon. I think almost the most exquisite piece of music I ever heard is Beethoven's Spring Sonata. The Adagio Molto Espressivo is espressivissimo indeed. I've got a good deal of Wagner, but not many songs. I'm waiting for them till the German records are released again.

I had seen a portrait of Charles Scott-Moncrieff by Stanley Mercer and thought I should like to have one of myself painted by him in the same style, a head and shoulders in Marine blues. Mercer arrived in March and was anxious to paint a three-quarter length portrait of me in the kilt; he was further taken with the notion of painting me in my study, which faced south. That involved being dependent on the sun's behaving itself, and sitting at irregular moments became a boring interruption of a new package of gramophone records. The portrait promised well, but as too often happens Mercer would go on trying to get an effect of more interest to other painters than to the sitter's idea of a likeness. Mercer was very good company, although he made rather a mess of my study with his paraphernalia and an enemy of Macdonald by letting one of his cigarettes burn the chimney-shelf which Macdonald had just made out of some rare wood. During the war Stanley Mercer had been in the R.N.V.R. and commanded one of the motor launches patrolling round Fair Isle, where the jumpers came from, one of which he obtained for me.

Bill Sells[1] came for a short visit and a letter from him written on May 1st from the Junior United Service Club, has survived:

I went to see the boat last week. . . . She is a fine craft and I think they have put excellent work and material into her . . . she seems exactly suited to your wants.

He then went on to suggest a few improvements.

----

[1] Vice-Admiral W. F. Sells, C.M.G.

There you are—a lot of guff, but there might be a grain of sense in it here and there. If you have time I'd like to know how the domain is getting on, and if the picture turned out well and how the young gardener is getting on with his roses and things. I hope you've had no more bad goes lately. Deadly weather here of course. Let me know when you come over—here or Admiralty. Good luck with the old book.

The "old book" was *The Seven Ages of Woman*, at which somehow or other I managed to work during that Spring. Faith wrote in *More Than I Should*;

"Life was becoming a huge, precarious and somewhat top-heavy structure. . . . Yet, however severe the financial crisis, he was always equal to it, alert and industrious to balance a charming extravagance which involved everybody round him in adventures of fantastic variety. To have lived with and worked for him makes ordinary life seem humdrum and ridiculous."

Orlo Williams was another visitor that spring. He was an ardent bird-watcher before bird-watching had become everybody's hobby. He was tolerant of my enthusiasm for the gramophone. I recall only one mild rebuke. I had played to him a Vocalion band record of the gods' entrance into Valhalla from *Götterdämmerung*.

"Yes," he murmured. "But it's a pity you never heard it played by a live orchestra instead of a recorded brass band."

Stephen Miall, a second-cousin of mine and editor of the *Chemical Age*, wrote to me early this year rather absurdly as "Dear Sir" and signed himself "Yours faithfully". The letter is an example of the pedagogic humour and condescension which some of my paternal relatives with the Symonds-Mackenzie blood affected. My mother used to find it trying, but used to enjoy laughing at it with her mother-in-law; even my father fell into it sometimes, which I found trying when I was a boy.

I have read a good deal of literature of which you are the author and my wife and myself were recently laughing over your Rich Relatives. It occurred to me that you might be diverted by the frivolous productions of one of your poor relations and I therefore send you a copy of the Chemical Age with an instalment of my latest effusion. It is a great many years since I saw you at your parents' house in West Kensington but I meet some of the various members of the Mackenzie family from time to time and hear most of the news.

Of course novels can hardly be compared with real literature such as I produce at rare intervals but novelists make up in quantity what they lack in quality. Euclid is read—I cannot say enjoyed—to this day but the Greek Sinister Streets have long since been forgotten!

Sometime when you are in London, if you are really at a loose end, I should enjoy discussing with you the relative merits of our literary styles or cigars or any other tokens of modern civilization. We authors suffer from too much isolation.

I wrote back to say I thought the *Electra* and *Ion* of Euripides might outlive his electrons and ions and would certainly outlive Euclid. I added that I disagreed about the isolation of authors; to my mind they suffered from too much congregation at literary sherry parties and from as much mutual back-scratching as the monkeys at the Zoo.

Later Stephen Miall and I became good friends and in another Octave I may tell of his meticulous research and consequent correction of our hitherto accepted Mackenzie line.

In that spring J. B. Pinker died of pneumonia on one of his visits to the U.S.A. He had been correspondent of one of the English dailies in Constantinople, from which he had gone on to edit the *Queen*. Then he decided to set up as a literary agent, to the indignation of A. P. Watt. Watt had been the first literary agent and he was inclined to regard Pinker's irruption into literary agency as a breach of copyright. In 1911, when my first novel was published, apart from Watt and Pinker, there were only Curtis Brown, Massie, and a charming fellow called Cazenove who was Masefield's agent and died young. The countless literary agents of to-day would have been unimaginable fifty years ago.

J. B.'s passion was driving a four-in-hand. I see him now beaming at me from the other side of his desk in Arundel Street. He is dressed in a grey frock-coat and on his desk is a grey top-hat; it is a fine Saturday morning and presently he will be driving a four-in-hand to Windsor. Pinker had what might almost be called a partnership with Methuen. Sir Archibald Methuen, whose real name was Steadman, had written successful schoolbooks before he started as a publisher. The three-book contracts which Pinker negotiated for his clients with Methuen were a feature of pre-First World War publishing. I owed much to Pinker's enthusiasm for my work; his death was a loss to me in every way.

By this time Martin Secker was finding it difficult to deal with the financial situation involved in our agreement, and when just before Pinker left for New York he renewed his offer to guarantee me £6,000 a year Secker and I agreed it would be wise for me to accept. I felt such an undertaking was too heavy a one for Eric Pinker to assume, but he insisted on his ability to do so. He was to be my sole agent for films, lectures, and all literary work, which was to guarantee him two novels a year. He was to receive 15 per cent. commission and at the end of three years we should settle up. I would repay him any debit and he would pay me any credit, after which we should revert to the normal 10 per cent. commission of an agent.

Nellie Boyte's mother had come to Herm and I realized that she was the very person to preside over the Mermaid Tavern. This was the new name I planned for the White House, which had once been known

as the Old Inn. Mrs Boyte was a personality in the grand tradition of
domestic service, which she had given up after she married a valet, also
in the grand tradition. From time to time she had returned to cooking
and housekeeping. Fyvie Castle in Aberdeenshire was one of her jobs;
another was looking after the author of *Vice Versa* for a time; her sister
was the housekeeper at Badminton. Mrs Boyte had a superlative
memory and her stories of girlhood in Suffolk and of domestic service in
her younger days were rich material. At this date she would be drawing
near to sixty. Mrs Boyte found for us the perfect cook in Hilda Everton,
whose young sister Honor came as parlour-maid when Dora Giles had
had to go back to Guernsey to look after an invalid mother. Honor was
given her room in the cottage and would remain with us for another ten
years until she married.

My mother came to Herm to discuss my project for turning the island
into a summer resort for trippers; the combined optimism of Mrs Boyte
and herself made it seem a successful certainty. I had decided to go to
Capri later in the summer. My mother found my passion for the gramophone beyond her. I recall my disappointment when after playing to
her some of John McCormack's records she said:

"Yes, yes, but you never heard Sims Reeves. There really was a great
tenor."

After my mother left I fell a prey again to doubts about the financial
future. I was finding it difficult to write with the continual interruption
of island problems; nor was I really enamoured of the tourist project. I
was at work in my cottage one day when suddenly three strangers
walked in. I explained that they were trespassing from the amount of
the island they were entitled to visit.

"Well, well," said one of them. "I thought England was a free
country."

I felt that ministering to the bellies of such people for the sake of
profit was an unworthy surrender to mammon. Nevertheless, I asked
politely enough how he would like it if I suddenly walked into his
drawing-room in England.

"Ah, that's different. I don't charge sixpence for walking round my
place."

It was about now that the Treasury made an offer to buy out the
Guernsey Treasury and substitute shillings and pence for francs and
sous. This would add appreciably to my wage-bill, but I cared less about
that than what seemed another menacing buzz from the hive of bureaucracy busy with the development of the Insect State.

The first major function of the Mermaid Tavern, which had been
granted a licence during the summer months for the sale of tobacco and
spirits, was an *al fresco* lunch for the directors of the Great Western Rail-

way. Every year before the holiday season arrived the directors made a
brief tour of the Channel Islands in their Weymouth packet. We had
not had the fine weather we had enjoyed in 1921, but the day of the
directors' visit was mercifully cloudless. The long table on trestles was
laid on the lawn just beyond the Mermaid; over a dozen directors sat
down to it. I think the reason for this large number was that every land-
owner who had yielded his property with good grace was made an
hereditary director when the G.W.R. was first being constructed. The
Chairman of the board of directors was the late Lord Churchill, from
whom I recall an amusing story that day. When Lord Riddell, the
owner of the *News of the World*, was created a peer, Lord Churchill was
asked by Lord Cholmondeley to join him in the formal introduction of
the new peer to the House of Lords.

"Made all his money out of c— and crime," Cholmondeley said to
me. "But he's quite a decent fellow."

I remembered this story when some years later at a dinner Lord
Riddell was begging novelists to keep sex out of their novels. Was he
afraid of their injuring the circulation of the *News of the World*?

The two outstanding personalities at that *al fresco* lunch were Lord
Inchcape and Sir Watkin Williams-Wynne. The latter was dressed in a
blue tail-coat suit and was wearing a dark-blue cricketing cap of the last
century. Lord Inchcape was the only great captain of industry I have
met who really looked the part, with his shaggy eyebrows, tufted ears
and dark compelling eyes he seemed as immovable as the Inchcape
Rock itself and Sir Ralph the Rover would have received as little mercy
from him as he got from the Rock. Yes, he certainly was "the real
Mackay". Inchcape and Williams-Wynne enjoyed teasing Lord
Glanely, who presented externally the comic figure of the rich parvenu
in *Punch* jokes of the 'eighties. He was wearing three or four large
diamond rings on his chubby fingers and had won the Derby with
Grand Parade in 1919.

It was soon after that visit from the Great Western board of directors
that toward dusk I walked along to the Common and as I reached the
dolmens was seized suddenly with a panic. It is hopeless even to try to
convey that peculiar feeling of terror which the Greeks recognized and
which the Psalms of David recognized. I hurried, half-running, back to
my cottage. I recalled what Countess Blücher had told me about the
prayer her sister had uttered to the spirits of the island that the next
tenant should be unfortunate.

Next morning I went back to where I had been seized by the panic
and prayed to the spirits of the island. I wound up by telling them if they
wanted somebody on whom they could vent their ill-will more appropriately than on me they should choose a profiteer of the war.

"Send a profiteer to Herm who will take over the lease from me and amuse yourselves with him," I urged.

I find it difficult to believe that it was mere coincidence which suggested to Major Elliott of Bucktrout, the big Guernsey tobacco shop, that he should invite Sir Percival Perry to visit Herm with him that very afternoon after lunch.

Sir Percival Perry had been Ford's representative in Great Britain before the war, but at the moment he was not on good terms with Ford. With financial backing from one of the big Scottish money-barons, he had recently bought the Slough Dump for the ridiculous price of £50,000. During the war the government had decided to turn some of the finest agricultural land in Buckinghamshire into a deposit for all the vehicles no longer capable of war service, to which were added tanks later. The train passed these disgusting acres of machinery out of action, the value of which merely as old iron was far in excess of what Perry had paid for it. These deals behind the scenes were characteristic of the Coalition Government. Perry had been at King Edward VI Grammar School, Birmingham, which he had left when he was 17 to acquire a small bicycle shop that was going cheap at the time, from which he was able to step into the motor-car business on the ground-floor. By now, at the age of 44, he was a director of several companies and a rich man, adding to his wealth by the way he was disposing of the Slough Dump. I have mentioned that Italian *pescecani* or profiteers did not feel assured of their status until they had acquired a *palazzo*, a large solitaire, and an obsequious secretary. British profiteers did not feel secure until they had bought a few race-horses, a grouse moor, or a yacht. Some of them had made enough money out of the war to acquire all these. Perry had decided to have a yacht, the expense of steaming about the Mediterranean in which had brought on a recurrent colitis due to the nervous strain of having to fork out all the time for doing something he did not enjoy doing.

While he was walking round the gardens of the Manor with me he asked if I had ever thought of selling my lease of Herm. The two outstanding features of Perry's personal appearance were a pair of grey eyes, the colour of granite in a rock pool, and a smile which was switched on like an electric lamp. I see now those grey eyes and that smile against a pink rhododendron in blossom as he asked this question.

Without a moment's hesitation I said I was prepared to sell the lease of Herm for a premium of £10,000, which was roughly the amount I had spent on it. I see now those grey eyes and that automatic smile as he said:

"I'm interested. I must think about it."

Sir Percival came over again next day with Lady Perry and his sister-

P

in-law Miss Meals, both of whom we all liked. Before they left, by which time, thanks to my own inability to be secretive about anything, Perry knew exactly what my financial position was, he suggested I should go back with him in the *Laranda* to Littlehampton, where we could talk business.

When the tide went out at Littlehampton the *Laranda* was aground in her berth and that business talk was carried through with us both sitting in the saloon at an angle of 45°, Perry managing to get himself higher than I was.

"First I ought to tell you something about my financial background," he said. "I think you'll appreciate what my position was at the Ministry of Munitions when I tell you that the Ministry sent me to the United States to buy three million pounds worth of agricultural machinery. Yes, I had a cheque for £3,000,000. And I must tell you something that will amuse you. By mistake the Treasury made out the cheque for thirty millions, but of course (with the automatic smile) I pointed out their mistake. Well, when I got to America I went at once to Mr Ford, with whom I was associated before the war until we had a slight disagreement. And I gave Mr Ford an order for two million pounds. He took it, and I wrote him out the cheque. Two millions! Then I waited, but Mr Ford said nothing. So at last I asked 'And my commission, Mr Ford?' 'Oh,' said Mr Ford, 'we don't pay any commission on orders for war material, Mr Perry.' So I consider," Sir Percival went on, his countenance expressing compassion for Mr Ford's unscrupulous greed, "yes, I consider that Mr Ford owes me £200,000. But I mustn't go on about my own worries. We must talk about Herm. I've been thinking over that £10,000 premium you are asking. Now, I've made a rule always to count my income as the £6,000 a year I get from my investments in gilt-edged securities. I don't count directors' fees and that sort of thing as income. You will have £6,000 a year from your writing; I have £6,000 a year from my gilt-edged securities. So really you are just as well off as I am. Still, I do want to help you as much as I can. And so I'm willing to pay £300 for a three-year's option on the lease of Herm, but I suggest that this £300 should be paid in tractors and agricultural machinery."

"From the Slough Dump?"

The automatic smile flashed for an instant as he went quickly on:

"And I suggest that Lady Perry and Miss Meals and my secretary Miss Howard and a friend or two from time to time should stay at the Mermaid Tavern, as you call it, when you go to Capri at the end of June. Then I shall be able to make up my mind about Herm. I shall be able to see further ahead than I can see at present. Then when you come back from Capri in September I shall be able to make you a firm offer. I'm going to give up this yacht. It's just an expense, just a waste of money, and I never like wasting money. Your new boat will be ready in July, won't it? And I dare say we shan't be coming until the end of July."

I went back to Herm and broke the news to Mrs Boyte. She was confident that the Perrys would enjoy themselves so much and be so well looked after that Sir Percival would not be happy until he had secured Herm for himself.

Frank Swinnerton came to stay for a few days with lots of good stories. The one that most amused me was of being given a bed in a friend's chambers. His host warned him that he was the victim of nightmares and that if Frank heard him screaming in the night he was not to be alarmed. Suddenly in the middle of the night Frank woke up to hear from the direction of his host's bedroom shrieks and then his voice moaning, "No, Frank. No, you mustn't."

"I left as early as I could next morning," said Frank Swinnerton.

He was full too of good stories about Arnold Bennett. Bennett was the only one of my seniors I never met, but Swinnerton's imitation of him was obviously as good as his imitations of those I had met, and I could fancy I really had met Arnold Bennett. He had a good story about a visit to John Galsworthy in Devonshire. He was received by Galsworthy at the end of a long room and as Swinnerton drew near to the table at which he was sitting Galsworthy rose and offered his hand from the other side of it.

"This is very sporting of you, Swinnerton, very sporting indeed," he said in his gravest voice.

Basil Leng and I went to Oxford for a weekend in that first half of June. Basil's younger brother Kyrle and Robert Gathorne-Hardy had digs in the High and to my pleasure I found that they were both gramophone enthusiasts. Bob Gathorne-Hardy with his roseate complexion looked about seventeen, but was already impressively *au courant* with the ways of the world; he and Kyrle had digs in the High familiar to me from twenty years earlier. Contemporaries of theirs at Christ Church were David Cecil and Eddy Sackville-West, both of whom I met. For me the meeting which brought back most vividly the Oxford of my youth was with Bob Boothby, who was in the rooms at Magdalen that were once Raymond Wavell's below my own. He was already the Bob Boothby of to-day and in that familiar "sitter" the twenty years since I had seen it became a mere twenty days. John Strachey came in on one occasion while I was there, but the most vivid arrival was of what was apparently a fifteen-year-old schoolboy smoking a very large cigar. He said a few words to Bob and was away almost at once.

"That's a hefty cigar for a schoolboy to be smoking," I observed to Bob.

He let out a loud Boothby laugh.

"That's Peter Rodd. He's in his third year at Balliol."

I recalled a visit of Peter Rodd to Capri some years earlier when his father was still Ambassador in Rome. On that occasion he had turned on all the bidets in the Quisisana Hotel to watch those jets of precious Capri water hit the ceiling. One day Peter would become a member of the Savile Club, where I have enjoyed with him as much good talk as with any Savilian. We have had only one disagreement in the course of a long friendship. This was an argument whether Montrachet should be pronounced Mont-rachet as I maintained, or Mon-trachet as Peter maintained. The wine-bibbers of the Savile were divided about this for some time, but lest any wine-bibbing reader should be misled by Peter Rodd's pronunciation let me set on record that my pronunciation proved to be the right one.

Returning to London from that all too brief Oxford excursion, I found myself in the same compartment as Bob Boothby's father and mother. Although this was the only time I had the good fortune to meet Sir Robert Boothby his personality is as clear to me to-day as that son of his with whom I have been intimate friends for over forty years. Sir Robert had been Captain of the Royal and Ancient and was the author of that famous song:

> *Jean, Jean, my bonny, bonny Jean,*
> *Come to my arms once again,*
> *They may say your feet are flat*
> *But they're nae the worse for that,*
> *You're my own sweet bonny Scottish lassie Jean.*

Lady Boothby, Sir Robert and I talked about Bob's future. They wanted to know what I thought about a political future for him, on which they had set their hearts. Bob had had a beautiful treble voice as a boy, and I have always regretted that he was warbling *O for the wings of a dove* before the recording of such a voice would have been a matter of course. No doubt I was full of confidence about Bob's political future, but what I ought to have advised was that he should make as much of his fine barytone voice as of his treble. In a way, like myself, he has eaten his cake and had it because we have both scored with our voices—on television. Nevertheless, it is a pity we never heard him sing Wotan's farewell on the stage of Covent Garden.

Before I left for Capri I went to see Sir Percival Perry at Ewell, near Epsom. I was amused by his library, which consisted only of sets of books in expensive bindings, not one of which looked as if it was ever

taken off the shelf. When the door was closed I was even more amused
to see that it was covered with the backs of books.

"That was my idea," Perry told me. "I thought it was such a pity to
spoil the look of my books with the bare back of a door.

We discussed Herm, and he asked if I should mind his bringing a
tank to the island. He had an idea that it might be used for collecting
the seaweed required to dress the fields.

"I'm getting a couple of ship's lifeboats, too, because your new boat
will be wanted to bring people over every day." He went on to say he
had been thinking over what he should be able to do to help me.

"My idea is that you should give me a three years' option during
which I should be able to make up my mind whether I can afford to pay
the premium you are asking. Mind you, I think it will be more satis-
factory for both of us if we nominate valuers. And now I'm going to
make a suggestion. It is important, most important, that you should be
able to carry on with the repairs and improvements you are making.
That row of four cottages, for instance, at the beginning of the road to
the Common is in a sad state. What I suggest is . . ." he broke off
suddenly. "Do you mind if I lie down on my tummy? I find it much
easier to talk about money matters when I'm lying on my tummy."

The automatic smile was switched on and the grey eyes were lighted
up by the excitement of talking about money as he lay down on the
hearthrug with a small notebook.

"I've been working out your expenses and what I suggest is that I
advance £6,000 which you will repay me at the rate of £2,000 a year
in half-yearly instalments. Most of this money of course will be spent on
island improvement. Should I take up the option sooner I suggest that
we form a company which will be responsible for your premium, half of
which you will invest in the company and from which of course you will
repay whatever I have advanced. Think over my suggestion during the
summer and when you come back in September we can have everything
put in proper legal form by Mr White. Mr White is my solicitor, a very
clever solicitor."

Perry scrambled up from the hearthrug and the grey eyes were now
beaming with benevolence.

"Well, good-bye. I hope you'll have a happy time in Capri. I know
we're going to have a very happy time on Herm. And I hope that one
day we're going to have a very happy partnership. By the way, I take it
Jethou will be included in the option?"

"No, it won't," I said quickly. "If we make such a success of Herm as
a tourist resort I shall want somewhere to retire to when I'm working
on a book."

"What a pity," Sir Percival sighed. "I had an idea we might grow poisonous plants on Jethou. I'm sure we should have a good market for them in the chemical industries. But I mustn't be greedy. I was too greedy when I asked if I couldn't have a K.C.B. instead of a K.B.E. 'Don't be greedy,' the Minister said to me when he was sending in his honours list."

I had had an idea of sailing the *Aphrodite* to Capri with Stanley Mercer at the helm, but when he could not manage to get away I gave up the idea. In any case, I knew that *Aphrodite* was needed for the trippers.

Thorneycroft's asked me if for her maiden voyage she might be entered for the British Motor Boat Club's annual race from London to Cowes. I agreed, and in the first week of July, with Mauger at the helm and Robertson in the engine-room, she left the Thames.

In the chronicle for July 6th the *Annual Register* noted:

"A gale swept across England, the wind reaching a velocity of 60 miles an hour; over $2\frac{1}{2}$ inches of rain fell in Hampshire."

Through that gale, in the course of which many of the competing vessels abandoned the race and made for harbour, *Aphrodite* held on and came in second, winning for me a large silver cup. By that time I was in Capri.

The Altar Steps was published in June. I was tepidly congratulated by some of the critics on what they evidently thought was an attempt to recapture the intellectual public after writing three books to amuse the general public. At the same time they almost all deplored paying so much meticulous attention to details of the religious life in the Church of England. There was a suggestion that in the enlightened and emancipated 'twenties nobody could any longer take religion seriously after *Eminent Victorians*.

One of the exceptions was Arthur Waugh, who gave the book a long and appreciative review in the *Daily Telegraph*. I wrote him a letter of thanks, to which I had the following reply:

I am awfully grateful to you for your charming letter. It really is a great pleasure if an author feels that some review has understood him; it helps one to buck up, and shoulder the day's work. Thank you very sincerely. "The Altar Steps" fascinated me. I have liked nothing of yours more. I know a good bit about the Anglo-Catholic crowd, and do in a way belong to it still myself, and I revelled in your portraits of the priesthood. I am sorry I did not say anything in the review about the Esther episode. I wanted to do so, and then found my space running out (I am restricted to a column). I hope Esther will appear again in "The Parson's Progress" to which I look forward enormously.

My very best wishes for your kind words.

Donald Rea wrote from the Theological College, Chichester:

"The Altar Steps" has created great joy here; what these reviewing fools mean by saying it is sparse of humour is to me unintelligible: the Tutor who sleeps next door to me was shouting with laughter well into the night on which it was published:

One letter, from Father J. H. C. Johnson, S.S.J.E., from Mission House, Society of St John the Evangelist in Boston, Mass., was a great encouragement. I still preserved a deep respect for the "Cowley Dads" as we called them in my time at Oxford.

In a remarkable way your books are refreshing and stimulating when life seems dull and futile. You make us feel that the world we actually live in is an interesting and romantic world, and that many tiresome things are amusing. You can help us priests very much by showing us how interesting and loveable people are: it must dawn upon the dullest of us, as we read your books, that the people we try to minister to are individuals and are amusing and pathetic and charming and important and have real dignity. . . .

Of course it is thrilling for us to read a novel like "The Altar Steps" in which our own world is really understood.

I wonder if you are getting any appreciation of that book in this country. I have been here six years: your book makes me realize in what a different world from ours the clergy have been brought up. . . . I know a community of sisters who have been reading "The Altar Steps" in Refectory. . . .

I was at New College when Michael Fane and his friends were at Magdalen. I was in Oxford last winter after five years. I sometimes found that the associations suggested by familiar spots came out of "Sinister Street" more readily and vividly than out of my own memories.

The Altar Steps was not reviewed more intelligently in America than in Great Britain, but George Doran did not grumble. Indeed, all the time I was being published by Doubleday, Doran there was never a grumble, though no doubt George Doran was disappointed that he could not make me a best-seller like Arnold Bennett or Hugh Walpole. It is ironical that I, who am half American, have never been able to attract the great American public. Somerset Maugham's *Of Human Bondage* never attained in England a fraction of the appeal that *Sinister Street* has had for fifty years: in the United States it is a classic, whereas *Sinister Street* is comparatively unknown.

The Seven Ages of Woman, which Secker planned to publish on the twelfth anniversary of *The Passionate Elopement*, that is upon my fortieth birthday, was held up by a strike in the book trade, to which W. H. Smith surrendered almost at once and so put less wealthy firms like

Simpkin Marshall in an impossible position. In the end *The Seven Ages of Woman*, which was in Secker's hands early that summer, was not published until March of the following year.

The Seven Ages of Woman was dedicated to Lady Algernon Gordon-Lennox. She wrote to me in Capri on June 15th:

My dear Friend,

Your letter from Herm has reached me to-day, having been returned from Capri. It is I who am proud! and I need hardly say how much I shall appreciate the honour, for you know your art has no sincerer admirer or well-wisher than I. . . . A rivederci.

Yours affly,

Blanche Gordon-Lennox

In London on my way to Italy I had some talks in the Savile billiards-room with Robin Legge, the musical critic of the *Daily Telegraph*. He and Percy Scholes were the only musical critics who had as yet recognized that such an instrument as the gramophone existed, and occasionally noticed some new record. Robin Legge, who had just potted the brown and won a game of snooker with Bill Orpen, said suddenly:

"Why don't you write me an article about the gramophone? Let me have it as soon as you can."

That suggestion from Robin Legge after he had just potted the brown made that moment one of the most decisive moments in my life, when I said lightly that I would write him such an article.

At the very end of June I was on my way to Capri. Passing through the customs when we reached the Gare du Nord in Paris, I told a young *douanier* as I managed to lift that weighty dressing-case up to the counter that I was *en route* for Rome; to my surprise he said:

"*Ouvrez ça.*"

I thought he could not have understood where I was going. If one was travelling round in the train to the Gare de Lyon to catch the night train to Rome the *douanier* used always to chalk one's hand-luggage and wave it on.

"*Mais, monsieur,*" I protested. "*Je suis en route à Rome.*"

"*Ouvrez ça,*" the young *douanier* repeated as gruffly and severely as he could manage.

I shrugged my shoulders and unlocked the case. As it happened the four boxes of my decorations, not yet strung together, were lying on top of my clothes; I had been asked to bring them because there was to be a *convegno* of all nations that summer, of which more anon. There they were—the purple box of the British Empire, the red box of the Legion of Honour, the blue and red box of the White Eagle and the pale blue box of the Redeemer.

The young *douanier* looked as ferocious as he could; picking up the red box he demanded in what he believed to be a tone of biting sarcasm:

"*Qu'est-ce que c'est que ça? Sont des cigarettes, hein?*"

"*Non, c'est la Légion d'Honneur.*" I murmured.

The young *douanier* dropped the red box as if he had been stung and slammed down the lid of the dressing-case. A grey-bearded Frenchman behind me with the rosette of the Legion in his buttonhole seemed on the verge of climbing over the counter to throttle the *douanier*, muttering in his wrath "*Ignoble! Infecte!*" and other adjectives of denunciation.

As for the *douanier*, he appeared to crumple up as he chalked my valise. Readers of my Second Octave may remember the customs-officer at Southampton who ruined my butterfly-collection on the way home from Brittany in 1894. At last, twenty-eight years later, I could feel those butterflies were avenged with poetic justice. That young *douanier* might have picked up the O.B.E. as a box of cigarettes and looked a little foolish, but it would not have been a gaffe that would seem a bad dream for the rest of his life.

Talking of dreams, I had a letter from Faith just before she left to say she had dreamt the previous night that a black beetle was running across the floor of the *salone* and that she had begged me to kill it, to which request I had replied, "I can't; it's on its way to keep an appointment."

Edwin Cerio, our landlord at Casa Solitaria, had become the *Sindaco* or Mayor of Capri in 1922, and put up the last fight to save Capri from becoming the Isle of Capree. The Milanese business combine had already done much to destroy the character of the island.

Faith would write in *More Than I Should*:

"Simple buildings were razed to the ground to make way for pretentious palaces. In some of the principal hotels were installed splendid bathrooms which lacked nothing but water. A clinic was opened, and patronized by very few invalids. . . . Business men from the north, ignorant of the subtleties of Capri, dared to think they could transform the paradise of lovers and poets into a profitable resort for smart people, with therapeutics as a side line. It was curiously depressing to see these egregious strangers poking about the place with an air of possession, to hear the smart, uneasy heels of their women folk on the cobbled streets, and it was with a sense of deliverance that one watched the handsome home-spun figure of Edwin Cerio striding along, his arms full of papers, his mind firmly fixed upon the project he had evolved, a project to save Siren Land from vandalism."

Cerio had organized a gathering of artists from all over Europe who were to urge upon the Italian Government the need to protect the domestic architecture and countryside of Capri from further destruction and disfigurement.

On the boat from Naples I was delighted to meet again the ebullient Marinetti, whom I had not seen since that gathering of the Poets' Club at which, under the disapproving eyes of Maurice Hewlett, I had composed and delivered an impromptu parody of Marinetti's Futurist hymn, for which Marinetti himself had embraced me on both cheeks.

Il Convegno delle Belle Arte opened early in July with an assembly of five hundred people, many painters, composers and writers among them, in the Giardino Augusto and was addressed by Marinetti at his most Futuristic. Ignoring the whole point of the Convegno, which was to protect the past, Marinetti pranced about, denouncing romanticism and *cinquecento* sentimentality. Going on with a paean to skyscrapers, he wound up by demanding a lift to a *cafeteria* on the top of the Faraglioni.

I have sometimes reflected with a smile that the pioneer of the self-conscious striving to be post-war and modern in the twittering 'twenties was Marinetti, a dynamic and lovable clown.

It may have been under the influence of Marinetti's passionate disposal of the past that when, soon after this, we were listening by moonlight on the terrace of Casa Solitaria to Alfredo Casella playing exquisitely a nocturne of Chopin, I heard a young Frenchman mutter, almost it seemed in agony, to another young Frenchman, "*Chopin! C'est dur.*"

Casella was modern enough himself in his compositions for the piano, but I never heard Chopin's music played better than by him. Another representative of music at the Convegno was the Venetian Malipiero, a descendant of Doges, whose ultra-modern compositions I found beyond my ear.

However, we did our best to be modern at Casa Solitaria by illuminating the Faraglioni with fifty Bengal lights on the parapet of our terrace when a cargo of distinguished guests were being taken round the island in a large boat under the full moon.

At a great supper held in the Quisisana I was called upon by Cerio to reply to the toast of the *stranieri*. I protested that I was not a stranger.

"You *must* do it," he insisted. "If I call upon one of the others it will create jealousy among the rest."

So I made a speech in Italian, ending up in English with Browning's lines:

> Open my heart and you will see
> Graved inside of it "Italy".

A member of the Government who made the next speech saluted me as a cross between Byron and Shelley!

"You see, *caro mio* Marinetti, it's no use. In spite of all you can say the past will keep cropping up."

Marinetti looked at me and shook his head.

"This Government is already dead," he declared.

And indeed Mussolini's Blackshirts were gaining more and more support all the time; Zanotti-Bianchi's Blueshirts had unfortunately faded away.

The Fascisti came to Capri that summer and demonstrated on the Piazza. Balbo was with them and that old aristocrat whose name eludes me. There was a lot of ceremonious bowing to one another and some impassioned speeches; more amusing were the less important Blackshirts who spent the evening sending messages round with an air of self-important conspirators. I was reminded of the way some of my agents used to behave in Athens until I dealt with it. But let us beware of laughing at Italians or Greeks: nobody who saw elderly Home Guards in Hampstead pretending that the enemy was round the next clump of bushes can afford to do that. Age cannot wither nor custom stale the game of cowboys and Indians for the male. I suppose my own dream of the South Seas had been another example of that.

A postcard from Lawrence written on August 20th came from Raratonga:

Calling here for the day—very lovely—Tahiti next—then 'Frisco. Wonder how you are. D.H.L.

A day or two later another postcard arrived from Raratonga.

If you are thinking of coming here don't. The people are brown and soft.
D.H.L.

My article on the gramophone in the *Daily Telegraph* brought me a number of letters. Robin Legge wrote on September 21st:

I was delighted to get your letter, because I had heard of the letters that had been received at the D.T. in consequence of your excellent article. . . . It would be a godsend to me if you, seeing eye to eye with me, would rub in the everlasting idea that there is now a multitude of reasonable folk—our noble selves to wit—who are keen on every improvement, whether of machinery or of taste in the recorded music— it will be a godsend indeed.

I began to wonder if it might not be a good idea to bring out a monthly magazine devoted to the gramophone. I recall that at about half-past five on the afternoon of this notion's occurring to me I saw the planet Venus over Monte Solaro; I thought at first she was an aeroplane. I was much excited by what must be a much rarer phenomenon than the flying saucers, which not long ago people were seeing so frequently, particularly in America, or even the Loch Ness Monster.

At the end of the month Bob Boothby, Bob Gathorne-Hardy and Kyrle Leng arrived in Capri. Bob Boothby was preoccupied with his future in politics. I remember his asking me when I thought a Labour Government would be in power and my reply that I saw no prospect of that for ten years at least.

Bob was laid low for a while with tummy trouble; I still have the letter he wrote me after leaving and here it is as the foundation of a friendship:

> Edenview,
> St Andrews,
> Fife
> *Oct. 2, 1922.*

Dear Mr Compton (Monty) Mackenzie,

I apologise very humbly for not having written before to thank you and your wife for being so kind to me in Capri.

One of my difficulties was that I didn't know how to address you. Every combination sounded too stilted or too familiar so I've put the lot in.

I took every train-de-luxe I could see till I got to Paris, and fell madly in love with a beautiful American heiress, whose name alas! I failed to discover, between Florence and Paris. On arrival in Paris I found I had enough money for a second-class ticket to London with a franc over. I paced the streets till midnight, drinking coffee at 50 centimes a glass and then took an omnibus train to Calais—a terrible night. Tipping nobody, I arrived in London at 11 the next morning, a shattered wreck!

Here in the intervals of playing golf, and lunching with the Prince of Wales, I have been dancing to a gramophone with fat married women who are all much appreciative of such assets as I possess, more attractive, and more amusing, than the debutantes.

Colonel Freddy Browning[1] tells me that when angered in the Levant you wrote your despatches in reverse, or sent telegrams to say you would probably be dead in another 6 hours! For which my congratulatioos!

Now I am going to bury myself in the north of Scotland to work for bar exams.

My love to Basil Leng if he is with you, and many many thanks to you and Mrs Mackenzie from

> *Bob Boothby.*

P.S. If you ever come to Scotland, remember

> *Beechwood,*
> *Murrayfield,*
> *Midlothian*

is where you stay.
Basil will tell you the water is hot.

---

[1] Amateur Racquets Champion, supporter of C, and father of the late Lt.-Gen. Sir Frederick Browning, G.C.V.O.

By the time those two letters reached me I was back in England, hoping Sir Percival Perry would solve the problem of Herm's future for me. Faith was to reach Herm by November. To some extent the worry of Herm dictated the mood in which I wrote an article for *The Times* about Capri, to which, although I should return for a while in the summer of 1924, it was really hail and farewell.

"Rare must be the man who, having spent an appreciable portion of his life in the Mediterranean, can stay satisfied with the English Channel for what remains . . . and however delightful may be my own island of Herm, I am convinced that I shall never complete a year there without craving for that other island in which, at the moment of writing, I most joyfully find myself again. Often during the weary English winter, more often during the laggard English spring, the lover of the South is tempted to hurry thither; as likely as not he will find that he has gained little by the exchange.

"The prudent lover will postpone his flight until the misery of an English summer gathers about him in swollen clouds. This year May gave us all that May can give; but those tempestuous morns in early June dear to Matthew Arnold, which revolt and justly revolt the cuckoo, revolted me this year, and, falling into as quick a despair as the bird, I was gone before him.

"Nor do I regret my lack of endurance, for since then I have sat here in a delicious complacency of mind, body and spirit, looking at pictures in the English papers of umbrellas intent upon the game at Wimbledon, of umbrellas betting at Ascot, of umbrellas cheering Leander to victory at Henley, of umbrellas—always and everywhere of umbrellas, umbrellas living, umbrellas loving, umbrellas newly born or lately dead, umbrellas murdering one another, divorcing one another . . . a black undulating world of umbrellas.

"Man requires the sun. Civilization requires the sun. It must have been the sun that first enticed the embryo of humanity from a gelatinous existence on the primeval foreshore. It was for a place in the sun that Germany fought; at the Peace Conference everybody fought for his neighbour's umbrella. It is humiliating to rule the sea and be ruled by rain. When I left London it was already drizzling; in Paris the drizzle was become a downpour; at Chambéry, next morning, the weather was only showery; on the other side of the Mont Cenis there was not a cloud in the sky; between Rome and Naples I had to swallow an ice at every stop to contend with the heat.

"Capri is never too hot. One might be disinclined to play lawn-tennis between twelve and five; one might think twice about a walk at such a time; but in the way that London can be hot, Capri is never hot. There is always a breeze from the north-west—a breeze that springs up about four o'clock and dies away at dusk. Occasionally there is a *scirocco*, which, in summer, means muggy and nebulous weather, bad for the temper—some say for the morals. You can read of its effect in *South Wind*. Mr Norman Douglas may invent, but he rarely exaggerates and the *scirocco* is, indeed, as detestable as he paints it. The only effect its victims outgrow is the first capacity for resistance they were able to muster when for the first time they were swathed in the vile folds. A summer *scirocco* turns the sea into platinum and human beings into thermogen; in winter, the sea becomes lead under that horrid influence, and human beings inert Gullivers, assailed by Lilliputian arrows.

"I have said so much about the *scirocco* because it would be dishonest to taunt England with her wet summers and claim perfection of climate for Southern Italy. Occasionally there is a *scirocco* . . . in fact to be candid, there is very often a *scirocco*.

.   .   .   .   .

"During the War, Capri suffered dreadfully from an eclipse of gaiety. Other islands might retort that such was the common lot. Capri, however, was not merely put out of action like an English seaside resort in winter. She had the air of a forsaken beauty, puzzled to know why she was being treated so. Moralists hoped that a lesson had been administered and that after the war the island would return to her primitive simplicity, chastened and humiliated by an experience of the fickle world.

"What actually happened was that the Neapolitans, unable to travel further afield, discovered Capri to be as perfect a summer resort as once was Baiae, whereupon a Milanese company bought all the hotels in the hope of persuading the rest of Europe that Capri was an ideal health resort for autumn, winter and spring. The abandoned beauty was to be dressed up as a nurse and readmitted to polite society. Luckily a *sindaco* was elected who understood that the true vitality of an island is less affected than an individual's by temperature, and that if that true vitality was to endure, it must endure by what it received as much as by what it gave. Capri had the *scirocco*; she did not require as well the agony of high-heeled shoes and a black cloud of compulsory evening-dress in the company's hotels. She was covetous not so much of *chic* as of distinction. She wanted visitors whose variety could compete with the variety of the natural scene.

"And how various that is! It pains me to declare that the charm of Capri is incommunicable. The landscape of Capri is really an inspired chromo-lithograph. Pen or brush that seeks to render its limestone and blue water is merely gilding the lily.

"I think of Monte Solaro's slow descent in a flood of oaks and olives towards Anacapri, and the sunset and the golden sea two thousand feet below; of those terraced vineyards and lemon orchards that end in the houses of the Grande Marina, brightly coloured and fantastically shaped as shells; of the diminutive port and the delicious bathing beach beyond; of the interior, with the countless peaks and precipices and the ruins of so many dominations, Phoenician, Roman, Saracen, even French and British; of that little town of Capri, with its shallow cupolas and rococo minarets, tumbled out in the middle of the island like a basket of mushrooms to which some child had added a few red and yellow toadstools; but all these pictures I make for my own pleasure, rather than with any expectation of informing, or even desire to inform a reader.

"And the flowers! There are nearly a thousand indigenous species on an island not five miles long and at the widest barely two miles across. When I remember those flowers I can believe that Capri really was Anthemoessa, that fabled flowery isle of the Sirens; and when I remember the sea-caves and arbutus groves, the myrtle thickets and drifts of rosemary, the cherry-trees of Anacapri that shade the young corn, the rocks under the blazing sun, and under the moon the velvety shadows and glittering fronds of palms—when I remember all these, wherever I may be, I hear again the voice of the Sirens, which, for me, is by day the drouthy piping of the cicadas, by night the liquid shrilling of the *grillo*.

"For the moment I have not to remember anything, for I am again in Capri. The cicadas, quiet for a space, have resumed their song. To-night I shall dine under an orange-tree hung with lamps; afterwards I shall sit in a *loggia* and listen to Casella playing César Franck, or to Marinetti reciting Baudelaire. The planet Mars will roll slowly down the southern sky, and the fishing-boats will twinkle until dawn."

In writing about Capri I omitted to say what a bad effect the *scirocco* had on my neuritis, nor did I reveal that by now I had decided that Casa Solitaria must be given up. I felt it would only be fair to Faith to keep it on for another two years until she had become fond of Herm. My habit has always been to live intensely in the present, and on account of my vivid memory my past remains as it were in the present. At the same time I am careful not to revisit the places of the past to indulge in senti-mental evocations of that past. I have never been back in Cornwall; I have never revisited Spain; I have not landed in Capri since I said a last farewell to it in 1925; I have never returned to the Channel Islands; I have spent no more than a week in Barra when the film of *Whisky Galore* was being made; forty years were to pass before I saw Greece again.

Mimi Ruggiero sensed that for me Capri was finished. I hear now the very tones of his voice as we came down through the grove of young pines we had planted above the beach of Ventrosa.

"Ah, *signore mio*, you are here, thank God, walking with me as we used to walk, but your heart is no longer here. *Suo cuore è lontano dall' isola nostra.*"

And as he said this the melody of the lyric in Boito's *Mefistofele*, *Lontan, lontan, lontano* on a red single-sided 10-inch celebrity record was singing soundlessly at the back of my mind.

I was deeply distressed that August by the Greek disaster in Asia Minor. Lloyd George had redeemed himself for me for his handling of Sinn Fèin by a speech he had made early in the month in which he had expressed a determination to stand by Greece. I might have known that the passion for Turkey by which so many British politicians and soldiers are obsessed would assert itself. At the end of the month came the defeat of the Greeks at Afium-Karahissar by Mustapha Kemal's Nationalist army, which ended in the Smyrna massacre, when the Turks nailed the Greek Archbishop to the doors of the Cathedral and pulled out his beard.

The French and the Italians had been trying throughout the First World War and ever since to gain control of Asia Minor and both could be blamed for arming Mustapha Kemal and the Ankara Nationalists. Nevertheless, if the Conservatives in the Coalition had not succeeded in ousting Lloyd George that humiliating surrender to Mustapha Kemal in October would not have happened.

When Bonar Law, with Lord Beaverbrook to feed popular opinion, funked war with Turkey the new Tory Government relegated the old British Empire to the past. It was the slipper-licking of the Turks at Chanak which made the rest of the world suspect that the British Empire was going the way of the Roman Empire.

On August 27th Sir Francis Elliot had written to me from Torquay:

Most of my private papers remained at Athens with my other possessions after I left; until I should acquire a permanent home. It was only last February that we began to occupy a villa I have bought at Cannes, and since then I have been gradually sorting out my papers and destroying many of them. Among them I have found a number of letters and memoranda of yours. Those which are principally concerned with reflections on individuals I am about to destroy, but there are some half dozen, mainly on political subjects, which will some day be of historical interest. I hesitate to keep them myself, because they will of necessity fall into other hands than mine, and they should only be used with discretion. Would you like to have them? Or have you kept copies of all your correspondence? In the latter case I will burn them. . . . Sells told me you had been reading my Father's "Some Revolutions etc" and had pointed out to him the analogy between my father's position at Naples and mine at Athens; it had not occurred to me before but it is quite true, up to a point.

On September 18th Sir Francis Elliot was writing from Cannes;

I can't help being sorry for the Greeks, even for Tino—not of course for Gounaris and Co., or Hatzanestis who is an ass of insufferable conceit—their misfortunes are by no means all their own fault.

Major antipathies were forgotten when I received a letter from Robertson to say that he was finding it impossible to work with Attewell and that regretfully he should have to leave Herm when I was able to get an engineer to take his place. He spoke with obvious pride and affection of the *Aphrodite* and of her fine qualities as a sea boat. *She has never given me the least bit of trouble.* I did not want to lose Robertson and I realized it was imperative to get back to Herm before disagreement between him and Attewell worsened. I thought it would be a good notion for me to know what the *Aphrodite's* sea-going qualities were and arranged that Mauger, Zabiela and Robertson should meet me at Cherbourg.

I certainly earned my experience; when we were in the Race of Alderney or the Swinge of Alderney in an equinoctial gale; I had not been so seasick since the waters of the Aegean and Ionian Seas. It was dark when we reached Herm, and I was thankful I had not been in the *Aphrodite* when she fought her way from London to Cowes in that July gale.

I was not too pleased by the report of the season at Herm which, for various reasons suggested by various people, had not been as successful as I had hoped. I decided that the real reason had been the wretched weather of that summer determined to make up for the glorious weather of 1921. Anyway, I was relieved to hear that the Perry party had enjoyed themselves, and hoped that when I went to London early in October matters would be settled satisfactorily between Sir Percival and myself.

I was invited to lunch with him at the Royal Automobile Club, where Mr White, his solicitor, would be able to explain the various clauses of the proposed agreement between himself and me.

It is a habit of men of business to give the most expensive lunch they can think of prior to a deal. The proposed victim is expected to be more malleable if he has previously been stuffed with caviare, oysters and grouse, and more pliable if moistened with champagne and brandy. As I knew that whatever Perry's terms were I should have to accept them, he could have spared himself that expensive lunch. Still, I enjoyed it. Afterwards we adjourned to the smoking room to find a comfortable corner for the fatted calf to be killed. Sir Percival's proposals outlined by Mr White began with the three years' option at the end of which Sir Percival would either take it up or not.

"I shan't ask for a renewal," he told me with a reassuring automatic smile.

A loan of £6,000 was to be devoted to improvements on the island; this would be repaid in half-yearly instalments of £1,000. As security for this loan I should hand over my Sun Life Endowment policy, the premiums on which amounted to £600 a year, and as a further security I should be required to give a bill of sale on the furniture in Herm, which would include my library.

So that was that, but next day I had a letter from Perry to say that he and Mr White had been talking it over and thought it might be easier for me if the repayment of the loan were made in quarterly instalments of £500. In other words, Sir Percival Perry would be able to foreclose in three months and not have to wait six months for me to default. It was a tough agreement but my financial position did not allow me to argue. I did refuse, however, to include Jethou. I recall only a sense of relief and a feeling that I could now get on with my plan to start a gramophone magazine.

One of the letters about the article in the *Daily Telegraph* had come from Percy Scholes. He said he had been trying to get into the heads of musical people the importance of the gramophone to the future of music and suggested our meeting when I came to London. So I asked Scholes to dinner at the Savile. When we sat down at the long table he said he was a strict vegetarian, and in the end chose two carrots for his dinner. Frank, who had been a page boy when Robert Louis Stevenson frequented the original house in Savile Row, could not restrain an expression of suppressed disapproval from flickering across his usually completely impassive countenance. However, he murmured a respectful "Yes, sir" and returned presently with two carrots on Scholes's plate. Nothing I could suggest would induce him to eat even a few walnuts.

If Scholes was a discouraging diner he was an enthusiastic encourager of my plan to start a monthly magazine devoted to the gramophone; his help and advice were invaluable that evening and for many years we could enjoy his sympathetic support. He would include *The Gramophone* in the *Oxford Companion to Music*, which helped me to achieve a record of being the only person alive to appear in all three of those Clarendon Press Companions—Literature and the Theatre being added to Music.

At the H.M.V. shop in Oxford Street I met Alec Robertson and Walter Yeomans, both of whom urged me to go on with my project. I was asked down to Hayes, where Alfred Clark, the Managing Director of the Gramophone Company, promised their practical help if I went on with my plan.

"And we'll let you call it by the title you suggest."

I did not understand what he meant.

"It is a copyright title, you know," he said with a smile. "By the way, there are already three magazines devoted to the gramophone," he added. "But they are really trade papers."

The *Talking Machine News* did not long survive *The Gramophone*; the *Sound Wave* held on for quite a long time; the third, I have forgotten.

I asked Alfred Clark if we might count on review records coming regularly from H.M.V.

"I ought to say that we shall review such records in the way a literary magazine reviews books. It wouldn't do for the public to think we just said what the gramophone companies wanted us to say."

Alfred Clark had been with the Gramophone Company since they started with headquarters in Maiden Lane. He can be considered the architect of what is His Master's Voice in Europe and Victrola in America.

"Oh no," he assured me on that October afternoon. "We shall welcome frank criticism."

I called next on the Columbia Company at Clerkenwell. When I asked Herbert Rideout, their Press Representative, the P.R.O. of to-day, whether in the event of my starting *The Gramophone* Columbia would send review copies he replied that it depended on what we said about them. I told him we should say what we thought and that if Columbia did not send review copies we should buy them and tell the public what we thought of them. Louis Sterling, the Managing Director, was as quick as Alfred Clark to see what an advantage to the record trade our proposed magazine might be. Rideout himself would become one of our most loyal and enthusiastic supporters.

I was amused by the general reaction at the Savile to the news that I was going to start a magazine about the gramophone.

"What an extraordinary chap you are! Who do you think is going to buy a paper about gramophones? I believe our maids have one in the kitchen, but I don't think they're likely to buy this paper of yours."

That member's remark was typical.

"Don't worry," said Robin Legge. "You'll pull it off."

I wrote to my brother-in-law, Christopher Stone, to ask if like myself he would put up £1,000 to start a magazine about the gramophone. He wrote back to wonder chaffingly what mad idea I should have next. Surely I must realize that with this new wireless the gramophone would soon be obsolete.

Another who had written to me about that article was Archibald Marshall; we met in London and on October 30th he was writing from Abbot's Lodge, Yoxford, Suffolk:

I shall come with a full-fledged proposal of our compiling a book together, which we could do on our heads, about the gramophone. Among other "dodges of a like nature" it might contain a series of say 12 programmes which it would be amusing to compile. . . . If we could adapt it for American use too it might be a big thing on our two names alone. Yours has the bulge over mine greatly in England, but in America I'm a seller.

A week later Marshall came to Herm and in a few days we had the records chosen for our programmes, of which I introduced half and Marshall the other half. I also wrote the introduction. The book was called *Gramophone Nights* and was to be published by Heinemann next year.

Archibald Marshall wrote novels about English country house life which suddenly caught the fancy of the American reading public. He had bought a small country estate but was already beginning to find it too much for him. Not long after this the American reading public dropped him as abruptly as they had taken him up. He was a burly man with a nervous temperament out of keeping with his appearance. I fancy there were domestic difficulties as well as financial. The gramophone had come as an anodyne to his worries. While we were picking our programmes Marshall insisted on laying the records all over the floor. He was a clumsy man and why he did not break more than he did in moving from one end of my study to the other was a wonder.

I had an omen when the *Aphrodite* came back after taking Archibald Marshall over to Guernsey on his departure. The tide was out when she returned and on such occasions she would be taken to moorings below the Rosière steps toward the southerly end of the island. I was working at a novel of mine to be called *Buttercups and Daisies*, which I had decided to write immediately instead of starting *The Parson's Progress*, the second volume of the trilogy begun in *The Altar Steps*.

Suddenly about eleven o'clock of a still night I had a feeling that the *Aphrodite* would slip her moorings and that she would be drifting with the tide on to rocks. Nellie Boyte went down as fast as she could to let Attewell and Robertson know what I feared. Both of them supposed it was my imagination, but they went along to Rosière steps and at that very moment the *Aphrodite* slipped her moorings and was carried along by the tide toward the harbour. For some reason the small boat usually moored close by was not there. Robertson and Attewell dashed along to the harbour, where they met Bannister, Sir Percival's engineer, who was looking after things for him. It was Bannister who managed to scramble aboard and start her engine just before *Aphrodite* struck one of the rocks outside the harbour.

I accepted my sudden premonition as a sign of good will from the spirits of the island. I felt that in offering them Sir Percival Perry I had at any rate halved the curse which Princess Blücher had laid upon the next tenant of Herm. I felt I was right when soon after this one of the tanks Sir Percival had landed for experimental agriculture blew up.

At the end of November Faith came to Herm with Isabella Caracciolo. Faith and Isabella had reached Rome two days after the famous march to Rome of the Blackshirts, Mussolini having arrived by train when all was safe. Like John Knox in days gone by, he believed in the *fait accompli* before he took any risks with his own safety.

Faith would write in *More Than I Should*:

"Monty and Hamlet were waiting for us on the pier, and we had a drink at the White House, now the Mermaid Tavern, before we walked up the hill to the Manor. The ugly house was transformed inside and the cottage adjoining where Monty lived and worked was snug and cheerful. Basil Leng was making a wonderful little garden for it. I was not surprised to see stacks of gramophone records in the study. . . .

"There were three gramophones already, an H.M.V. of the latest type in his study, the original Vocalion in the dining-room, and a huge instrument called the Ochestraphone in the billiards-room. . . .

" 'I've got twelve hundred records now. Some of the orchestra and chamber music records have got rather a scratch. The best thing is to think it's raining and then you hardly notice it.'

"I soon got used to thinking it was raining, and sometimes it was a downpour."

One evening when Hamlet was dozing with his head on Isabella's knee he woke suddenly and snapped at her face. Once before he had woken from sleep and snapped at Quilter. I knew that he must be put away. Big dogs like Great Danes and Alsatians are subject to sudden attacks of hysteria, and whatever their owners may declare can *never* be trusted. No more lovable dog than Hamlet could be imagined, and we all mourned him. That people should be allowed to keep Great Danes and Alsatians in cities when cats still have to undergo six months of quarantine is one more example of what to me is the mysterious phenomenon of the bureaucratic mind.

The first volume of Charles Scott-Moncrieff's translation of Proust's *À La Recherche du Temps Perdu* had been published that September by Chatto and Windus, and in the hope of drawing critical attention to it in Great Britain Scott-Moncrieff was gathering a symposium of various writers, including myself, which Chatto's were going to publish. His translation had been well reviewed and I told Charles I did not think the proposed symposium in a limited edition would help the sales of the book. In saying that I was probably influenced by my own anxiety to get out of contributing. All my life these forewords and introductions and expressions of opinion have hung over me. At this very moment a foreword to which I am committed lies heavily upon me. For me foreword is a synonym of *mañana*. Scomo, as we called him, was worried because Chatto and Windus had not decided whether they would publish the *Jeunes Filles* volume, of which Scomo was writing in January:

I am tired and unwell and angry and have done about 130,000 words for which I haven't yet had a penny, which is galling; however I am determined that this book shall come out in English.

I doubt if I should ever have succeeded in making my contribution to that symposium if Hope-Johnstone had not been with us that winter. In spite of his own indolence Hope-Johnstone was the most stimulating of all my friends.

I had felt I must have his conversation again when a letter arrived from him in that autumn of 1922; it must have been the longest letter he ever wrote. Of a new young laurel in the Bloomsbury shrubbery he observed:

It is a novel of the E. M. Forster school—I expect you know the type. They say —the critics—I believe, that Forster has discovered the human soul—it is an unfortunate discovery. I thought we were going to be allowed to forget about our souls. Behaviourism is the only doctrine. There is, it appears, no need to assume even consciousness to explain behaviour—we have certain "language habits". But E. M. Forster writes about high-toned bourgeois with refined souls and what they think when they cross the field on their way up from the station, and it is, to me at least, of an unconvincingness—the day dreams of the cultural sedentary. I used to wonder once how this kind of book was written. I believe I know now. It is automatic writing! Anna Karenina or Education Sentimentale are not automatic writing.

There was a lot more in that letter which made me long for Hope-Johnstone's talk, and I was delighted when he arrived in that December for a long stay. Not only did he give invaluable help with the preparation of the first number of *The Gramophone*, which was planned to come out on the First of April, but he also went through Dean Jeremie's library and discovered enough rarities to justify ten times over what I had paid for those 4,000 books. He was lodged in the tower of the Manor House, which was where Prince Blücher had lodged himself.

Harding used to tell of having one day been sent for by the Prince;

"'Come in, Harding,' he shouted when I knocked at the door. "And my goodness, did I feel awkward when I went in and saw him standing up in his bath as naked as an egg."

Hope-Johnstone was full of a recent swindle in which a party of gullible dreamers of adventure had been lured into sailing to the South Seas in a decrepit vessel which sank in the Thames before they reached Gravesend. This gave me the notion for my book *The Old Men of the Sea*, which was serialized by Cassell's. I abandoned *Buttercups and Daisies* and sat down to write it on New Year's Day of 1923, reading the *North Atlantic Pilot*, the *South Atlantic Pilot* and the *Pacific Pilot* before I navigated the *Octoroon* to the Kermadec Islands, which I called by another name. I knew all there was to know in print about the Kermadec Islands because it was for them I had tried to obtain a lease from the New Zealand Government through Pember Reeves. *The Old Men of the Sea* was called *Paradis à Vendre* in the French translation. This was the title of one of the chapters and when the book was reissued in 1963 by Macdonald's it was called *Paradise for Sale* to avoid confusion with Ernest Hemingway's *The Old Man of the Sea*. Lloyd Osbourne was much taken by the book and made a great effort to get it bought by Hollywood for a film, but without success.

Sir Percival Perry came for a couple of days soon after Hope-Johnstone had arrived and I can see that underlip of his twitching when Perry said at some meal:

"I suppose one ought not to say this but you know we were all a teeny-weeny bit disappointed at the Ministry when the Armistice was proclaimed. Yes," and his voice took on a kind of remote and sorrowful dreaminess. "Yes, we had a new tank and we were never able to know how good it was because the war came to an end."

His voice died away in a deep sigh of regret. I had not words, but H-J was equal to the occasion.

"Yes, it must have been very disappointing," he agreed, his mouth twitching. "Except of course for those who were fighting."

"Oh, of course, we were all glad at the Ministry when the war was over," said Sir Percival quickly. "We were only so disappointed that our new tank wasn't ready sooner."

H-J and I were fascinated by the speed with which Sir Percival could do ready reckoning and we agreed that the foundation for a commercial career in the grand style was the ability to say what one herring cost quicker than anybody else, coupled with complete shamelessness.

In that December I received a typewritten note signed in the clear hand of that preposterous Satanist, Aleister Crowley, about whom Somerset Maugham once wrote a novel called *The Magician*.

> Collegium ad Spiritum Sanctum,
> Cefalù,
> Sicily.
>
> Dec. 3, 1922.

Dear Sir,

Do what thou wilt should be the whole of the law. I was told that Mr Norman Douglas could be reached by addressing a letter simply to Capri. I did so, but it has come back. I believe I am right in supposing that he is a friend of yours as of mine, and that you may be able to give me an address which will find him. If you can do so I shall be very greatly obliged.

Love is the law, love under will.

> Yours faithfully,
> *Aleister Crowley*

Just before Christmas came a picture postcard of the Gothic building in Cefalù where he had started a sort of Agapemone with a bunch of absurd women. On this was written in a feeble feminine hand:

> *Do what thou wilt shall be the*
> *whole of the law*
> *Many thanks for your note of Dec. 14 re*
> *Norman Douglas.*
> *Love is the law, love under will.*

followed by the firm signature

> *Yrs.,*
> *Aleister Crowley*

I am always expecting that some enterprising literary archæologist will dig him up and write *In Quest of Crowley.*

FORTY YEARS OLD: 1923

M Y fortieth birthday fell on a mild January day with a pale blue cloudless sky, and I was presented with a silver ash-tray subscribed for by the island people. It was celebrated by sports—a three-legged race, a sack race, an egg and spoon race, even an obstacle race; and in the evening we had a dance. By now both H.M.V. and Columbia were sending me their dance records, which made our Saturday night dances merry affairs throughout the rest of the winter and spring. Those dances had to be paid for by husbands and wives having to listen beforehand to half an hour's talk by me about music. I was pleased when some educational records arrived from H.M.V. with the instruments of the orchestra, so that I was able, as I hoped, to teach my people the difference between a violin and an oboe. The problem instruments in those days for the recorders were the double bass and the cor anglais. I recall being taken to see a dance-band recording at Hayes with a tuba all by itself at the far end of the recording room, pretending to be a double bass.

Those Saturday evening dances were the only evenings I took off from writing very hard at *The Old Men of the Sea*, sometimes until dawn broke.

Somehow I had managed to produce my contribution to the Proust symposium. Charles Scott-Moncrieff wrote on February 1st:

All your good gifts were assembled to greet me at Printing House Square last night, three letters and your quite charming article, which makes me sorry you spend so much time writing novels, and your novel which makes me ashamed of having made you waste a few hours on an article.

The novel was *The Seven Ages of Woman*, which was published in March. Of it Charles Scott-Moncrieff wrote:

What I admire most is the cyclical effect of the close; I see on my own poll a fresh streak of silver every morning, but your repetition of the adoptive grand daughter theme is so beautifully and satisfyingly done that it reconciles me to my approaching dissolution; only in my case it'll be nephews: nice creatures, one of them at Lancing already; not that any of my uncles ever thought me a nice creature: that I am quite sure of.

The Old Men of the Sea occupied my night; by midday I was concentrated on *The Gramophone*. H-J went to London and came back with the welcome news that all three recording companies would advertise at a rate of seven guineas for a page; Hudson and Kearns would be the printers.

We decided to print 6,000 copies, and the first number of *The Gramophone* appeared about April 20th, three weeks later than we had hoped.

I wrote practically the whole of that first number under different signatures—my own name, C.M. and Z. In the Prologue I announced that the magazine would have nothing to do with wireless.

"Our policy will be to encourage the recording companies to build up for generations to come a great library of good music." I urged people to realize that the gramophone was to music what the invention of printing had been to literature. As Z. I reviewed at length the records of the first quarter of 1923. Under my own name I wrote the first instalment of a musical autobiography. As C.M. I wrote on "The Practical Utility of Chamber Music". Hope-Johnstone reviewed the latest records as "James Caskett" and Faith wrote about "Good Singing" as F. Sharp. Kind Mark Hambourg gave us an article on piano recording. Almost half a dozen gramophone societies sent in their news, about all that existed of gramophone societies in April 1923.

We had an accommodation address at a friend's house in London and presently he was writing to say that his letter-box could not deal with the letters pouring in. We decided to give up any idea of a May number and to concentrate upon a June number's coming out promptly on the first of the month. When the returns of unsold first numbers began to arrive on Herm I thought we had over-estimated our success and cut the printing order for the June number to 3,000; this contained an examination by "James Caskett" of all Galli-Curci's records and became a sought after rarity.

I wrote to Christopher and asked whether he would not like to reconsider his unwillingness to invest £1,000 in *The Gramophone*; this time, still with a hint of indulging one of my mad schemes, he agreed but was able to put up only £300 in cash. Then he visited Herm and we decided we must get hold of premises in London. Faith, not sorry to be away from the problems of Herm, volunteered to find them, and went up to London. On June 30th Christopher wrote from the Arts Club:

I've just been with F. to see some rooms at 25 Newman Street which will do excellently; a bedroom for her and two small rooms for office and a sitting-room ready to go straight into. They belong to a maisonette belonging to a charming woman who calls herself Iris Norton, dressmaker. I fancy F. will get herself set teas, and other meals out. Rent £150 a year for 6½ years. Only extras are light and gas and water and of coourse a charwoman. F. is delighted with it and I really believe it will suit all our purposes. I must clinch the matter on Monday and will

take it on myself, but I am counting on you to see me through. A line confirming this
would relieve my mind. . . . Don't worry about us at all. I expect you are having
enough to think about at Herm.

Gramophone Nights was published, in my introduction to which I had
written:

"At the present moment we are, all of us who earn a living by entertaining the public, wondering what is going to be the effect of the
broadcasting boom on our sales, and the great recording companies
must be wondering more anxiously than any of us. I do not think that,
if they will follow a strict policy of building up for the public a great
library of good music, they need be afraid of wireless competition; but
if they issue nothing except rubbishy so-called ballads, schoolgirls'
violin pieces and hackneyed orchestral compositions, they will not be
able to compete for long with the rubbish that is being buzzed into the
ears of the public every day by the broadcasting companies; poor
material soon wears out, and the public are not going to pay for records
of rubbish when they can get a change of rubbish daily."

Presently I received a latter from Mr John Reith,[1] the Managing
Director of the British Broadcasting Company, which had just moved
from its original headquarters in the Strand to Savoy Hill. Mr Reith
said he had been pained to read my remarks about wireless in my book
and suggested a meeting at which he should like to tell me some of his
ideas about the future of broadcasting.

So when I was next in London I went to see him in Savoy Hill. Mr
Reith was then 34 years old, an engineer who after being wounded in
the war as a Major in the Sappers had worked with the Ministry of
Munitions and in the previous year had been appointed General
Manager of the British Broadcasting Company. That was a fortunate
day for the B.B.C.

I see that tall gaunt figure with the scarred cheek banging his fist
down upon a very large glossy table devoid of papers as he growls "The
Press think that they can smash the B.B.C. The Press will find they are
mistaken."

I put my money on Mr John Reith at that moment, and came away
from that interview convinced that his broadcasting policy was going to
make the gramophone and wireless to a large extent a mutual help to
one another. I was determined to spur the recording companies into a
bolder policy over good music; Mr John Reith was equally determined
to pay no attention to the quacking of Fleet Street about the miseries of
chamber music and Bach cantatas being allowed a place in the programmes of the B.B.C. against the aim of Fleet Street to give the public

[1] The Rt. Hon. Lord Reith of Stonehaven, G.C.V.O., G.B.E.

what the public wanted. As I was leaving him with an assurance that my magazine would recognize the value of broadcasting to the gramophone Mr Reith told me he was hoping to bring out a little weekly paper in September which was to be called *The Radio Times*. Mr Bernard Shaw, Mr H. G. Wells and Mr Arnold Bennett had promised to contribute articles about broadcasting; he hoped that I would contribute an article some time. I promised to do so, and should keep my promise next spring.

About the same time as I was in London Sir Edward Elgar suddenly grunted to me in the Savile billiards-room:

"I hear you've started a paper about the gramophone. No doubt your clever young critics will try to teach me my job. Fortunately I don't take the least interest in music any longer."

I do not recall what I said, but whatever it was Elgar's grumpiness stopped.

"In the future you'll find you've outlived your day. You'll feel out of touch with the present. The critics will wonder why you were once taken seriously. Take my advice and have another interest. You'll be tired of books. Did you ever have a microscope?"

I told him about that microscope of mine I wrote of in Octave Two.

"I don't know that I should be much interested in looking at the hairs of a kangaroo. What I look at are diatoms. Those exquisite fossil deposits at the bottom of the sea. Looking at them I can enter fairyland when I wish."

There was a note in his voice that seemed to be revealing a mystical beauty to which he had penetrated and to which he was showing me the way.

Suddenly he said he was thinking of going up the Amazon next winter as far as Manaos.

"That is if I can get a cabin to myself," he added.

I thought then at forty what an absurd qualification for going up the Amazon was a cabin to oneself: I understand that qualification better at eighty.

Nevertheless, in spite of his declaration of having lost all interest in music Elgar did talk about it from time to time. I wish I had noted down his *obiter dicta*. I remember only two. One was that by far the greatest musical brain of our time was Busoni; the other was that it was a pity Schubert used so often to write in an exhausted key.

It may have been that year but more probably it was the following year that on a Saturday afternoon, after sitting next to Elgar at lunch, I sat with him afterwards in the billiards-room.

From the further end of the long settee came the voice of W. J. Turner saying that he was off to the Queen's Hall to hear the *Symphonie Fantas-*

tique; at this date Berlioz was still regarded with condescending superiority by the Brahmins. Suddenly and sharply Elgar said to me:

"What's that about the *Symphonie Fantastique*?"

When I told him it was being played that afternoon in the Queen's
Hall he asked me if I had ever heard it.

The *Symphonie Fantastique* was still a long time from being recorded
and it was rarely played at concerts. When I told Elgar I had never
heard it he asked me if I would like to go with him to the concert.

"A lot of it is rather theatrical rubbish, but there is one thing in it
which is really tremendous, and that is the March to the Guillotine.
Tell the porter to telephone to Queen's Hall for a couple of seats for me
and call a taxi."

When we reached Queen's Hall I paid off the taxi and went to the
box-office.

"You have two seats in the circle for Sir Edward Elgar?" I asked the
clerk.

He pushed them across to me, saying:

"Twenty-five shillings."

"They're for Sir Edward Elgar," I reminded him gently.

"Twenty-five shillings," he repeated.

He had apparently never heard of Sir Edward Elgar. So I put down
the money and rejoined the great composer without telling him that the
box-office clerk at Queen's Hall had never heard of him.

We had seats almost at the end of the third row of the circle on the
right. The concert began with Strauss's *Don Juan*, during which Elgar
sat looking gloomily bored, but when the Berlioz symphony began he
was lost in emotion, mopping his forehead from time to time and almost
it seemed groaning under his breath. When the long third movement
was over Elgar turned to me and said:

"Now I am going to mark for you the rhythm of this astounding
March to the Guillotine."

And mark it he did by thumping my knees and digging me in the ribs
with his elbow. Then he got angry because the cymbalist was not handling his cymbals in the way they ought to be handled.

"No, no," he muttered and started waving his arm over to his
shoulder, whereupon a floppy young woman in front of us turned round
and said, 'Hush!'; she evidently thought Elgar was a Philistine colonel.
She might as well have tried to hush Vesuvius in full eruption; the
merciless rhythm of that march was having such an effect upon him
that I should hardly have been surprised if he had suddenly leapt from
his seat, vaulted over the floppy young woman in front, and landed
down on the conductor's dais in order to make that recreant cymbalist
handle his cymbals in the way Elgar thought they ought to be played.

The crisis was reached just as the egg-faced clarinettist put his instrument to his mouth to play that phrase which signifies the last agony of the man about to be executed. He must have caught sight of Elgar in the circle at that moment; whether he thought it was Elgar himself or his ghost I do not know. His egg-shaped face expressed horrified surprise and when I saw Elgar's eyes flashing down upon that clarinettist I feared his mouth would dry up and the phrase never be heard. However, he managed to make his clarinet speak.

During the Dies Irae movement Elgar sat back mopping his brow, apparently exhausted by the emotion of the music; at the end of the symphony he rose abruptly.

"You're not going to stay for the Rachmaninoff Concerto?" I asked.

"No, no," Elgar replied. "As I've told you, I no longer take the slightest interest in music."

With this he hurried away up the aisle; the glances of the floppy young woman in front and others who had only come to the Queen's Hall to adore Rachmaninoff followed him indignantly.

For me with Elgar's departure the atmosphere became so ordinary as to seem heavy; Rachmaninoff himself was playing, but I longed for the concert to finish.

"When I was a small boy," Elgar once told me, "I said to my mother that one day just my name on a letter would find me; a little while ago I had a postcard from the other end of the world simply addressed to me by name with no place or even country."

The critics in to-day's mood of musical fashion write of Elgar as if he were a faded Edwardian beauty whose figure was now out of fashion; the critics in my youth wrote of Mozart with a kind of patronizing tolerance. The musical critic of *The Times* once wrote that the music of Berlioz was like the novels of Mr Compton Mackenzie. He meant it as an academic sniff at Berlioz; he would not have relished my gratification.

On Herm we had a visit from his Excellency the Lieutenant-Governor and Lady Capper that spring. The General had directed the Tank Corps in the latter stages of the war but he had not otherwise been touched by modernity. I recall asking him if he would like to hear some Wagner.

"Isn't that rather unhealthy music?" he asked. "I've always heard that Wagner's music was rather unhealthy."

So I put on instead of the Löhengrin wedding-march a record of Caruso singing *Le Régiment de Sambre et Meuse*.

The General shook his head.

"Yes, that was always our trouble with the French. They were too excitable."

I decided it was unfair on the General to play any more records and the conversation came round to my time in Greece. I recall telling him of the first time I had landed on the Asia Minor coast and saying what a thrill it had been to reflect that there was nothing but land between where I was standing and Peking.

"Yes, well, of course our soldiers didn't have time to think about that sort of thing. That was poor Johnnie Hamilton's trouble. His dispatches were too high-falutin'. After all, Gallipoli was a bad mistake which couldn't be put right by fine words."

I forget what I said to this; probably I just shrugged my shoulders and asked his Excellency if he would like to walk round the garden.

It was sometime about now that in addition to all my worries about the future of Herm I received a letter from Newman Flower enclosing a letter from somebody in Glasgow called Waterbury.

My attention has been called to an article which appeared in your magazine "The Story-Teller" of July last, in which a most unwarrantable and libellous use has been made of my family name.

Your author Mr Compton Mackenzie, not content with using my surname must needs introduce my late wife's Christian name, and also that of my housekeeper into this squalid fabrication.

You will please note that I shall hold your firm responsible for this: and intend to take whatever action may be necessary to indicate [sic] my family honour.

I cannot remember what the story was about, but the rough draft of my reply to Newman Flower has survived.

I have never heard of any person who was called Waterbury; the only Waterbury I know was a watch which was with me at my prep school. The story itself is a fairly common one. Such trimmings as distinguished it from many others were entirely my own invention. There are no imaginable grounds for legal action. It looks like an attempt at extortion, or else the fellow is a lunatic.

The next communication was a long letter from a firm of solicitors in Glasgow to Cassells' solicitors:

Our client Mr L. B. Waterbury, has handed us your letter to him with copy of the story entitled "Never Say Die", as to which he complains.

We may explain that in 1901 at the request of Mr John F. Waterbury, a prominent member of the New York Chamber of Commerce, an investigation was undertaken from London as to the family name Waterbury, and it was found that the family of our Client was the only one bearing that name in Great Britain. We note that you state that the use of the family name is pure coincidence, but the matter does not end there, and there are no less than four distinct points in the story which point to our Client and which have caused his friends to make remarks. These are:

(1) The name Waterbury is not known in Great Britain apart from our Client's family, but is nevertheless used as the name of one of the principals in the story;

(2) The name of our Client's wife was Emily Waterbury. That name is also used for one of the characters;

(3) The name of our Client's housekeeper is Miss Wilson. That name is again used;

(4) Some years ago, on account of an unfortunate attack of skin trouble, our Client had to wear gloves at all times, and the person referred to as Waterbury in the story has to do the same.

.   .   .   .   .

There is no doubt that our Client has been very much annoyed and distressed by the association of his name with such disreputable characters of a story, especially when the association did not stop at the name alone, but imparted various other items pointing to him and, in these circumstances, we shall be glad to know what your Clients are prepared to do about it.

Cassells' solicitors, like most solicitors who act for publishers, were frightened by the prospect of an action for damages and earnestly recommended that everything should be done to avoid such an action, which, after the Artemus Jones case, they thought might involve heavy damages.

I wrote to Newman Flower that I was willing to apologize for an unwitting series of coincidences, but that if Mr Waterbury went to law and was awarded damages against me I should treat those Glasgow solicitors as Mr Pickwick treated Messrs Dodson and Fogg and go to prison rather than pay a farthing. I had not known anything about a Waterbury from New York digging into his origins 21 years ago and that if I was to be sued for using the name Wilson, one of the commonest names in the world, and lose my case, authors in future would have to stick to single letters for their characters.

In the end the matter was closed with an apology and by Cassells' paying Mr Waterbury's costs.

There was quite a racket among solicitors at this date after the ridiculous damages awarded in the Artemus Jones case. Someone wrote in a book something about little Artemus Jones on a weekend with a girl in Ostend. Artemus Jones was a barrister who soon afterwards became a County Court Judge. The author had obviously used the name unwittingly, but the jury gave Artemus Jones £2,000 damages. The real Artemus Jones could not have conceivably suffered the least material damage and an apology should have been ample. However, it could be argued that the author had been negligent in not checking to see if what he thought was an imaginary name was in fact a real one.

I finished *The Old Men of the Sea* toward the end of March and started immediately to write a book for children called *Santa Claus in Summer*, which was the first and last time I have ever really enjoyed writing a book—it remains to-day my own favourite book. I had arranged with Michael Sadleir that *Santa Claus in Summer* should be published by Constable and that I should find an illustrator.

The moment I had finished *Santa Clause in Summer* in May I started *The Parson's Progress*. Although *The Altar Steps* had played havoc with my circulation, I was determined to carry on with what was called a trilogy but was in fact a single book which, were it ever published in one volume, I should call *Faith, Hope and Charity*.

The Perrys had all arrived, and in the middle of May Sir Percival himself told me he had decided that a partnership between us to run Herm would not work out because our ideas for its development were too different. However, as soon as possible he was willing to take up his option and would accept the valuers' estimate of the premium he should pay. I had paid back the first two £500 instalments of the loan and I knew I was going to have difficulty in finding the money to repay the third instalment. If I failed with the June instalment Sir Percival would be able to foreclose and I might have to lose my insurance policy and my library. The financial situation was growing worse and worse, and in Nottingham my mother was losing a lot of money. Indeed, things were so bad that I volunteered to play there in a season of Shakespeare—*Hamlet, Richard III, Henry IV*, and *Antony and Cleopatra*. I was even prepared to go on tour. Fortunately the situation in Nottingham was saved by help from the Nottingham magnates. So work on *The Parson's Progress* did not have to be interrupted by acting.

As June came in and Sir Percival still showed no signs of taking up the option I went down one day to the Mermaid Tavern, to which he seemed to feel it was more dignified to refer as the White House. Perry took me to his bedroom, from which a cat came out as we entered. He looked at it sadly.

"Oh dear, what a pity it is that dear little kittens grow up! He was such a dear little kitten and now he's grown into a great cat and I have to spend eighteenpence a week on food for him."

On one wall of his bedroom there was a picture of a girl in a sunbonnet leaning over a stile and feeding a donkey with carrots or something; on the other wall there was a picture of a lady with very little on, lying on a hearthrug in front of a glowing fire, the pervading illumina-

R

tion of that fire giving her limbs so much colour that she looked as if she was wearing almost nothing at all.

Sir Percival made his usual excuses for not taking up the option immediately and when I went back to my study that evening I read gloomily through that option in which all that Sir Percival could bring to the island in the shape of people and things was meticulously noted. Hope-Johnstone had gone to London to grapple with the July number of *The Gramophone*; Faith had just discovered those ideal headquarters for the paper in Newman Street, which would give both her and *The Gramophone* accommodation.

Suddenly I realized that Mr White, the clever solicitor, had made what I hoped might be a fatal slip in that option he had drawn up. I sent for Attewell and told him to ask Sir Percival to look in on me at the cottage to-morrow round about noon. Then I packed myself into my chair, and putting the future of Herm out of my mind, settled down to *The Parson's Progress* while Nellie Boyte played the latest H.M.V. gramophone.

When Sir Percival arrived next morning I asked him again if he could not give me a positive date for taking up the option. He switched on the smile and told me in the kindliest of tones how anxious he was to give me a definite date but that as he had told me yesterday he was not yet in a position to do that.

"And I have done all I could to help you, haven't I?"

Those grey eyes were wide open as if they were astonished at my failure to appreciate his magnanimity.

"I've been reading carefully through the option agreement, Perry." He looked as grave as if I had told him I had just been reading through one of St Paul's Epistles. "You have provided for various people to stay on the island whenever you wish during the time you are waiting to make up your mind about the option." Sir Percival nodded. "You have provided for bringing furniture to the Mermaid Tavern, or the White House as you prefer to call it." He nodded again. "You have provided for bringing three tanks and other relics of the Slough Dump to the island for which, in the event of misappropriation, as it is called, I am to be responsible. But you or Mr White or both have made one serious omission. You have not provided for yourself personally to stay on the island. Now, either let me know whether you wish to take up the option at once or else I'm afraid I shall have to ask you to leave Herm this afternoon and not come back again until you have decided to take up the option."

Sir Percival jumped up from his chair and went across to the door, which he flung open in a gesture of rage. I thought he was going to slam it and disappear, but abruptly he turned and said:

"I'll take up the option. My valuers will be Knight, Frank and Rutley. You will let me know the name of your valuers within twenty-four hours."

He slammed the door behind him and vanished.

I went over to Guernsey and arranged with Lovells to act as my valuers on the day fixed, which was finally decided for some date early in July. I sent an appeal to Mr Ridley, the Manager of what was still called the London and Counties, Parr's and Westminster Bank, which would presently become the Westminster Bank. I knew that he had been indulgent over my overdraft. Would he be still more indulgent and honour the cheque for £500 which I had to send to Sir Percival Perry as another instalment towards repaying his loan to me. I explained about the option and dear Ridley as always stood by me. Where I should have been without Ridley's support during the next few years I shudder to think. I hear now the General Manager of the Westminster Bank asking me if I knew what I owed to Ridley.

"I've known him come down to London from Oxford and refuse to go back until I'd agreed to the extension of your overdraft."

I should dedicate one of my books to Ridley in a poor attempt to express my gratitude for the way he stood by me in the difficult times ahead. The picture in my mind's eye is of him and his wife sitting on either side of the fireplace in his room above the bank in the High, both of them listening to the faint wireless of the time with earphones.

When the day came for the valuers to do their job the weather was glorious throughout the two days. Hope-Johnstone was back and we asked Knight, Frank and Rutley's man to dine with us. Later I should hear that this was regarded by Perry as a kind of bribery. He had himself charged the valuer for his meals.

At the end of the second day young Lovell told me that his valuation had been a thousand pounds more than that of Knight, Frank and Rutley. Would I agree to split the difference? I was willing, and Knight, Frank and Rutley's man went along to the Mermaid to ask if Sir Percival would agree to this. It was half-past ten; Perry had already gone to bed. He needed all the sleep he could get before he was woken up like David Garrick according to Samuel Foote by the ghost of a halfpenny he had spent the day before. Sir Percival was not at all pleased by being woken. He came out on the balcony in his pyjamas and told Knight, Frank and Rutley's valuer that he did not employ dogs to bark for him and bark himself. That observation cost him £500, for the valuer came back and agreed to Lovell's valuation.

I had already paid back £1,500 of the £6,000 Perry had advanced me and in the end Perry or Trust Management (Ltd) had to part with £3,000 in cash; like other financial experts he had disguised himself as a Limited Company registered in Guernsey. Yet it was December before that sum was paid in full. Every payment of an instalment involved pettifogging little arguments. Even when the final instalment was paid the new tenant of Herm kept back £10 *in escro* in case too much had been paid for something and discovered later. I had never heard the phrase.

Sir Percival had secured some bargain of his own in the way of boats; he did not want the *Aphrodite* included in the valuation. I remember telling him that I should not include the pheasants, which were thriving, and I hear now the "Thank you very much" uttered in a tone of tristful gratitude as if my generosity had just saved him from bankruptcy.

At spring tides it was the custom on Herm for everybody to go down to Belvoir and reap a harvest of sand-eels; these were not eels but small fish which buried themselves in the sand and when cooked were like whitebait. Perhaps the final action on my part which made Sir Percival Perry feel that a partnership between us would be impossible was when I refused to make everybody surrender his catch of sand-eels in order that the whole of the catch might be sold for some trifling sum in Guernsey next day.

Sir Percival Perry and I lived in different worlds. He once said how much he envied the advantages I had enjoyed of school and university.

"I left school when I was seventeen to start life with a little bicycle shop," he sighed.

"But you hadn't got to leave school. You could have stayed on if you had wanted to," I pointed out.

"Oh, but I felt it was my duty to take advantage of that little bicycle-shop."

When he was given a peerage Lord Perry of Stock Harvard chose for his motto "Look Beyond"; if I were choosing a motto I should prefer "Look Round".

I had decided that if and when Perry took up the option I would move to Jethou. My next Octave will begin with my going to Jethou in that July of 1923 and will end with my leaving it at the end of 1930.

I have never put foot on Herm since I walked down the Rosière steps and embarked in a small boat to be rowed across the Percée to Jethou on that tranquil summer morning. As I write these words over forty years later I can still hear my footsteps crunching on the beach of that dearly loved little island.

APPENDIX A

FIRST DESPATCH

THE FIGHT FOR ACHI-BABA

LIGHT AND SHADE IN GALLIPOLI

"LANCASHIRE LANDING"

BATTLE IMPRESSIONS

We received yesterday the following telegram from Mr Compton Mackenzie, the well-known novelist, who has temporarily replaced Mr E. Ashmead-Bartlett at the Dardanelles. The latter, having lost the whole of his kit in the Majestic, was obliged to return to England in order to obtain another outfit. He is again on his way to the East.

MALTA, *June 14*

We boarded our ship and travelled for nearly an hour towards the sound of guns, coming down through a grey and indeterminate day that was very slowly changing to a clearer atmosphere. A northerly wind was blowing, such a wind as might shatter the chestnut blossom in England on the Fourth of June. Therefore most of us stayed in the wardroom, until we were off Cape Helles among the transports and trawlers and various craft at anchor.

A small green whale, all that is now visible of the Majestic waited motionless upon the water. She was subsiding rapidly, they said, and already, in the watery sunlight, she gave the illusion of slowly assuming to herself the nature of the waves that splashed against her still rigid sides. Such a dream of a ship's transmutation to her own element vanished in the billows of dust ashore, vanished in that queer heartlessness of war that is really the desperate occupation of the mind with something to do and therefore no time to dream.

ON THE BEACH

"Lancashire Landing"—the glorious name of that beach is the climax of all the castles in the sand that were ever built. No children at Blackpool or Southport could imagine, in their most ambitious schemes, such an effect of grown-up industry. Inevitably the comparison with a seaside resort on a fine Bank Holiday arrives, so inevitably as really to be rather trite. Yet all the time the comparison is justifying itself. Even the aeroplanes on the top of the low cliff have the look of an amusement to provide a threepenny or sixpenny thrill. The tents might so easily conceal phrenologists or fortune-tellers. The signal station might well be a *camera obscura*. The very carts of the Indian Transport, seen through the driven sand, have an air of waiting goat-carriages.

We walked up the slope from the beach, and suddenly there broke upon one the realization that all this time the guns had been thundering. Suddenly an empty stretch of desiccated scrub rolled on before us. The homely chatter of the beach was forgotten. There was nothing but a noise of guns and wind, and, for the eye, nothing but the black and white telegraph poles, the wires winking in the sun, and the imperturbable larks rising and falling. This empty stretch began on the sky-line, and it was necessary to enter a trench originally dug by the Turks and good enough it seemed to withstand any but the heroes of that imperishable assault upon April 25.

We hurried on, here and there almost sticking in rank clay, which was sometimes even wet enough to want a mattress of boughs for its passage. Finally we came to the shelter, considerably labelled "Low Doorway" upon the lintel. The walls were hung with canvas, and each of the low oblong windows gave us, as we leaned upon their high sills, a new aspect, framed in branches, of the battle of the hill.

Somewhere behind, a 60-pounder crashed at intervals, and we could hear the moan and rattle of the shell go forward on its way. In front of the shelter the country dipped gradually down, to rise again more steeply beyond a wide and partially wooded hollow. Here, through the glasses, could be seen a number of mules, tranquil enough, notwithstanding the concentration of shell-fire that was sweeping, and shrieking, and buzzing over their heads, to explode halfway up the opposite slope. Every shell burst with its own shape of smoke, and so substantial was the vapour that the wind could only carry it away bodily, unable for a long time to disperse it. The shrapnel puffs materialized from the air at first as small and white as wads of cotton wool, then growing swiftly larger and turning to a vivid grey, then fainter again and travelling across the view like tadpoles of cloud, until at last they trailed their tails in a kind of fatigue, before they dissolved against the sky. Heavy shells created volcanoes all along the line, and from the sea, like drums solemnly beaten, came the sound of the ships firing.

It seemed very calm in the shelter, as the wind fretted the grass and fluttered two magenta cistus flowers immeditaely outside the window, and as a tortoise crawled laboriously past our straining binoculars. It seemed very calm, as one looked at the maps pegged out upon the trestle tables. But it was 10 minutes to 12, and at 12 o'clock the advance would begin.

THE ATTACK

The gunfire lessened, and from the whole line the noise of musketry and Maxims came sharply, a noise that was tenser than the guns and more portentous. It was as if one had been listening to a change of orchestration in a symphony, as if, after a heavy and almost dull prelude, the strings were leading to a breathless finale.

Yet as one gazed through the glasses there was scarcely a visible sign of action. Once indeed a large body of men were visible, as they climbed the green slope. But they were soon lost, and, notwithstanding those angry rifles, we had nothing at which we could look except the mules standing motionless in the hollow, and once, down a ribbon of road, an orderly galloping. Yet all the time messages were coming in along the wires. All the time it was possible to mark with green, and red, and blue pencils a redoubt gained, a trench occupied, or, at some point perhaps, a check.

One message brought news of 50 prisoners, coming in, up on our left, and a Staff officer went off to meet them. It happened to be my chief, and I was glad of the excuse to go with him. The greyness of the morning had quite gone by now, and the air was brilliant, after the damp and gloom of the shelter. The road towards the line of battle ran by the cliff's edge, and out at sea, escorted by destroyers, two battleships, with guns and turrets in blackest silhouette against the flashing sea and the silver fume of the horizon, went backwards and forwards at their slow and stately business and their solemn firing.

We met the escort just where a Red Cross flag was flying above the cliff-burrows of the Field Ambulance. Some of the prisoners were badly wounded, and these were at once taken off for medical attention. The rest were halted, and several of the escort really danced round us, talking and laughing, not yet free from that first wild elation of the charge. The dust and sweat caked upon their faces made it almost impossible to see where the khaki ended. They were like the clay models of a sculptor, and their bayonets lacked even so much lustre as tarnished foil. They were children intoxicated with some splendid adventure, as they stood round us, laughing and chattering of the deeds of their regiment; and the plaster of dust, obliterating all lines, all hair, all signs of age, made them appear more than ever like children.

The Turks were very glad to have been taken, and when another Staff officer came up and spoke to them in their own language they were enthusiastically anxious to be pleasant. One felt a fresh rage against the Germans for having been able to dupe such fine fellows, for they were fine fellows, as they squatted there, many of them wounded, but none complaining, and all of them beaming at the cigarettes our soldiers offered them. It was, of course, impossible to examine the prisoners here more than cursorily, because a group so large might have drawn the enemy's fire. So down they marched toward "Lancashire Landing" and the accommodation of the Assistant Provost-Marshal.

When we were back in the shelter there was still nothing visible, and two of us went down to one of the Headquarters, where, heralded by the telephone's petulant and gnat-like summons, more news came back of the progress of the battle.

It was true then that the Worcesters had captured three lines of trenches, and I thought of the men in that escort, who had danced about in the roadway by the sea-edge and chattered all together about their exploit like children. The Indian troops had suffered severely, but the Sikhs and the Gurkhas had made a desperate advance. The Gurkhas had pressed on. It was magnificent to watch a thin red line of pencil symbolize and record their achievement. The Naval Division had lost heavily, having come up against three trenches, banked one above the other on the slope. But, nevertheless, a blue line showed where and with what valour they had held their ground against a bloody enfilade.

We emerged from the dugouts and passed along the paths that wound among the tents and cavities which the Irishmen had found time to decorate with white stones. Once more returned that sensation of being near the seaside and of all this noise of battle being but a dream.

The rifles and Maxims had begun again when we reached the shelter. A second advance, timed to begin at 4 o'clock, was already in full swing.

Again we tried to see the figures of men in their bayonet charges up the slope, and still there was nothing visible except the mules and an ambulance wagon galloping up the ribbon of road.

UNTIL THE EVENING

The sun was by now westering fast, and when the result of the second advance arrived we hurried back along the trench toward "Lancashire Landing". Birds were twittering in their flight through the radiant air, and beyond them three biplanes were winging homeward, one behind the other, as birds fly across the sunset to roost. The 60-pounder was still moaning on its way to the enemy's lines. But not even guns could destroy the golden peace of that evening of the Fourth of June.

As we waited on the lighter to go aboard our ship some of the wounded able to walk were coming down to the beach to go on board a hospital ship. These were the red and blue lines marked on the maps upon that trestle table. They were tired and silent, strangely different from the jubilant men of the escort at noon, who had shown their triumph in every movement. They were tired and silent, and the sight of that company was almost intolerably moving, not from any vulgar pity for their suffering, but because they were so wonderful and so calm coming down to the edge of the sea in the evening after the battle.

APPENDIX B
SECOND DESPATCH

ALEXANDRIA, *June 30*

The battle of June 4 ended with substantial progress on our centre, although on our left and on our right (notwithstanding the most violent charges and countercharges) we were unable to consolidate some of our initial gains. The reason of this may be found in the natural strongholds of the Turkish flanks—natural strongholds that are helped by the most elaborate fortifications. The British and the French line on Gallipoli Peninsula, from the Aegean to the Dardanelles, is confronted by rising ground that culminates in the centre with the flat summit of Achi Baba, 800 feet high.

On either side the ground falls away to the sea in ravines and dry watercourses called "deres", which the Turks have had time to make impregnable to any except those superb troops that are now fighting to pass over them. There is no room upon the Gallipoli Peninsula to find weak points; and we are now in the position of having to storm an immensely strong fortress, the advanced works of which, by an amazing feat of arms, we already hold, and the glacis of which has to be crossed before we move forward to the assault upon the bastion of Achi Baba and beyond to the final assault upon the very walls of that fortress.

Further up the coast the Australians and the New Zealanders have made a lodgement upon one of the strongest advanced works of the Kilid Bahr plateau, as seen from the north-west.

KILID BAHR THE KEY

Here they threaten the communications of the fortress, and are drawing against them a large part of the garrison. This is composed of the flower of the Turkish army; and, notwithstanding casualties that must already amount to 70,000, the enemy troops are fighting with gallantry —with desperation, indeed—because they realise that when the bastion of Achi Baba falls the occupation of the Kilid Bahr plateau becomes a mere question of time; and that when Kilid Bahr (which dominates the Narrows of the Dardanelles) falls the doom of Constantinople is at hand.

In view of the difficulties—were it not for the landing, one would be tempted to say the "impossibilities"— which confront our men the gain of a score of yards in the Gallipoli Peninsula may fairly represent for the purposes of comparison a gain of 500 yards in the western theatre of war. Therefore, to find its importance, the gain of 500 yards on June 4 must be measured with affairs like Neuve Chapelle; and the few quiet days that succeeded may be accepted as repose after a violent effort.

On the night of Friday, June 11, there was a brilliant little action by the Border Regiment and the South Wales Borderers, which resulted in the gain of two trenches.

On Wednesday, June 16, the enemy, led by a Turkish officer and a German, made an assault on the trenches of the 88th Brigade, but were driven off with loss. However, that night, the trenches gained by the two regiments on the 11th were heavily bombed—so heavily that our men were forced to retire about 30 yards and dig themselves in.

DUBLIN FUSILIERS CHARGE

At dawn we were able to enfilade with machine guns the vacated trenches. Then the Dublin Fusiliers charged with the bayonet; and once more gave us possession of our gains at heavy cost to the Turks, whose dead filled one trench.

On the evening of the centenary of Waterloo, Friday, June 18, the enemy bombarded very heavily another portion of our trenches on this side of the line. They were evidently attempting in miniature our own methods of Neuve Chapelle and of June 4, for immediately after the bombardment they were seen to be massing for an attack. However, the imitation ended rather abruptly at this point, and the affair petered out into discretion.

GLORIOUS, SUCCESSFUL ATTACK

On the evening of Saturday, June 19, the Turks, by a fierce attack, managed to get into an awkward salient which had remained in our hands after June 4. For some time there was great difficulty in recovering this, but the 5th Royal Scots, and a company of the Worcesters, led by Lieut.-Colonel Wilson of the former regiment, made a glorious attack and drove out the Turks.

Of the Royal Scots one can add nothing but that they are Edinburgh Territorials, brought in by the fortune of war to make the twelfth Regiment of the immortal 29th Division, whose deeds since April 25 may have stirred the ghost of Homer to sing their valour.

BATTLE OF THE LONGEST DAY

Mention has been made already of the difficulties that oppose our advance upon the two flanks. On June 21 it was determined to straighten the line upon the extreme right and at 4.30 a.m. the preliminary bombardment began. The dawn had been clear, but soon a curtain of silver, through which gleamed the ghost of the rising sun, hung over the Kereves Dere. This was the smoke of bursting shells.

Slowly, as the sun climbed up, the curtain became more substantial; then it seemed to droop and sweep along the hollows like a vanishing mist of dawn; and during a respite the thin blue smoke of the bivouac fires came tranquilly up into the still air. The respite was very brief; and the bombardment began again with greater fierceness than before. The 75's (three-inch guns) drummed unceasingly, the reverberation of the 125's (five-inch) and of the howitzers shook the observation post over the Kereves Dere, and beyond, upon the sloping shoulders of Achi Baba, the curtain became a pall.

The sun climbed higher and higher. All that first mirage of beauty had disappeared, and there was nothing but the monstrous shapes of giants of shell smoke that appeared one after another along the Turkish lines.

All through the morning the cannonade went on.

By noon, the 2nd Division of the French had on the left stormed and captured all the Turkish trenches of the first two lines. Even the Haricot redoubt, with its fiendish entanglements and its maze of communicating trenches, was in French hands.

On the right, however, the French 1st Division, after reaching their objective, had been counter-attacked so effectively that they had fallen back.

TAKEN, LOST AND RETAKEN

Again they advanced, again they took the trenches, again they were driven out; it began to look as if the victory on the left would be fruitless, that the position would become an untenable salient and the Haricot redoubt revert to the enemy. At this moment a message was sent to say that the trenches MUST be recaptured; and when recaptured, HELD. There were still five hours of daylight for this battle of the longest day.

British guns and howitzers were asked for and sent at once. The bombardment was resumed throughout that afternoon. At half-past five it seemed as if every gun on earth were pouring shells on the Turkish lines.

At six o'clock the third assault was delivered. In one trench there was a temporary shortage of ammunition, but the enemy fought even with stones and sticks and fists. A battalion came hurrying up from the Turkish right to reinforce. It was caught on open ground by the drumming 75's and it melted away. Thus 600 yards of Turkish trenches were taken; and still the bombardment continued in order to ward off the counter-attack that was anticipated.

The smoke of the shells, which at dawn had been ethereal, almost translucent, was now in the sunset dun and sinister, yet the sunset was very splendid, flaming in crimson streamers over Imbros, tinting the east with rosy reflections, and turning the peaks of Asia to sapphires. It had a peculiar significance on this day of the Solstice, crowning as it did those precious five hours of daylight that for the French had been fraught with such achievement. Slowly the colour faded out, and now, minute by minute, the flashes of the guns became more distinct, the smoke was merged in the gathering dusk, and away over the more distant Turkish lines the bursts of shrapnel came out like stars against the brief twilight.

TURKS LOSE 7000 IN ONE DAY

One knew how anxious would be the darkness that now was falling upon this 21st of June, but in the morning we heard gladly that the enemy's counter-attacks had failed, and that our Allies were indeed firmly established.

The Turkish casualties were at least 7000. One trench 200 yards long and ten feet deep was brimming over with the dead.

They had been valiant, those dead men. French officers who have fought in the West say that as a fighting unit one Turk is worth two Germans; in fact, with his back to the wall the Turk is magnificent.

The French casualties were few considering what a day it had been, what an enemy was being attacked, and how much had been gained. The right of the line now commands Kereves Dere and the profile of Achi Baba seems to write itself less solidly against the sky.